WITHDRAWN

HARVARD LIBRARY

WITHDRAWN

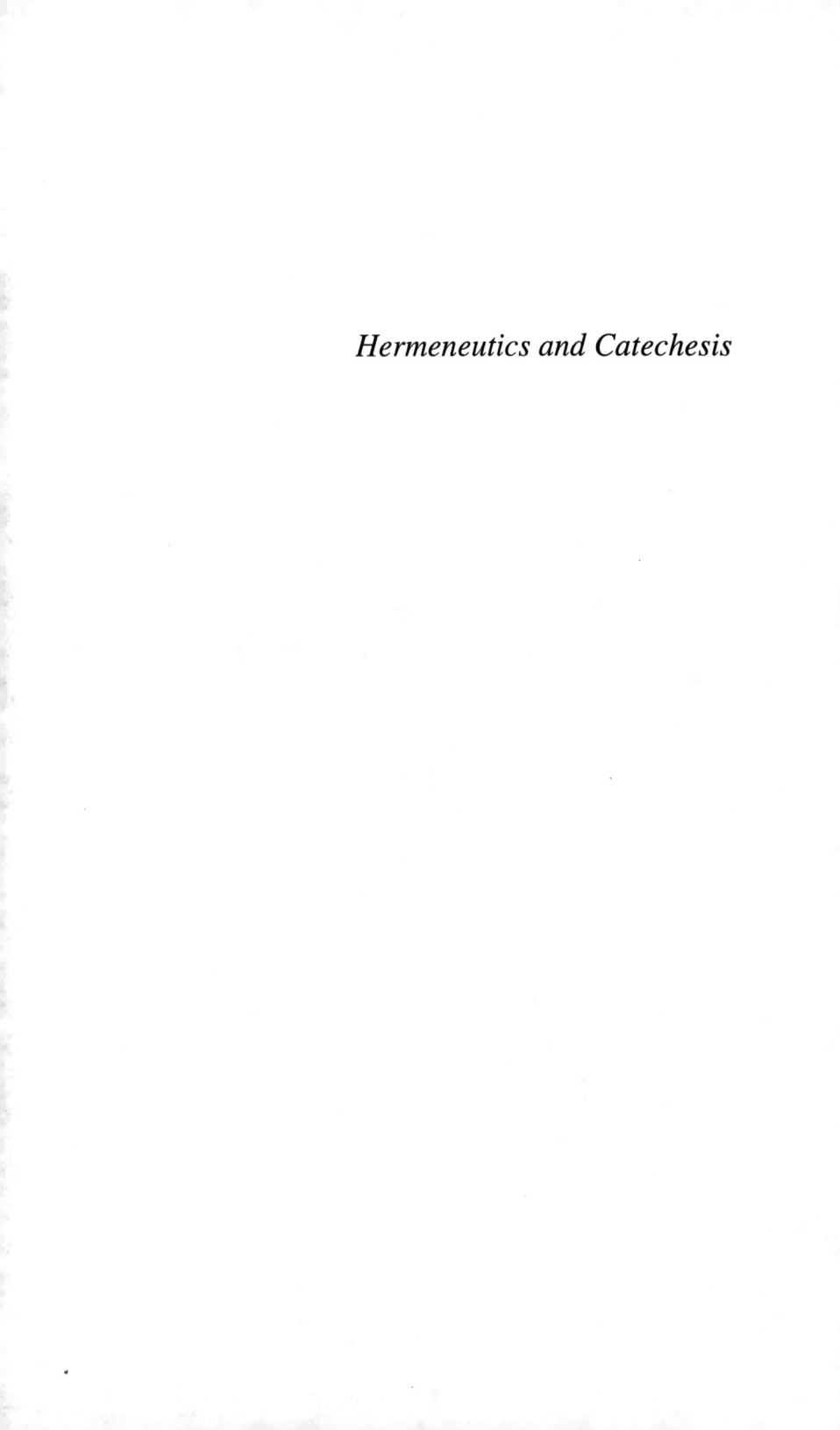

Hermeneutics and Catechesis

HERMENEUTICS AND CATECHESIS

Biblical Interpretation in the *Come to the Father* Catechetical Series

Foreword by

Gregory Baum

Robert J. Hurley

University Press of America,® Inc.
Lanham • New York • Oxford

Copyright © 1997 by
University Press of America,® Inc.
4720 Boston Way
Lanham, Maryland 20706

12 Hid's Copse Rd.
Cummor Hill, Oxford OX2 9JJ

All rights reserved
Printed in the United States of America
British Library Cataloguing in Publication Information Available

Library of Congress Cataloging-in-Publication Data

Hurley, Robert J.
Hermeneutics and catechesis : biblical interpretation in the Come to the Father catechetical series / Robert J. Hurley ; foreword by Gregory Baum.
p. cm.
Originally presented as the author's thesis (Ph.D.)--McGill University, 1994.
Includes bibliographical references and index.
1. Vien vers le père. 2. Catholic Church--Catechisms--French--History and criticism. 3. Christian education--History--20th century. 4. Bible--Criticism, interpretation, etc.--History--20th century. 5. Catholic Church--Education--History--20th century. I. Title.
BX1962.H87 1997 268'.8271--dc21 97-18444 CIP

ISBN 0-7618-0873-6 (cloth: alk. ppr.)
ISBN 0-7618-0874-4 (pbk: alk. ppr.)

☉™ The paper used in this publication meets the minimum requirements of American National Standard for information Sciences—Permanence of Paper for Printed Library Materials, ANSI Z39.48—1984

To my beloved Chantal

CONTENTS

FOREWORD _____ xi

ABBREVIATIONS _____ xiii

ACKNOWLEDGMENTS _____ xiv

INTRODUCTION _____ 1

    A New Catechism: Mixed Reactions _____ 3

    The Problem Described _____ 6

    A Clarification of Terms _____ 8

    Reading the Bible in the Catholic Tradition _____ 10

    The Plan of the Book _____ 13

1. THE CATECHETICAL HERITAGE OF *VIENS VERS LE PÈRE* _____ 15

    The Middle Ages _____ 15

    Protestant Reformation _____ 17

    Catholic Reformation _____ 18

    The Counter Reformation _____ 19

    The 20th Century _____ 21
        The First Half of the 20th Century _____ 24

Prelude to Reform _____25
The Liturgical Movement _____27
The Biblical Movement _____29
Catholic Action _____30
Theological Renewal _____32

2. A HISTORY OF *VIENS VERS LE PÈRE*: EUROPEAN AND CANADIAN INFLUENCES _____38

Catechetical Renewal in France _____39
    A Return to the Bible _____42
    Liturgy as a Source of Catechesis _____45
    New Methods and a New Task _____49
    The Intellectualist Strain _____57

Signs of Renewal _____58
    New Institutions _____58
    The Influence of Lumen Vitae _____60

International Catechetical Meetings _____64
    Kerygmatic Catechesis and Religious Experience _____64
    The Catechumenal or Anthropocentric Stage _____69
    The Anthropological Phase _____71
    Summary _____73

The Catechetical Renewal in Quebec _____73

3. PEDAGOGY AND HERMENEUTICS IN *VIENS VERS LE PERE* _____97

PART ONE _____98

The Scope and Sequence of *Viens vers le Père* _____98
    The Primary Years _____98
    The Elementary Years _____100

Three Centres of Interest in *VVLP* _____102

Methodology and Content	103
Child Psychology and Scripture	107
Profile of the Six to Seven Year Old Child	108
Six Year Olds Reading Scripture	112
Doctrine and the Reading of Scripture	116
The Primary Years	116
The Elementary Years	119
Progressive Revelation	123
PART TWO	126
The Role of Experience in *VVLP*	127
Education as Legacy	131
Education as Achievement	135
The Integrated Approach of *VVLP*	139
Conclusions	142

4. THEOLOGY AND HERMENEUTICS IN *VIENS VERS LE PERE*   148

A Situation Calling for Reform	152
VVLP: Major Theological Influences	155
Joseph Colomb	155
Marcel van Caster	162
Historico-Prophetic Catechesis	165
"Experience" in Recent Catholic Theology	167

De Lubac's *Surnaturel* _____167
Karl Rahner _____170
   Faith and Experience _____170
   Rahner's Understanding of Revelation _____174
   The Divine Presence as Manifested in Day-to-Day Life 177
   Summary _____179
Gabriel Moran _____181

Connections to the *Viens vers le Père* Series _____182
   Pedagogical Inspiration Predominates _____182

A Theological Profile of *VVLP* _____187

Interpretation Scripture in *VVLP*: Preliminary Conclusions __194

5. HERMENEUTICAL OPTIONS IN *VIENS VERS LE PERE* 200

The Concept of Revelation in *VVLP* _____202

Three Hermeneutical Approaches _____205
   VVLP and Meaning "Behind the Text" _____207
   VVLP and Meaning "In Front of the Text" _____216
   The Idea of the Subject in Ricoeur _____219
   The Consequences of the New Ontology for Hermeneutics 223
   VVLP and Meaning "In the Text" _____236

Conclusions _____253

CONCLUSIONS _____259

WORKS CITED _____268

INDEX _____286

FOREWORD

The reform of the traditional catechism took place in the 1960s—a time when the whole of Catholic life and thought were experiencing a profound renewal. The new tools of religious education issuing from that reform played a significant role in bringing the laity at large into contact with the fruits of the broader renewal. In Canada and the United States, the long-lived *Viens vers le Père—Come to the Father* Catechetical Series enjoyed great success, allowing the theology and educational praxis of European catechesis to take root in North-American soil. Robert Hurley's *Hermeneutics and Catechesis* represents the first in-depth study of this landmark series and offers a unique look at the several popular movements and individuals, at home and abroad, which gave rise to it.

Although this book provides the historian with a wealth of new information about the *Come to the Father* Series—gathered through many hours of interviews with the principals involved and a critical scrutiny of the relevant documentation—the work seeks first and foremost to provide an analysis of the use of the Bible and biblical scholarship in a popular, confessional setting. This book may be identified with a growing number of interdisciplinary works, in that it required expertise not only in the areas of exegesis and hermeneutics but also in curriculum theory and educational praxis.

One of the dangers of interdisciplinarity is that the author-researcher may shine in one field and be found wanting in the other. Happily, this is not the case here. Hurley's doctoral programme in New Testament Studies complemented his field-experience as a catechist and religious education consultant. It should not be surprising then, that this author has been able to disentangle the strands of the various disciplines underlying this catechetical series.

Educators will profit from the discussion of the major trends in curriculum theory and practice—developed between the 1930s and the 1960s—which have affected virtually all contemporary programmes of religious education. Specialists in hermeneutics and biblical scholars will be interested to discover how the fruits of biblical scholarship have been translated into a popular context. The latest theories affecting biblical hermeneutics and general hermeneutics are discussed. Theologians may be interested to see how a single theological idea such as the concept of revelation—even though it remains entirely implicit—manages to exercise tremendous influence on the shape this catechesis assumes.

In the end, the reader comes to appreciate the degree to which pedagogy, theology and biblical studies have all, each in their own way, made a turn towards the subject and to the question of reception theory over the course of this century. Showing just how parallel trends in various disciplines resemble one another is surely one of the advantages of such interdisciplinary study.

Like all good scholarship, this books raises as many questions as it answers. How should today's educators approach the question of religious education in those schools where it is still taught? The social space occupied by the churches in Quebec and Canada has shrunk and religion seems far less important to the average citizen than it did in those days when *Viens vers le Père* first appeared. While the way forward may not be obvious, *Hermeneutics and Catechesis* suggests several paths which ought to be avoided.

Gregory Baum

List of Abbreviations

ACEBAC	Assoication catholique des études bibliques au Canada
CCC	Canadian Catholic Conference (of Bishops)
CCD	Confraternity of Christian Doctrine
CTSN	*Critical Theory Since 1965.* Tallahassee, 1989.
DTF	*Dictionnaire de théologie fondamentale.* Montreal, 1992.
ISPC	Institut supérieur de pastorale catéchétique (de Paris)
LThK	*Lexikon für Theologie und Kirche.* Freiburg, 1961.
NORE	National Office of Religious Education
NT	*New Testament*
OCQ	Office de catéchèse du Québec
ONC	Office national de catéchèse
OT	*Old Testament*
SOCABI	Société catholique de la Bible
TRE	*Theologische Realenzyklopädie.* Berlin, 1988.
VVLP	The *Viens vers le Père (Come to the Father)* Catechetical Series

ACKNOWLEDGEMENTS

This book was originally written as a Ph.D. thesis (McGill University, Montreal, 1994). Like all writers of dissertations, I find myself indebted in manifold ways to mentors, family and friends. Professor Frederik Wisse, who directed the thesis, offered judicious insights and encouragement throughout the entire project. In the many warm conversations we shared, surprising similarities emerged as we reminisced about the catechesis we had received inside two radically different traditions, Reformed and Catholic. Professor Gregory Baum kindly reviewed the entire work and offered helpful suggestions for the revision of the fourth chapter which deals specifically with theological concerns. Professor Martin Jeffery, one of the authors of the *Viens vers le Père—Come to the Father* series, was invaluable as a guide in the early stages of research. Richard Topping, a doctoral candidate at St. Michael's University in Toronto, shared a paper with me which inspired the structure of the fifth chapter.

While researching this book, I had the opportunity to interview many of those directly involved with the production and evaluation of the *Viens vers le Père—Come to the Father* series. I would like to take this opportunity to thank them all for their kind cooperation, especially Françoise Bérubé, Jean-Paul Bérubé, Bishop J.-M. Coderre, Norbert Fournier, Julien Harvey, Philip Hoyoux, Jacques Laforest, Gilles Raymond and Jean-Paul Tremblay.

Many thanks to my friend Todd Blayone, who provided much-needed help in the preparation of a camera-ready version of *Hermeneutics and Catechesis*.

Funding for the publication of this book was provided by a grant from the *Fonds Gérard-Dion* at Laval University in Quebec City.

I also wish to express my appreciation to the Sisters of Mercy in Newfoundland. It was in large part thanks to the award of a scholarship established by this congregation (the *Sesquicentennial Doctoral Scholarship*: $32,000.00) that I was able to pursue the studies which led to the production of this book. The Sisters, several of whom were my school teachers, have done much more than simply offer financial support for my education.

Finally I thank my family: my mother, Regina, for her unwavering support; my children Jacques, Marie-Chantal and Oliver for their patience with a dad who was too often buried in books, and above all, my spouse, Chantal Tanguay, for her patience, her joy and her love. It is to her that I dedicate this book.

INTRODUCTION

> Of no profit to me will be the ends of the world and the kingdoms of this age; it is "better for me to die" to Jesus Christ than to rule the ends of the earth. I seek him who died on our behalf; I want him who arose for our sake. The pains of birth are upon me. Indulge me, brothers: do not prevent me from living, do not want my death, do not give to the world one who wants to be God's, nor deceive him with matter; let me receive pure light—when I am there, I shall be a human being....For I write to you (fully) alive, longing to die. My longing has been crucified, and there is no matter-loving fire within me. There is water living and speaking in me, saying from within me, "Come to the Father."[1]
>
> Ignatius of Antioch

Spanning the globe and an abyss of time, centuries wide, these words of Ignatius became the signature of the *Viens vers le Père (Come to the Father)*[2] catechetical series. Grade One of the six-grade series derives its title from the enthusiastic words of the second-century martyr and later, the entire series became popularly known under this name.[3] The last sentence of this excerpt stands in the origi-

---

[1]. Excerpts from Chapters 6 and 7 of Ignatius' "Letter to the Romans." Translation from William Schoedel's *Ignatius of Antioch: A Commentary on the Letters of Ignatius of Antioch*, ed. Helmut Koester, Hermeneia Series (Philadelphia: Fortress Press, 1985), 181-182. In his commentary on these and adjacent verses, Schoedel notes the Gnostic flavour of the oppositions between, on the one hand, world, matter and corruption and, on the other hand, pure light and true human being. Hints of Gnostic influence also appear in the general notion of a total rejection of the material world: To live in this world is death, and to die "to" Christ is birth.

[2]. In English translation, this catechism became known as the *Come to the Father* series. In deference to the French origins and inspiration of these resources, we retain the original title, *Viens vers le Père*, throughout most of the book. Considerable detail regarding the composition and evolution of this catechism for 6-12 year olds will be provided in Chapter 2.

[3]. When the Grade One portion of the programme (as distinct from the series as a whole) is referred to, our text will indicate it. As we will see be-

nal French version of the Grade One Pupil's Text, where it serves as both inspiration for and summary of its catechesis. In a manner reminiscent of the liturgical use of psalmody, the redactors respond to the words of the saint, embracing them as an expression of their own intentions: "Faire écho à cet appel que l'Esprit murmure au coeur de tout enfant baptisé, tel est l'unique but de ce petit livre."[4] Theological elements discernible in this passage (and elsewhere in the extant writings of Ignatius), find an echo in the leading intuitions of the concept of revelation underpinning the *Viens vers le Père* series; a concept which we will demonstrate, fundamentally shapes its praxis of biblical interpretation.[5] In the pages which follow, I will attempt to elucidate the biblical hermeneutic underpinning the 1960s catechetical series, known variously as *Initiation chrétienne, Catéchisme canadien* and the *Viens vers le Père* series.

The inchoate Trinitarianism suggested in Ignatius' *Letter to the Romans* depicts the Christian message as an invitation to humanity to share the inner life of God.[6] The catechesis proposed in Grade One, *Viens vers le Père*, explains its overall objective in similar terms: to help children "enter into a personal relationship with the triune God, by initiating them into the fundamental movement of Christian life."[7] This ancient epistle, rife with the flavour of a world-negating Gnosticism, may be understood to recommend social and political acquiescence. Ignatius was not trying to change the world in which he found himself, but rather to change himself and ultimately to escape the

---

low, the official French nomenclature of the series changed as the intended audience of the catechism grew.

[4]. OCQ—Équipe, *Viens vers le Père: Initiation chrétienne des enfants de 6-7 ans, Livre de l'enfant* (Montreal: Fides, 1964), 3.

[5]. A particular idea of revelation is implicit in the writing team's response to these prophetic utterances. The Spirit murmurs "to the hearts of baptized children." This choice of vocabulary leaves the impression that only the baptized can hear the call of the Spirit. The writing team's reception of the words of Ignatius points to an extrinsicist idea of revelation (see Chapter Four below) which remains consistent throughout the series.

[6]. Schoedel contends that the "water" in this passage is especially reminiscent of the living water in John (4:10 & 7:38) and is apparently to be identified with the Spirit. Schoedel, 185.

[7]. Collaboration: OCQ—NORE, *Come to the Father: Teacher's Manual—Grade One* (Toronto: Paulist Press, 1966), 9.

world. The *Viens vers le Père* series cannot be said to counsel a flight from the world. In contrast to Ignatius' pessimistic world view, this series exudes the optimism which was so typical of the liberal North American scene in the 1960s. The social and economic ills which plague developed societies, while referred to occasionally in this catechesis, are kept on the periphery as the reader is presented a generally optimistic view of the state of human affairs. All but absent from this series is the idea that sinfulness may be systemic in our social and political institutions and that such sinfulness might be adversely affecting the lives of its audience. One is left with the impression that all that is required for the world to improve is the personal transformation of individuals. Jean-Henri Dunant, founder of the Red Cross, numbers among the inspired individuals held up as personal models for the children to imitate.

If the "things of God" and the corrupt world appear mutually exclusive in Ignatius, the *Viens vers le Père* series imagines a world of boundless possibility. Despite such radically different attitudes towards the world, the *Viens vers le Père* series shares with Ignatius an understanding that the Christian message intends primarily the spiritual transformation of men, women and children by inviting them to enter into a relationship with God. Ancient and modern, these texts present revelation first and foremost as a story about God's relationship to human persons. What revelation has to say about life-in-the-world is a second-order affair. Our study will attempt to demonstrate that the theological concept of revelation underpinning this series plays a central role in its hermeneutical agenda.

A NEW CATECHISM: MIXED REACTIONS

There were those who decried the new Quebecois catechisms of the 1960s and 1970s as the "Gospel of Satan" and proof that the clergy had been infiltrated by communists.[8] In addition to these assaults from the fringe, a more serious challenge was mounted from within Quebec's episcopate. Despite its critics, the *Viens vers le Père* series was

---

[8]. For an entertaining account of the attacks on the new catechisms by fringe elements see: Jean-Louis d'Aragon, "Marx ou Satan?", *Relations*, 385 (September 1973): 252.

hailed by most as a great step forward for catechesis in the 20th century. Its methods and goals represented a major change in catechetics and its publication registered a profound change in the way the Church in Quebec understood its relationship to the world in which it lived. Other than the articles which appeared in catechetical and theological journals around the time of its publication, no major study of this important publishing effort has been undertaken. Its history has not been mapped, its methodology has been given no in-depth analysis.

Viens vers le Père introduced (or reintroduced after centuries of absence) welcome new elements in its catechesis. Its pedagogy incorporated the major insights which curriculum theorists had developed in the first half of the 20th century. In stark contrast to its long line of predecessors, this catechism attempted to address the whole child and not simply his/her intellectual capacities. *Viens vers le Père* reflects a balanced understanding of the psycho-social characteristics of young children informed by the behavioural sciences. This grounding in the behavioural sciences set the series apart from its predecessors on the North American continent and elsewhere.

As it moved beyond the purely cognitive aims of notionally-abstract catechisms, *Viens vers le Père* set for itself an ultimate goal which lay in the realm of the spiritual. The catechesis of this series intended to do more than simply fill a child's head with correct doctrinal formulæ. Its writers sought nothing less than the spiritual conversion or formation of the child. In this sense, one might describe the overall intent of the series as pastoral. They were well aware that faith, as such, cannot be taught and that the family and parish play a key role in the catechetical process.[9] The authors clearly understood faith to be a free gift which God alone can bestow as God sees fit. *Viens vers le Père* was an attempt to communicate the contents of the Christian faith in terms which 6-12 year olds are capable of understanding. It offered a faith-witness to the children it addressed and tried to remove the intellectual and psychological obstacles which might block a response to God's offer of faith.

The theological climate in Quebec immediately prior to the publi-

---

[9]. The new religious education programmes which have replaced the *Veins vers le Père* series in Quebec define their overall objectives in educational rather than in pastoral terms.

cation of *Viens vers le Père* was resistant to change and suspicious of subjectivism. Given this context, the move which the *Viens vers le Père* series made in the direction of the human subject was significant. This series introduced the audience as an important element in its catechetical discourse. In catechisms inspired by Neo-Thomism, the same content was delivered to all audiences with the same teacher-centred model of pedagogy. By shifting the focus of catechetical activity to a consideration of the psychological requirements of the student, the *Viens vers le Père* series shows signs of being caught up in that broad-ranging concern for the human subject which has characterized intellectual life throughout the 20th century.

From the time the redactors of this series first took up their pens a great deal of scholarly reflection has been devoted to the question of the foundations of human language. As a consequence of this research, the capacity of human language to express true and accurate ideas about reality has been thrown radically into doubt, and even the foundations of the idea of the human subject have been shaken. The critical evaluation which follows, evaluates this series in the light of scholarship not-yet available (or not yet in wide circulation) at its time of publication and as a consequence may seem at times harsh. Clearly, in its day, this catechism occasioned a great deal of justified excitement, breaking much new ground and implementing many improvements to catechesis. If we are to learn from its example, however, we must describe *both* its strengths *and* its weaknesses.

An international catechetical movement gave rise to this series and others like it, and permanently changed the face of modern catechetics. Hence, a contemporary discussion of catechesis involves at least three disciplines—educational theory (informed by the behavioural sciences), theology and biblical interpretation. While *Viens vers le Père*'s main contribution appears to have been its adaptation of the findings of educational psychology to the needs of religious education, it also adapts significant theological insights for catechetical use. Although we will also have occasion to discuss other aspects of the *Viens vers le Père* series in the course of our work, they will be developed with the ultimate goal of throwing light on the series' approach to interpreting the Bible.

THE PROBLEM DESCRIBED

An underlying assumption of our research is that readings of the Bible which do not bracket questions of faith are guided by theological options which condition the scope and results of their interpretations. For theologically-interested readings of the Bible, the operative notions of christology and revelation as well as the interpreter's perception of the relationship between divine message and human situation ineluctably influence interpretative choices. Agreeing with Norbert Lohfink, René Marlé contends that the whole problem of the Christian interpretation of the Bible turns on the identity and mission of Jesus Christ.

> Le problème biblique, pris dans sa totalité...renvoie ainsi directement au problème christologique: Qui est Jésus-Christ, qui "accomplit" le dessein de Dieu manifesté dans l'Écriture, dans lequel, et dans lequel seul, cette Écriture trouve son sens dernier, dans le mystère duquel uniquement elle peut être "comprise"?[10]

Methods of interpretation which understand the meaning of a text to be primarily related to the circumstances of its production have dominated the field of biblical criticism since its inception. Any question of establishing the supernatural aspects of the origins, identity or mission of Jesus Christ as truth claims are ruled out in a critical, historical research model. Other approaches to the biblical text, which are not centred on the historical, have begun to exert considerable influence in critical circles today. What began with historical questions about the literary forms, genres and structures of the Bible's literature, has grown into a wide range of methodologies which are distinct from historical scholarship. In recent decades, methods developed for the study of secular literature have been applied to the study of the Bible.

Even as the variety of approaches to biblical interpretation has proliferated, especially since World War II, most critical reading remains confined to what one might call "hermeneutical laboratories." Critics study the Bible in academic settings, employing methodologies which, to the degree humanly possible, attempt to overcome the subjective influences in the reading process. In North America, the paradigm of the natural sciences has often provided the scale against which

---

[10]. René Marlé, *Herméneutique et catéchèse* (Paris: Fayard-Mame, 1970), 74.

biblical studies has gauged its procedures and products. Of late, a new perspective has emerged in the field of literary studies which influences the core concept of biblical criticism and focuses on today's reader. Scholars who champion this new emphasis agree with historical critics that it is impossible to entirely remove subjective influences from the reading process.

New approaches attend to the subjective factors which influence the way in which a given audience or individual reader receives the biblical text. Many scholars of all persuasions have become aware of the ways in which theological, philosophical and ideological presuppositions shape their interpretations of Scripture. This thorough investigation of the act of reading has given rise to the development of a discipline which in its original German setting is called *Rezeptionstheorie*. This term has been variously rendered in English as *Reception Theory*, *Reception Aesthetics* or *Reader Response Theory*. Whatever the nomenclature, Nigel Watson proffers a definition for this new discipline; it is "the rigorous study of the act of communication from the standpoint of both author and recipient."[11]

This new discipline allow scholars to focus on the ways in which those outside the guild of professional critics take up the task of reading the Scriptures. To date, meta-critics working in this field have applied more energy to deconstructing the work of their colleagues than to examining readings done outside the academy.[12] While not deriving its methodology from any of the established branches of Reception Theory, the plan and scope of our inquiry constitutes an exercise in meta-criticism in that it offers an interpretation of the hermeneutic underlying the *Viens vers le Père* series.[13]

The Bible continues to be read most frequently in the setting of or-

---

[11]. Nigel Watson, "Reception Theory and Biblical Exegesis," *Australian Biblical Review* 36 (1988): 49.

[12]. A salient example may be found in the work of Mieke Bal, *Lethal Love* (Bloomington: Indiana University Press, 1985). See also Robert M. Fowler, *Loaves and Fishes* (Chico: Scholars Press, 1981). Fowler, however, does report on empirically-based models of reader-response criticism.

[13]. For a discussion of the origins, goals and applications of Reception Theory see Gilles Routhier, *La réception d'un concile* (Paris: Les éditions du Cerf, 1993), Chapters 1 and 3. Routhier provides an extensive bibliography, 243-261.

ganized religion. Scripture reading in Churches, synagogues, confessional schools, Bible-study groups and the like, rarely, if ever, have the luxury of attending to exegetical concerns of the philological, historical or literary variety. In communities for which the Bible functions as Sacred Scripture the question of the pertinence of the text to the lives of contemporary people stands front and centre. Theirs is not an antiquarian interest in texts from the first century of the common era. Moreover, in the pulpit and in the catechetical classroom, exegetical concerns must be reconciled with the demands of pedagogy and theology. The list of disciplines vying for a place on the catechetical agenda does not end there. Today, social and political analyses assert their indispensability for religious and ethical reflexion.

To investigate the biblical hermeneutic at work in a contemporary catechism will mean to investigate the interaction and overlap of the disciplines which nourish its catechesis. In order to isolate hermeneutical choices, one must be able to identify and trace the provenance of the various strands which combine to produce a modern religious education programme. We have already mentioned the influence which theological concepts exert in the process of interpretation. Educational principles underlying a catechesis prove no less crucial for the role they play in shaping the reading process. One must try to determine what in the course of a lesson corresponds to a demand of educational psychology, what to a demand of theology and finally what to a requirement of hermeneutics. Below, Chapters 3, 4 and 5 will attempt to throw light on these questions respectively.

A CLARIFICATION OF TERMS

Biblical critics have traditionally associated hermeneutics with the tasks of preaching and catechesis. The notion was widely accepted that exegesis was the business of the academy. Objective and scientific, exegesis establishes the facts, i.e., what was written. Subjective and intellectually-interested, hermeneutics determines what the text means for today's reader. A generation or two ago, hermeneutics, described as the "science" of theoretical reflections on meaning, was divided into three areas: 1) noematics, which dealt with the various senses of scripture, 2) heuristics, which explained how to discover the sense of a passage and 3) prophoristics, which offered rules for communicating the sense of a scriptural passage to others.[14]

In recent decades, voices have begun to question whether the task of interpretation is finished once the exegete has established the "facts." Scholars such as Ricoeur maintain that interpretation is incomplete unless it includes both objective and subjective elements. The ancient senses of *hermēneia*, the original Greek term from which "hermeneutics" is derived, offer no help in resolving questions about disciplinary boundaries separating hermeneutics from exegesis, since it includes at once the notions of explaining, interpreting, proclaiming, discoursing on and translating.[15] The field of general or philosophical hermeneutics has recovered a sense of *hermēneia* which had disappeared from view for centuries. Raymond Brown, with an admirable economy of words, describes this sense, once implicit in the ancient Greek term and now revived:

> ...it can refer to interpretation by *speech* itself, inasmuch as language brings to expression and interprets what is in one's mind (conscious and unconscious), or even what constitutes one's identity, being, person. (We should conceive of this process dynamically, not statically; for not only does an established intention or identity find precise expression in language, but in the very act of linguistic communication one's identity and intention can grow or even come into being.)[16]

These reflections suggest that the process of interpretation cannot be complete with an objectivizing, historical methodology. The intellect of the interpreter, his/her judgment and personality are necessarily called into play in the act of interpretation.[17]

---

[14]. Raymond E. Brown with Sandra M. Schneiders, "Hermeneutics," *The New Jerome Biblical Commentary* (London: Geoffrey Chapman, 1990), 1146. Brown notes that these distinctions, having been found unwieldy and overspeculative, are rarely used today.

[15]. Walter Bauer, (Wm. Arndt, F. Wilbur Gingrich) *A Greek-English Lexicon of the New Testament and Other Early Christian Literature* (Chicago: University of Chicago Press, 1979), 310.

[16]. Brown, 1146. Other modern uses Brown attributes to *hermēneia* are 1) to translate from one language to another and, 2) to offer interpretation by formal commentary or explanation.

[17]. Marlé, *Herméneutique*, 67. On the role of subjectivity in biblical interpretation, Bultmann rightly emphasized that a true encounter with Jesus implies an engagement of one's subjectivity, an engagement of one's whole

Considered broadly, hermeneutics refers to a general orientation of research, characterized by a preoccupation to establish the meaning or truth about any object.[18] As a theory of interpretation, hermeneutics is better thought of as an *ars interpretandi* than as a science. It requires the use of judgment and a weighing of possibilities and implies much more than the mechanical application of various sets of rules. The problem at the heart of hermeneutics crosses disciplines and finds applications in the study of literature (both religious and secular), theology, philosophy, psychology, linguistics and sociology. In the context of this research , the branch of hermeneutics which holds our attention will be the interpretation of written texts, especially religious texts.

READING THE BIBLE IN THE CATHOLIC TRADITION

Wittingly or unwittingly, religious communities create and uphold traditions. Nowhere perhaps is this clearer than in catechesis, the means by which communities hand on their beliefs to a new generation. In the case of Catholicism, *Tradition* is understood not simply as a reliable guide but also as an authority in matters of faith.[19] With other Christians, the Catholic community holds that the Word of God constitutes the norm of Christian faith. For Catholics, the Word of God is understood to have been expressed historically in two important instances, in the Bible and in the Church's faith tradition. While the biblical witness to Jesus has priority over the Church's tradition of faith, the latter also remains authoritative in the Catholic community.[20] That the Bible possesses such priority in the norms of faith may not have been evident to an observer of the Roman Catholic Church when Neo-Scholasticism was its dominant theology. It is not surprising then,

---

self in faith, lest the encounter lead to unbelief. Marlé concurs: *Herméneutique*, 59.

[18]. Marlé, *Herméneutique*, 10.

[19]. By Tradition, one understands principally the biblical witness, the articles of the Creed(s), the statements of ecumenical councils and excathedral pronouncements.

[20]. For a brief but lucid presentation of the concept of Tradition in Catholic thought see Hermann J. Pottmeyer, "Tradition," *Dictionnaire de théologie fondamentale*, under the direction of René Latourelle and Rino Fisichella (Montreal: Bellaramin, 1992): 1429-1437. (Hereafter: *DTF*).

INTRODUCTION 11

that catechisms inspired by neo-scholastic theology gave only a minor role to the use of the Scriptures.

The *Viens vers le Père* series represents the first serious attempt by the Catholic community in Quebec and Canada to develop a catechesis which incorporates the witness of the Scriptures as something more than proof texts in support of doctrinal abstractions. Consonant with the Catholic ethos, the Bible is read in the *Viens vers le Père* series in the light of the Church's faith tradition. The Scriptures are understood against the backdrop of a rich Patristic heritage, the Creed(s), the pronouncements of ecumenical councils and that most rare instance of authoritative tradition, the excathedral statement. *Viens vers le Père*'s reading of the Scriptures respects this long history of the Church's faith tradition and shows itself to be in agreement with the important interpretations of Scripture which characterize that Tradition.

One of the dangers inherent in an institution which values tradition is that it might value it too highly. The risk is that the past might impose a virtual tyranny and paralysis on the present. The Reformation aside, the history of the Catholic Church has witnessed time and again a push to reform, often inspired by (those later recognized as) its greatest saints. In the case of the Church's doctrinal heritage, the danger persists that an exaggerated respect for the particular formulations of dogma might lead to a lack of respect for persons.[21]

Historically, the Church has formulated the meaning of the Scriptures in different ways. The Church's reading of the Bible has been adapted so as to keep its preaching and teaching of the biblical message vital and actual for successive generations. The acceptance of the methods of biblical criticism in the Catholic community has had the effect of highlighting a development in the Church's hermeneutical methods. By contrast, a sense of permanence and immutability seems to have settled upon the Church's formulations of doctrine. Because of the interplay of doctrine and Scripture in this series, the role *Viens vers le Père* assigns to doctrine will affect its biblical hermeneutic.

Many theologians hold that treating dogmatic formulations as immutable is doing the Church a disservice by making them more an obstacle than an aid to faith. Writing several years ago, René Marlé posed the danger as a tension between an active, searching faith and a

---

[21]. In the ecumenical dialogue, an intransigence regarding the particular wording of given beliefs has proved at times to be a stumbling block.

problematic expression of that faith's content:

> N'y a-t-il pas opposition irréductible entre le dogme, qui définit, établit, "fixe" de manière définitive l'objet de la foi, et la préoccupation herméneutique qui part de la conviction que cet objet est le lieu d'une interrogation, et que sons sens ne peut pas se dévoiler en dehors d'une recherche active du sujet qui s'y intéresse?[22]

Marlé went on to call for an examination of the Catholic community's concept of dogma as well as the epistemological assumptions guiding its approach to dogmatic reality.

> L'importance de cette mise au point pour la catéchèse ne saurait échapper, s'il est vrai qu'une catéchèse catholique doit s'employer à transmettre la vérité révélée, non seulement en se souciant de sa réception véritable dans l'esprit et le coeur de ceux auxquels nous nous adressons, mais encore en opérant cette oeuvre de transmission dans le respect fidèle du cadre dogmatique dans lequel l'Église formule sa foi.[23]

The question of the interaction between doctrine and biblical hermeneutic in this catechetical series is crucial to understanding the latter. Is Scripture used (as in earlier catechetical programmes) in a narrowly supportive role for traditional doctrinal formulations or does it provide a new optic through which these doctrinal statements may be better integrated into life? Are Scripture and doctrine ends in themselves, or are they at the service of a larger process of evangelization and catechesis? Does catechesis intend primarily to throw light on the doctrinal tradition of the Church or does it intend primarily to elucidate the lives of those it addresses? In either scenario, i.e., in either a content-centred catechesis (intended to elucidate tradition) or a person-centred catechesis (intended to elucidate life), an explanation of doctrine takes place. Content-centred catechesis relies on a strategy of transmission while person-centred catechesis is a process best understood on the model of the conversation. Person-centred catechesis intends to bring the doctrinal tradition of the Church into conversation with the life experiences[24] of the listener. Catechesis in this sense is a

---

[22]. Marlé, *Herméneutique*, 109.
[23]. Marlé, *Herméneutique*, 110.
[24]. Or in gadamerian terms, "with the pre-understandings and prejudices of the listener."

hermeneutical endeavour and the conversation it engenders should allow for both a hermeneutics of suspicion and a hermeneutics of retrieval, for the use of both explanatory methods and understanding. Since doctrine and the believer are brought together in all catechesis, the question which interests us here is the character of that encounter.

THE PLAN OF THE BOOK

Of the book's five chapters, the first two present an historical analysis which helps clarify the form and content of the *Viens vers le Père* series. The third and fourth chapters, respectively, assess the pedagogical and theological influences on the programme's biblical hermeneutic. The fifth and final chapter, presents three contemporary hermeneutical strategies which serve as an interpretative grid in our evaluation of this series.

Chapter One has three goals: 1) to introduce the catechisms and catechesis in use immediately prior to the catechetical renewal and the publication of the *Viens vers le Père* series; 2) to highlight the antecedents in the history of catechesis of the "new" elements which characterize this programme: liturgical emphasis, biblical foundation, existential reference; 3) to situate *Viens vers le Père* in those larger theological and pastoral movements within the Church which gave rise to the ecclesial reforms of Vatican Council II.

Chapter Two tells the story of the *Viens vers le Père* series, tracing its inspiration to the European catechetical renewal of the first half of the 20th century. Of particular interest in this regard is the influence exerted on the North American scene by the catechetical movements in France and Belgium beginning in the 1950s.

Even a cursory treatment of the background of this series reveals that the principal influences which preoccupied its redactors were educational psychology, theology and biblical interpretation. The writing teams borrowed elements from these disciplines which would allow them to communicate the vital character of the Christian tradition to the children who were the intended audience of their catechism. It is our hope that an investigation of the background of the *Viens vers le Père* series will yield insights into the relative weight one ought to assign the various disciplines which influenced its catechesis. While one might profitably consider this series from other angles—from a sociological perspective, for example—the present study will limit its investigation to the three disciplines suggested by the series itself.

Chapter Three describes *Viens vers le Père* from the perspective of curriculum theory. In Part One of the chapter, a profile of the series' pedagogy is presented which sets the series against the backdrop of the renewal in educational theory and methods. Part Two of the chapter, evaluates *Viens vers le Père* using "heritage " and "achievement" models of education as reference points. It is our contention that by distinguishing those elements in this programme which originate in educational theory and practice, we will be better able to isolate and identify its hermeneutical options.

Chapter Four examines this series within the context of 20th century Catholic theology. Given that the catechetics of Joseph Colomb inspired much of the renewal in France and directly influenced the education of several members of the writing teams, his writings will be of particular interest to our study. The concept of revelation is central to any theologically-interested reading of the Bible. In Catholic circles, few theological concepts have received more attention in recent decades. The concepts of nature and grace have figured prominently in discussions of the idea of revelation; both are discussed in Chapter Four using the work of Henri de Lubac and Karl Rahner as reference points.

Finally, Chapter Five relates the contents of the *Viens vers le Père* catechism to three fundamental options within biblical and general hermeneutics today. In briefest terms, one may speak of meaning as construable in one of three loci: "behind the text," "in front of the text" and "in the text itself." Elements of each of these options are evident in this series and we attempt to weigh the influence of each in light of the pedagogical and theological options outlined in earlier chapters.

To examine the texts of *Viens vers le Père* through the optics of educational theory, theology and hermeneutics forms the basis of our methodology—a methodology which has as its ultimate goal the elucidation of the biblical hermeneutic at work in the *Viens vers le Père* series. We turn now to that task.

Chapter 1

THE CATECHETICAL HERITAGE OF *VIENS VERS LE PÈRE*

In matters ecclesial, a grasp of present realities inevitably demands that one situate the subject matter in the long and varied history of the Church. The physiognomy of catechesis in the first half of this century still bore the battle scars incurred in the polemics of the Reformation period. To gain even a rudimentary appreciation of the debates of that era, however, a few remarks about catechesis in the Middle Ages are required.

THE MIDDLE AGES

After the collapse of the catechumenate in the 6th century, catechesis became a summary and an explanation of the Christian religion for baptized adults.[1] Formal catechesis was *rare* in the Middle Ages and what there was of it, was communicated orally, using formulas and other mnemonic devices. From the seventh to the thirteenth centuries, catechesis remained a dominical activity at which Church-goers heard explanations of the Creed and prayers such as the Our Father and received instruction regarding the principal duties of the Christian.[2] Points of doctrine and morality were gathered in groups of 7, 10 or 12 and memorized: 7 deadly sins; 7 petitions of the Lord's prayer; 7 gifts of the Holy Spirit; 7 works of mercy; 7 beatitudes; 7 sacraments; 10 commandments of God; 12 articles of the Creed, and more.[3] The *historical-liturgical* orientation of the Patristic era all but disappeared, leaving the quotidian, communal and ritual Christian experience shrouded in ignorance and neglect. Instruction became more standard-

---

1. Joseph Colomb, *Le Service de l'Evangile*, I (Paris: Desclée, 1968), 34.
2. Colomb, *Service*, 34.
3. G. Emmett Carter, *The Modern Challenge to Religious Education* (New York: Sadlier, 1961), 58.

ized with the appearance of manuals, which in this early stage of development, were intended as guides for the catechist rather than as texts for those seeking instruction.[4]

Towards the end of the Middle Ages, a gradual decline in preaching and catechesis was accompanied by a preoccupation in daily life with religious matters and a penchant for translating thought into images.[5] Every act of life was related to a belief in Christ and to one's salvation. J. Huizinga describes the spirit and thought of the late Middle Ages thus:

> All thinking tends to religious interpretation of individual things; there is an enormous unfolding of religion in daily life. This spiritual wakefulness, however, results in a dangerous state of tension, for the presupposed transcendental feelings are sometimes dormant, and whenever this is the case, all that is meant to stimulate spiritual consciousness is reduced to appalling commonplace profanity, to a startling worldliness in other-worldly guise....
>
> The spirit of the Middle Ages, still plastic and naive, longs to give concrete shape to every conception. Every thought seeks expression in an image, but in this image it solidifies and becomes rigid. By this tendency to embodiment in visible forms, all holy concepts are constantly exposed to the danger of hardening into mere externalism. For in assuming a definite figurative shape thought loses its ethereal and vague qualities, and pious feeling is apt to resolve itself in the image.[6]

This was the age of indulgences sought through good works—pilgrimages, eucharistic processions, Benedictions[7], veneration of relics and all manner of pious practices. In the post-Constantinian era, the shift in the position of the Church vis-à-vis the larger society had already contributed to a decline of preaching and teaching.[8] In the early Church, the decision to become a Christian was both personal and voluntary and implied a counter-cultural stance in the face of a pagan society. For medieval Christians, on the other hand, one entered

---

4. C. E. Roy, *L'organization catéchétique* (Paris: Casterman, 1938), 52ff.
5. Johan Huizinga, *The Waning of the Middle Ages* (Garden City, N.Y.: Doubleday Anchor, 1954), 151.
6. Huizinga, *Waning*, 151–152.
7. Benediction is a religious service at which the consecrated host is adored and prayers of intercession offered. It is rarely seen today.
8. Colomb, *Service*, 35.

the Church and society at the same moment, at birth. Baptism became not only the sacrament of admission into the believing community but served also as initiation into the political structures of society. Hence, the liturgy and Christian life, which appeared to need substantial explanation in Patristic times, now appeared self-evident in the enveloping Christendom. The role played earlier by the catechumenate fell now to the Christian environment, the principal agent of which was the family.[9] The medieval family, however, given the paucity of catechetical instruction, was ill-equipped to assume this role and the situation which ensued was one of ignorance compounded by a distance from the essential sources of the Christian life, the liturgy and the Bible.

Theology too took a new path during the Middle Ages; a move which may have contributed to the decline of "life-centred" catechesis and preaching. R. M. Grant chronicles the change.[10] For the Church Fathers, theology consisted largely in commentary on the text of Scripture. Teachers often wrote their biblical commentary as interlinear annotation or as marginalia. With time, theological questions were added. Eventually, the marginalia proved so cumbersome that theological questions began to circulate on separate sheets. Professors no longer relied principally on the biblical text for lecture material, preferring to allow theological questions to preponderate. With the rediscovery of ancient Greek philosophy, the move away from theology as commentary on the meaning of Scripture and toward a philosophically-inspired consideration of Christian doctrine established itself. In retrospect, it is hardly surprising that life-centred preaching and catechesis declined, as theological teaching became more immediately interested in relating the Gospel to Aristotle and Plato than to the average illiterate, lost somewhere in the nave of the Church.

PROTESTANT REFORMATION

The intent of Luther and Calvin was to return to "theology by exegesis," a direct rejection of medieval trends which had grown so conversant with philosophy.[11] The catechumenate, hymnology and

---

9. Colomb, *Service*, 35.
10. Robert M. Grant and David Tracy, *A Short History of the Interpretation of the Bible*, edition no. 2 (Philadelphia: Fortress Press, 1984), 83–84.
11. See Grant and Tracy, Chapter 10.

preaching were the three practical means adopted to carry the message of the Reformers into the lives of their followers.[12] In 1521, Calvin published a catechetical manual in Geneva, intended for children and employing a question and answer format. Luther followed with a Small and Large Catechism in 1529, texts which survive in use in many parts of the Lutheran Church in the 1990s. Christians today are apt to conceive of catechesis as a puerile activity limited to prescribed curricula and closely associated with the use of text books. The modern tendency to reduce the loci and scope of catechesis by identifying it exclusively with the use of catechisms dates from this period.[13]

Luther's texts, which enjoyed wide circulation in Lutheran parishes, were less intellectually rigorous than the earlier Roman Catholic teacher manuals. His manuals were meant to be used directly by children and adults, rather than as guides for catechists. With regard to both their method and content, these books were very similar to existing Catholic manuals. Like their predecessors they explained the Apostles' Creed, the Lord's Prayer, the Ten Commandments, Baptism and the Eucharist.[14] Luther and Calvin produced the first popular manuals of catechesis with content adapted to children. Developing appropriate methods for teaching children, however, fell beyond the possibilities of 16th century pedagogy.

CATHOLIC REFORMATION

The Jesuit, Peter Canisius, delivered the first serious response to the very popular catechisms of Luther and Calvin. In 1556, Canisius published his *Summa doctrinae christianae*, a homologue to Luther's Large Catechism, intended for use in the universities and higher levels of education. He followed this extensive work with the *Catechismus minimus*, a counterpart to Luther's *Little Catechism*, aimed at children and uneducated adults. Finally, in 1558 he published *Catechismus minor seu Parvus Catechismus catholicorum*, an intermediate text for

---

12. Pierre Lestringant, *Le ministère catéchétique de l'Église* (Paris: Éditions «Je sers», 1945), 51.
13. Carter, 61.
14. Hans-Jürgen Fraas, "Katechismus: I. protestantische Kirche I/1 Historisch (bis 1945)," *Theologische Realenzyklopädie*, XVII, ed. Gerhard Müller (Berlin: Walter de Gruyter, 1988), 713. (Hereafter cited as *TRE*.)

use in German schools.[15] This text was translated for use throughout Europe and dominated some areas for nearly two hundred years.

It is worth noting that, Canisius' catechism was nourished by the Scriptures and writings of the Patristic era. It contained some 2000 citations from the Bible as well as 1200 from the Church Fathers.[16] While Canisius was concerned to offer a corrective to the catechisms of Luther, he did not become so preoccupied by the Reformers as to let his work become a stilted or truncated presentation of the faith.

The next work, aimed at reforming the catechetical ministry within the Roman Catholic Church, was published in 1566 in response to a decree of the Council of Trent. The *Catechismus Romanus*, as it came to be called, was intended for use as a source book for those whose responsibility it was to explain the Christian faith. Its catechesis was christocentric.[17] The writers of this catechism were explicit in their wish that the contents of their work be adapted to the age, education, intelligence, mores and general living conditions of each particular audience.[18] Described as a guide for preachers, the catechism issuing from the Council of Trent referred frequently to the Scriptures, retaining an interpretation that was both authoritative and traditional. This biblical focus faded as the tenor of the Catholic Reformation slipped into the acrimony of the Counter Reformation.

THE COUNTER REFORMATION

In the decades following the Council of Trent, the face of Catholic efforts in popular religious education changed considerably. The catechetical enterprise would not remain the exclusive province of parish priest and parent. Increasingly, this educative task was being handed over to lay people, school teachers and the several new religious congregations of brothers and sisters, formed especially with the religious instruction of children in mind.[19] Adult instruction was given new attention as well, as catechetical classes targeting a mature audience proliferated.

The upshot of these developments was the proliferation of

---

15. Gerhard J. Bellinger, "Katechismus II: römisch-katholische Kirche," *TRE:* XVII, 730.
16. Colomb, *Service*, 37, note 1.
17. Colomb, *Service*, 38.
18. Colomb, *Service*, 38.
19. Colomb, *Service*, 39.

catechetical manuals. In Italy, Robert Bellarmine published two manuals: his *Dottrina cristiana breve* (small catechism) in 1597 and his *Dichiarazione più copiosa* (large catechism) in 1598.[20] These manuals, in which instruction took the form of question and answer, achieved considerable theological clarity and precision. While the catechetical task might have managed just as well with far less abstraction and rigor, the deepening rift between Catholic and Protestant ignited a zeal for eradicating—what the forces of the Counter Reformation considered—heretical thought. Such an environment did not foster a balanced and well-rounded treatment of faith concerns. The excesses and omissions which this period spawned continued to plague catechetical efforts well into the 20th century. The relegation of the Bible to a secondary role in the catechetical task was one such regrettable outcome of this polemical pedagogy. The passion for theological correctness—which dates from the age of catechisms—also had the lamentable consequence of the abandonment of a principle which had been known in catechesis since the days of Augustine's *De catechizandis rudibus*, viz., instruction in the faith ought to accommodate the audience's age, education, intelligence and general circumstances of life. The new manuals, obsessed as they were with accuracy of expression, with "truth," flattened the catechumenate. Now old and young, educated and ignorant would adhere to the *unerring* formulations of the manuals. Before long, these manuals had worked their effect and the truth about the matters they contained became more or less reduced to the terse formulations contained within their pages.

The antagonisms entrenched in ecclesial relations from the 16th century on, presupposed that occidental society was and ought to be Christian in character. The real arguments between the parties revolved around orthodoxy and the authority to determine such. As the decades went by, social changes would alter these assumptions irrevocably. This was nowhere truer than in France. Enlightenment and Revolution had lead people to organize outside the auspices of the Church. By the early decades of the 20th century, the seeds of secularization, planted centuries earlier, were to suffocate Christendom, as the Church assumed a humbler position vis-à-vis the larger society. In the wake of social and political revolutions, catechesis stood essentially unchanged and could remain so, largely because its conception was a-historical. The content it intended to transmit was "unchanging" and

---

20. Bellinger, 730.

"immutable"; it intended to transmit the truth about God. There were some notable exceptions to this monolithic vision, but these catechisms never enjoyed international circulation and by the turn of the 20th century they had all but disappeared.[21]

THE 20th CENTURY

By the beginning of the 20th century, several traits might be considered typical of the catechetical scene throughout most of the Catholic world.[22] Outside Sunday preaching, adult catechesis was practically non-existent. Catechesis was considered a childhood activity, identified with catechetical manuals which followed a question and answer format. The work of the catechist most often consisted in an explanation of the catechism's answers to its own questions. Catechisms had evolved into doctrinal summaries that were replete with abstractions, far beyond the psychological capacities of children in primary and elementary grades. These texts, tending towards rationalism and legalism, were often tainted with anti-Protestant polemics. The catechetical

---

21. Of note here are: the catechism of Bishop Harlay (1687) which centred on Scripture and the Church Fathers; the four catechisms of Bossuet, also from the 17th century, which re-emphasized the role of parents as the first and principal catechists of children; the method of St. Sulpice, which graded the instruction to the age level of children; the efforts of John Baptist de la Salle who modified the Sulpician method with considerable success.

22. The aims of the present study are limited to an elucidation of the *Viens vers le Père* series of catechetical resources. Thus many aspects of the larger history of catechesis in Europe and Quebec fall beyond our scope. For a thorough treatment of the history of catechesis in Quebec, the principal work of reference is Fernand Porter`s *L'institution catéchistique au Canada. Deux siècles de formation religieuse, 1633-1833* (Montréal: Les Éditions franciscaines, 1949). See also: *Une inconnue de l'histoire de la culture: la production des catéchismes en Amérique française*, ed. Raymond Brodeur, Jean-Paul Rouleau (Ste. Foy: Éditions Anne Sigier, 1986). See also: C. E. Roy, *L'Organisation catéchétique* (Paris: Casterman, 1938). For a more complete treatment of the history of the catechetical scene in France see: A. Boyer, *Un demi siècle au sein du Mouvement Catéchistique Français* (Paris: Editions de l'Ecole, 1966); Marie Fargues, *How to Teach Religion [D'hier à demain, Le Catéchisme* (1964)], trans. Sister Gertrude (Glen Rock, N.J.: Paulist Press, 1968), 5-50; Joseph Colomb, *Le Service de l'Evangile* (Paris: Desclée, 1, 1968), Chapter III; Pierre Ranwez, *Aspects contemporains de la Pastorale de l'enfance* (Paris: Les éditions du vitrail, 1950).

process was cut off from the child's family life and was most often considered the task of professionals in the field, such as priests, sisters, brothers and lay teachers. Moreover, catechesis had become estranged both from the parish and from the rhythms of the liturgical year.

The teaching methodology used at this time has been referred to as "magisterial" because it assumed an authoritative position for the catechist within the double contexts of Church and school. This method assumed that verifiable information would be taught in a didactic fashion by a competent instructor.[23] The traditional method depended almost exclusively on the memory, intellect and will of the learner. This system favoured a view of the Christian life as a life of duty; the teacher's duty was to instruct in the faith, the student's duty was to learn the truths of faith. No further motivation was considered essential in a world defined by ecclesial membership.

Catechisms of this type were essentially the same the Catholic world over. René Marlé offers an eloquent and succinct evaluation of the theology which marked these "bellarminesque" treatises. Although the analogies he chooses spring from his native France, the substance of his remarks fits almost any of the old catechisms.

> The foundation of the whole edifice was the existence of a sovereign God, who established an order of reality into which man, as a rational being, could not fail to integrate himself. Faith was presented as the submission of the mind and will to this divine order, maintained in and by the Church. The sacraments came to sustain man's efforts or to mend his weaknesses. The elements of this doctrine were admirably jointed together. Since they were all of equal importance, they formed together a perfectly coherent system....In this solid edifice there was not a single crack through which a question could pierce. Everything that could be known—for essentially it was a question of knowing— was properly located, outside the questioning and believing subject, in a kind of being in itself, an absolute objectivism.
>
> The contents consisted of ideas, representations. In this flat landscape where notions and propositions were laid out, clearly delineated, and followed one another, there quite naturally operated a quantitative, additive logic: yes, a "quantity" of things were learnt....
>
> And the beautiful order in which the religious truths were then proposed to the understanding was in many respects analogical to the one

---

23. R.M. Rummary, *Catechetics and Religious Education in a Pluralist Society* (London: Our Sunday Visitor Press, 1975), 5.

that defined the cultural universe within which it had first been elaborated: it was the order of the 17th century classical style and its neatly tailored gardens. Similarly the sovereign God of Christian doctrine still bore some resemblance to the God of rationalist theism which, since the late 18th century, he has (sic) been striving to combat. In other words, the ideas brought into play in catechesis were perhaps not as "pure" as they might have seemed, or at least their "purity" was perhaps not a gospel purity; it could also, or principally, be identified as the purity of the "clear, distinct ideas" of Cartesianism, or of the rarefied air of the Enlightenment.

The abstract quality which, in the final analysis, means the emptiness of the formulæ, was bound to become more perceptible as the important social movements of the 19th century and early 20th century (Marxism, Nietzchism, psychoanalysis, and so on) took root and developed. The catechism still continued to function because the Church nonetheless retained from the past an appreciable social solidity, but what the catechism handed on was becoming increasingly alien to the newly emerging society. Could it continue to show its film of remote ideas to children whose parents in many cases, were unbelievers?[24]

In the first half of the 20th century, Quebecois society was very supportive of the work of catechesis. In this setting, the Church continued to have reasonable success with catechisms inspired by Neo-Scholasticism. This was not the case in an increasingly de-christianized France, however, where the constitution enforced the strict separation of Church and state. There the distance between life and catechesis was felt more keenly and more quickly.

Other than scriptural references inserted as proof texts in support of an article of doctrine, there was little evidence of any serious reflection on the Bible. In their neglect of the Bible, the catechisms of this era reflected the neglect of the Scriptures within the Church at large. The reaction to the Protestant emphasis on the Bible had stilted the liturgical and theological life of the Roman Catholic Church, and forced the Bible, the primordial source of doctrine and inspiration for Christians, to be relegated to a secondary role. Shaken by the cataclysms of the 20th century, theological terms of reference which divided the world along confessional lines appeared antiquated and irrelevant.

---

24. René Marlé, "A New Stage in French Catechesis," *Lumen Vitae* 36 (1981): 64-65.

The First Half of the 20th Century

After centuries of virtual stagnation in catechesis, momentum for change gathered as a reluctant Church came face to face with modernity. The confrontation was to transform the face of the Church and with it, the face of catechesis.

With the population of France and Germany largely de-Christianized by the end of the Second World War, catechists in Europe turned to newly published translations of Patristic catechesis for inspiration. In one respect, the experiences of the Churches of post-war Europe resonated with those of the early Church. Although to different degrees, both contexts lacked that very sympathetic Christian environment which buttressed the Church's catechetical efforts in the Middle Ages and up to the 18th century. It might even be argued that in the history of the Church, only the pre-Constantinian Church knew a more diminished sociological status than the Church of the second half of the 20th century. As Christendom waned and public religious culture declined, elements of Christian tradition could no longer be taken for granted. Rather than Christian apologetics as the principal explanation and defence of religion, the socio-religious conditions demanded a fundamental theology which could assume little or no direct contact with ecclesial structures or the Gospel. To a large extent, it is in the intellectual ferment of post-war France and Belgium, as we shall see later, that the Quebecois/Canadian inspiration for *Viens vers le Père* would be found.

The seeds for a movement of rapprochement among Churches were sown in the wake of the devastation of Europe. All sides had claimed God as their own in the fighting. Warfare among nations that maintained at least a Christian veneer had led to unthinkable destruction and attempted genocide. Confessional differences were dwarfed before such fundamental crises of meaning. A heretofore halting ecumenical movement, present only in liberal-minded Churches, gained new vigour, and spread to Roman Catholicism. Given the fate of the Jews, the need for the Church to rethink its position vis-à-vis world religions was evident. The ecumenical movement rallied support.

The process of African, Asian and South American de-colonization which took place in the decade following World War II, served as an unexpected catalyst in the process of catechetical renewal. After centuries of occupation, Europe vacated its colonial premises, leaving behind a ponderous occidental heritage, surviving especially in colonial public institutions. Christianity, clothed in western cultural garb, was now firmly ensconced in many of the former colonial possessions. Indigenous adaptations of Christianity had been discouraged under colonial rule— once independence was achieved, a hidden legacy of dissonance and tension surfaced. This tension was symptomatic of a religion that had failed to become integrated with its host environment.

Churches were patently not immune to the imperialistic tendencies of European society. The clash between occidental and non-occidental cultures, which surfaced in the post-colonial period, paralleled another clash of cultures. The distance separating European and non-European culture could not be greater than that separating medieval Europeans from modern Europeans. Historically, Catholic Christianity has emphasized the transmission of dogma. While a great deal of the Church's dogmatic heritage had been translated into the thought-world of medieval Europe, it remained stagnant in that form for centuries afterwards. However brilliant the work of Aquinas and his contemporaries may have been, it was defined by the social, religious, economic and epistemological conditions which obtained in the context of medieval Europe. The estrangement of modern Europe to a medieval mind set, must surely be an apt analogy for the estrangement of indigenous cultures to European hegemony. A modern inculturation of dogma was never considered necessary, or at any rate, never undertaken before the 20th century.

The impact of urbanization, secularization, technical progress, progress in the human sciences, and the birth of many new nations combined to make the 20th century a time ripe for ecclesial reform. For the Catholic Church at any rate, that reform would not take place in the first half of the century. From the 1930s onwards, the ground work was being laid for the decisive reforms that would take shape in the 1960s.

Viens vers le Père was shaped by a complex of forces, both secular and ecclesial. The particular factors significant for its development were present in several contexts; in the social and ecclesial life of Quebec, in the domestic and catechetical reforms in France and Belgium, and in the rapidly evolving situation in the missions.

The Prelude to Reform

The history of catechetical renewal is of course bound up with the history of that wider renewal in Roman Catholic ecclesial life which eventually precipitated the Second Vatican Council. Catechisms most often mirror dominant trends at work in the intellectual and social life of the Church. Joseph Colomb considers a series of secular and ecclesial factors which converged, making the renewal of catechesis both possible and necessary:[25]

Secular Factors

1. Studies in psychology demonstrated modes of thought proper to childhood and adolescence. For example, the inability of young, school-aged children to handle intellectual abstractions became evident. Moreover, it was made clear that as children grow their exceptional requirements for development evolve. As an example, we may look to the needs of children in the primary grades. It was established that five to eight year olds learn most effectively in situations which incorporate gross motor activity; a requirement which diminishes as children advance in age.

2. The spread of compulsory education in the industrialized world called for a system of catechetical formation that offered more than one or two years of pre-sacramental instruction.

3. Work in sociology was drawing attention to the influence of the child's milieu in the learning process. There was a heightened consciousness of the fact that one no longer lived in a Christian society and the importance of the role of the family in the learning process of the child was recognized.

Ecclesial Factors

1. The biblical movement emphasized the importance of Scripture; it reminded catechetics of the need to teach a "History of Salvation."

2. The liturgical movement stressed the link between catechism and liturgy, as well as the importance of liturgical celebrations and liturgical texts.

3. Informed by a new appreciation of the Scriptures, the theological renewal zeroed in on the core of the Christian message: the place

---

25. Colomb, *Service*, 50.

of the resurrection, the mystery of the ecclesial community, and so forth. Theology began to appear increasingly like a call to conversion and less like a purely intellectual explanation of doctrine.

4. Parish renewal and the branches of Catholic Action helped to place catechetics in the overall framework of the pastoral action of the Church.

In a subsequent chapter, the advances in the human sciences which underpin the pedagogy of *Viens vers le Père* will be considered in some detail. For now, a brief introduction to the ecclesial factors leading to the renewal of catechesis should illuminate the context in which this programme took shape.

Reform in the Catholic Church in the 20th century crystallized in the liturgical and biblical movements, in Catholic Action and in theological renewal. These developments spread throughout western Europe, and the influence of each is reflected in the catechism under study here. In the earliest stages of development, the biblical and liturgical movements were frowned upon by the Bishops, as they challenged the status quo. In France, the prodigies of *La nouvelle théologie* attracted more than frowns from Rome; several were sternly reprimanded and some were deprived of their university chairs.[26] Catholic Action was a different story. The name became synonymous with Church efforts to re-establish a Christian society in a Europe that had become largely de-Christianized by the early part of this century. Catholic Action flourished in France where secularization had made rapid inroads.

The Liturgical Movement

Movements characteristically lack a geographical centre of development. Converging trends developing concurrently in varied cultural settings, over time, began to cultivate a climate for change at the grass roots level. These movements were heavily interdependent; innovations in one area often spurred them in another. Liturgics was the first area to register a significant thrust towards renewal. The flourish of activity in liturgical thought which took place in several Benedictine monasteries in Europe in the second half of the 19th and early 20th

---

26. Henri Rondet, "La nouvelle théologie," *Sacramentum Mundi*, ed. Karl Rahner, 4 (Montreal: Palm Publishers, 1968), 234.

centuries had considerable effect on liturgical renewal.[27] Although the first results of this movement were pushed aside, its enduring legacy lay in its revival of the ancient traditions of the Latin Church, the rediscovery of the Church year and of the traditional spiritual wealth contained in the ancient liturgical texts. Notably, Gregorian chant underwent a revival at this time. Pius X, with his *Motu proprio* dealing with Church music, *Tra le sollecitudini* (November 22, 1903), assured the survival of these early fruits of renewal by mandating their use.

In response to this word from the Pope, several Benedictine abbeys—clustered at first around abbeys in Western Europe—set in place a wide reaching effort for renewal. The Viennese Augustinian, Pius Parsch, built on these early efforts and published many popular writings which quickly spread internationally in translation. This movement culminated in new bilingual texts for worship,[28] vernacular hymnals, renewal of the Holy Week and Easter services at the parish level and a host of other changes.[29] As reform reached North America, the concept of a community gathered around the altar, collectively exercising the priesthood of Christ was being affirmed.

Another important element in the success of the liturgical movement was its link to the many youth movements of Catholic Action. From its beginnings, Catholic Action sought to establish a sense of community solidarity through the liturgy, bridging the gap between ecclesial ritual and secular experience. The leadership in these movements began to sense a contradiction between their ecclesial and public roles; now passive spectator, now agent of social transformation. These tensions led Catholic Action to sponsor liturgical conferences

---

27. Here, we follow J.P. Michael's synopsis of developments in the area of liturgy found in "Die liturgische Bewegung," *Lexikon für Theologie und Kirche*, ed. Josef Höfer, Karl Rahner (Freiburg: Verlag Herder, 1961), 1097. (Hereafter cited as *LThK*.)

28. In 1954, Pius XII authorized the use of bilingual rituals (French-Latin) for French Canada. See Jean Hamelin, *Histoire du catholicisme québécois*, 2 (Montréal: Boréal Express, 1984), 217.

29. Here, one sees the degree to which lay Catholics had slipped to the margin of Church life. Prior to these reforms and for centuries earlier, the celebration of the passion, death and resurrection of Jesus had been limited to a fraternal celebration of bishop and priests and to those lay spectators who lived close enough to the cathedral church to attend. It is worth noting in this context that, even if reforms had begun earlier, the decisive reform of the liturgy did not take place until Vatican Council II.

and study days, supplying members with literature on the subject.[30] A growing awareness of the collective character of salvation, coupled with a realization that gospel values can only be lived in communities of faith, spread beyond the circles of Catholic Action. The Church in Quebec, attuned to these international developments, focused considerable energies on a renewal of the liturgy. As timid reforms began to appear, it became evident that not all sectors of the Church were clamouring for the changes pressed for by activists. Many directives were met with considerable reserve and the need to educate Church-goers soon became evident. Within the framework of liturgical renewal, a centre for Bible and catechetics was created in the diocese of Montreal—evidence of the extent to which the biblical, catechetical and liturgical movements were understood to be interdependent.[31] Centres such as the one established in Montreal proliferated as the biblical movement took hold.

The Biblical Movement

The term biblical movement refers to the Church's efforts to bring its members closer to the Scriptures. This was accomplished by supplying inexpensive Bibles and teaching aids, by staging dramatic performances, by sponsoring Bible days, Bible circles and the like. These initiatives were meant to lead to frequent, if not daily reading of the Bible and thereby to a deepening of the faith. The biblical movement was closely linked to both Catholic Action and the liturgical movement. In fact the resurgence of a biblical emphasis in theological education and in pastoral work was translated to the Church at large by means of these kindred movements.

The biblical movement varied, dependent upon the national settings in which it grew. In Germany "das Katholische Bibelwerk" appeared in 1933.[32] In Austria, "das Volksliturgischen Apostolat," linked to Pius Parsch and the Klosterneuburg Abbey, stimulated great interest in the Bible. Through the efforts of this liturgical apostolate, a journal entitled *Bibel und Liturgie* appeared and many ordinary Catholics gained access to the Scriptures through the inexpensive editions of the Bible it published. In Belgium and France, the biblical movement had no organizations of its own but took shape alongside

---

30. Hamelin, 221.
31. Hamelin, 221.
32. Here we follow J. Kürzinger, "Bibelbewegung," *LThK*, 344-345.

the liturgical renewal. Of great influence in this regard was the popular French biblical literature, which reached a wide audience through the work of such notable figures as H. Daniel-Rops.

An active biblical movement developed in Quebec, where the *Jeunesse ouvrière catholique*, an arm of Catholic Action, was responsible for its initial penetration. *La propagande biblique romaine de la Bible*, began in this context and in 1940 was renamed *La société catholique de la Bible* (SOCABI). The society functioned at the level of popular promotion of the Bible while the *Association catholique des études bibliques au Canada* (ACEBAC) became the principal organization dealing with modern critical scholarship. A Canadian translation (French) of the New Testament appeared, along with a periodical called *Bulletin biblique*. Short biblical notes were submitted to newspapers and most dioceses added a Bible society to their diocesan structures to encourage the reading and understanding of Scripture.[33]

Catholic Action

Clearly, Catholic Action assumed an important role with respect to the popularization of both the political and ecclesial agendas of Church leaders. Its development merits attention here. In response to speeches by Leo XIII and Pius X, which called on Catholic lay people to assume the task of re-establishing a Christian culture, Catholic Action took shape as a visible organization during the pontificate of Pius XI.[34] Since the beginning of the 20th century, in areas where insufficient numbers of priests were available, certain tasks were handed over to lay people. The notion that lay people would be the carriers of the Christian message to the estranged world, *extra muros*, was taking shape in these years. The task of Catholic Action was described essentially as the furtherance of the Kingdom of God through a participation in the apostolate of the hierarchy. As a means of spreading the kingdom of God it also had a social dimension. Its three word motto—*See, Judge, Act*—suggests the concern it held for the welfare of the society it wished to transform. The movement promoted out-reach in the everyday life-settings of its adherents, striving especially to attract lapsed Catholics.

In the French speaking world, Catholic Action became particularly politicized. Those who took part in Catholic Action preceded the great

---

33. Hamelin, 63.
34. J. Verscheure, "Katholische Aktion," *LThK*, 74.

majority of other Catholics in their critical stance toward the dominant society. Most Catholics simply identified with and were assimilated into the dominant culture.

While Pius XI frequently referred to Catholic Action as the "collaboration and participation of the laity in the hierarchical apostolate of the Church," this formula left his successor, Pius XII, wary.[35] The latter soon clarified his predecessor's statement in a way that largely returned the laity to their erstwhile role of docile followers of the episcopacy. The matter was hardly closed as debate in France became heated. In Quebec, a notable incident reached public attention. At the 1939 National Congress of *La Jeunesse étudiante canadienne-française*, Simone Monette, one of the groups leaders, declared publicly that the group no longer saw itself as "le prolongement du bras et du sacerdoce de l'évêque." Later she added, " nos messages doivent être conçus et exprimés par nous."[36] Episcopal reaction to her statement ranged from accusations that she was a "freemason in germ" with a spirituality suffering from a "Protestant deviation," to quiet encouragement behind the scenes to continue her work.[37]

Throughout the 1930s and for part of the next decade, Catholic Action in Quebec suffered from a lack of doctrinal clarity and from a rivalry among the various religious orders shepherding its several constituent organizations. In an atmosphere heavy with ultramontanist sympathy, the apostolic delegate was permitted to foul organizational efforts by founding an unnecessary "oversight committee," intended to unify the branches of Catholic Action. It did little more than duplicate the work of an already existent provincial committee. Despite these peripheral difficulties, an even more serious problem plagued the early efforts of Quebec's Catholic Action.

In Europe, the movement and its organizations functioned against the backdrop of a secularized and increasingly de-Christianized society. The Quebec of the 1930s-1950s might well be described as hyper-Christianized in its public life. Few indeed were the areas where ecclesial power did not play a significant role, and participation in the public aspects of Church life was near universal. Quebec did not need to be re-Christianized, and so it took some time for the work of Catholic Action to become clarified on Quebecois soil. At first, the chaplains

---

35. Verscheure, 74.
36. Hamelin, 71-72.
37. Hamelin, 72.

for the branches of Catholic Action met around issues of public morality: temperance campaigns, dress on public beaches and so forth—an agenda which betrayed a profound misunderstanding of the original goals of Catholic Action.

By the mid 1940s, the Quebec Bishops acted to streamline the organization of Catholic Action. Better organization prepared the many youth groups for the important work they would undertake in the 1950s. As it came of age, Catholic Action in Quebec presented both a social and a nationalist axis. Hamelin comments upon the significance of this movement within the Church and within a rapidly-evolving Quebecois society.

> L'intégration de l'action catholique dans l'appareil de l'Église insère dans le catholicisme québécois un ferment porteur de tensions, voire de ruptures. Par sa méthode du «Voir, Juger, Agir», l'action catholique s'ouvre aux réalités urbaines c'est-à-dire sociales, et recourt à la rationalité scientifique pour les comprendre; par son insistance sur la vocation apostolique de tous les baptisés, elle privilégie la dimension engagement social, fondée sur les valeurs de responsabilité et de solidarité. Elle introduit un nouvel agent: le laïc, ce chrétien non tonsuré mais autonome, responsable, ayant ses droits et une mission propre. Ce nouvel acteur, qui s'efforce de distinguer une évaluation morale d'une démarche analytique de dissocier le social du national, le spirituel du temporel, la responabilité du laïc de la soumission passive du fidèle, pose problème. Il dérange les clercs et heurte les nationalistes, qui regrettent qu'on dissocie le religiuex du national, comme si l'Église universelle n'était pas une idée incarnée dans ces Églises pariticulières.[38]

Theological Renewal

Responding to the Zeitgeist of a new century, the grass roots movements within the Church were informed and guided by the work of innovative theologians. The synergism of biblical renewal, liturgical reform and Catholic Action created an atmosphere in which these movements both fed on and nourished theological reflection in the 1930s and 1940s. Early on, the *Verkündigungstheologie* or kerygmatic theology of the Faculty of Theology at Innsbruck stirred great interest.

The liturgical-historical works of Josef Jungmann, not only guided the liturgical movement, but blazed the trail of a theological renewal

---

38. Hamelin, 74-78.

as well. *Die Frohbotschaft und unsere Glaubensverkündigung (The Good News and Our Proclamation of the Faith)*, a seminal work by Jungmann, was to be a key inspiration for catechetical and theological renewal. Pushed aside by ecclesial authorities when it first appeared in 1936, *Die Frohbotschaft* forcefully argued the case for a return to the sources of faith. Jungmann wished to return to the biblical roots and the zeal of the first Christians who responded to the primitive kerygma. This focus on the Bible grew out of efforts to renew the liturgy. To rediscover the biblical source was to rediscover the key to a fuller understanding and experience of the centre of Catholic life, the liturgy. It was to bring new emphasis in the Mass to the "Liturgy of the Word" which had been overshadowed for centuries by the Liturgy of the Eucharist. In reaction to the biblical emphasis of the Reformers, Catholics had allowed this fundamental aspect of communal Christian worship to fall into neglect. The medieval model of theology, which had to some extent lost touch with the biblical sources, prevailed.

The influence of neo-scholastic theology in catechetics led to an inordinate preoccupation with exactitude in theological formulæ; the concern was to pass the immutable message, pristine from age to age. One captures the aridity of this approach in Jungmann's response to his contemporaries who lamented the "terrible ignorance" of Catholics with regard to the doctrines of the faith:

> And this "ignorance" despite the fact that countless Catholics have received in our schools a more extensive and conceptually precise exposition of the doctrines of faith than did the priests in the Early Church and well on into the Middle Ages! But, even if such instruction did succeed in imparting a flawless knowledge of all the individual doctrines one has in mind, would it produce the fervour of the Christian life, the joyous pride, the enthusiastic response of the early Christians to the Good News? Far from it....Perhaps it is Christ himself who has given us the decisive answer to the problem in the episode of the disciples going to Emmaus....What was his remedy for the dullness of faith of these disciples? A vital understanding of the scriptures as they unfolded His role of Suffering Servant in the Father's merciful plan of salvation.[39]

While it is clear that the *Summa* of St. Thomas took great pains to produce a coherent and integrated picture of the significance of reve-

---

39. Josef Andreas Jungmann, *The Good News Yesterday and Today*, edition no. 2, trans. & ed. Wm.A. Huesman (New York: Sadlier, 1962), 5.

lation and faith, it has become equally clear that a popularization of theological tracts was not likely to produce any such coherence for lay audiences. What preacher could summarize the *Summa*? So overwhelming had the heritage of St. Thomas become in Roman Catholicism, that it must have appeared wholly implausible to Jungmann that it should be supplanted by another theological system. His solution, and he was supported in this by other theologians on faculty at Innsbruck, was to introduce a project of kerygmatic theology which would supplement the pastoral lacunæ of the scholastic model, i.e., a kerygmatic model that would revitalize preaching and teaching within the Church.[40] The immediate goal of the kerygmatic theologians was to develop a theology of Gospel proclamation that would allow ordinary people to grasp the Christian fact as an integrated and coherent whole. This approach was meant to supplement rather than to supplant the scholastic model. The line-up of theological erudites who objected to the double theology implied in this critique included Rahner, Urs von Balthasar, Stolz, Schmaus and Daniélou. They argued that the rupture which already existed between the study of theology and life would only be exacerbated by this bifurcation. It was feared that kerygmatic theology would lapse into subjectivism and irrationality, leaving the scholastic model intact but lifeless.[41] The stage was set for fundamental change; the monolith of Scholasticism would be replaced by a plurality of new responses to a world, very different from the one in which Thomas had formulated his *Summa*.

In the long run, kerygmatic theology was defeated, but not without bequeathing a rich legacy to theological renewal. As the significance of the *Verkündigungstheologie* sank in, it became increasingly clear that theology must be at the service of proclamation and directed towards a deeper living of the Christian life. Despite a move by the superior of Jungmann's own religious order to remove the book from circulation, it was not possible to closet its ideas.[42]

The theological renewal, which was about to flower, depended heavily for its inspiration on a revival in the use of two fundamental

---

40. Domenico Grasso, "The Good News and the Renewal of Theology," *The Good News Yesterday and Today*, 204. This is an essay in appraisal of Jungmann's *Die Frohbotschaft*.

41. Grasso, 205.

42. Johannes Hofinger, J.A. Jungmann (1889-1975): "In Memoriam," *The Living Light* 13 (1976): 354.

sources of Christian understanding, Patristic writings and the Bible. In France, work continued throughout the Second World War on *Sources chrétiennes*, a comprehensive collection of Patristic sources presented with a French translation. This behemoth among publishing enterprises (a projected 4000 volumes) took shape under the editorial guidance of the noted scholars De Lubac, Daniélou and Mondésert. In the sphere of biblical scholarship, the 1943 encyclical of Pius XII, Divino afflante spiritu, opened a new era in biblical criticism for Catholics.[43] Scholarship, that had proceeded quietly for years previous, now received approval. Soon Catholic scholars became respected members of the guild of biblical experts.

If the shift from medieval to Patristic sources appears at first glance retrograde, it was in fact to unearth a wealth of long forgotten tradition within the Church.[44] The concern within Catholicism to remain faithful to tradition, both apostolic and Patristic, is of ancient vintage and a defining feature of its ecclesial ethos. In fact, respect for our forbears produced a situation where true innovation was considered at least suspect, if not heretical.[45] And so, predictably, the road forward took a detour, rediscovering paths that had earlier been travelled.

Scholasticism proved to be a formidable fortress. Its fortifications, mortared with tradition and reason, could repel virtually any direct assault. Its walls would have to be skilfully sapped. Burrowing beneath these walls unearthed ancient but forgotten traditions and gave rise to arguments from Tradition capable of challenging later medieval developments. In the end, the critique Jungmann had begun in *Die*

---

43. Grant and Tracy, 125.
44. See the section dealing with sources of renewal in the liturgy (above) for an example of how Patristics provided fresh inspiration.
45. See G. Emmett Carter's work, cited above, for a salient example of this attitude. Written before ecumenical thought took hold, Carter uses words such as "revolt," "innovation," and "heresy" when referring to the Protestant Reformation. When he desires to critique any element that has grown up within Catholic tradition, he takes great pains to illustrate that his critique is founded within a still older and more venerable tradition of the Church, which has been lost sight of. While the ecumenical movement has practically eliminated this antagonistic style, Catholic theologians continue to affirm the value of Tradition, the record of the experiences of those Christians who have gone before us in the faith.

Frohbotschaft, would prove devastating.[46] He made a simple yet profound observation regarding Scholasticism: "Theology is primarily at the service of knowledge; hence it investigates religious reality to the outermost limits of the knowable (*verum*)...The proclamation of the faith, on the other hand is entirely oriented toward life."[47] Scholasticism was framed in the philosophical tradition of classical realism and as such, sought epistemological certainty, free of the vicissitudes of historical circumstance. It was not directed at life. While adjustments and minor developments may have occurred from time to time within this theological system, its method reflected none of the major historical changes which had taken hold in the societies in which it functioned over the centuries. It concerned itself rather with a reasonable consideration of the facts of revelation and dogmatic pronouncements as they had been preserved in the Tradition of the Church. Theological renewal attempted to redress the ignorance of the human side of the divine-human relationship upon which the process of revelation depends.

Bernard Lonergan characterized the shift that occurred in theology as "The Transition from a Classicist World View to Historical-Mindedness."[48] Scholasticism may well have conceived of its theological method as a-historical but it was in fact as historically contingent as any other model of theological reflection. Lonergan cites a letter from James Coriden which makes this point:

> It seems to me that the transition of organizational and structural forms in the Church is a pattern that parallels the transcultural transmission and consequent development of dogma. The changing laws and forms and methods in the Church down the centuries, the borrowing from different cultures and civilizations and adaptation to altered circumstances in the world—all these seem to be more than mere facts of history, they seem to be a theological requisite....This point seems to me to be much more than a nice theological observation. It seems to be central and synthetic. It is the motive for the whole effort toward

---

46. In this context, Chapter Four of Die Frohbotschaft presents Jungmann's critique of Scholasticism, underlining how Scholasticism's focus of study had become divorced from the concerns of everyday Christian life.

47. Jungmann, 33.

48. Bernard Lonergan, "The Transition from a Classicist World-View to Historical-Mindedness," *A Second Collection: Papers by Bernard J.F. Lonergan, S.J.*, ed. Wm. F.J. Ryan, Bernard J. Tyrell (London: Darton, Longman and Todd, 1967), 1-9.

renewal and relevancy...[49]

From this very productive period of theological renewal in the Roman Catholic Church, theologians emerged who combined the strengths of Scholasticism's philosophical penchant with a new historical-mindedness. Karl Rahner, a prominent representative of this shift, resisted involvement in the kerygmatic school at his faculty and began a dialogue between fundamental theology and the existentialist philosophy of his professor at Freiburg, Martin Heidegger. This dialogue lead Rahner to conclude that all human history has been marked by the grace of God. Daniélou, de LuBac and others opened up the rich Patristic record, drawing inspiration from it in their own reflections and rendering it accessible to theologians at work in other specialities. Of particular interest for our inquiry, Patristics drew attention to salvation history, a theme of biblical theology prevalent among the Church Fathers. In the biblical sphere, Historical Criticism was drawing the attention of the new guild of Catholic scholars to the wealth of information "behind-the-text." Moral theologians, in casting their attention to history-in-the-making, began to critically examine the findings of psychology, sociology, economics and other secular fields, incorporating those elements into their reflections which they judged worthwhile and capable of explicating the Gospel in today's context.

The twin influences of biblical renewal and the rediscovery of Patristic sources effected a metamorphosis of the theological scene within the Roman Catholic Church. As we have seen, this move to the sources accompanied a move to an historically-minded model of theological reflection. The 20th century may be described as the age in which Catholic theology focused its gaze on history, dialoguing critically with the many new intellectual, social and political developments of our day in an attempt to have the Gospel heard. As we shall see, catechetical renewal was profoundly shaped by this theological reform.

---

49. James Coriden as quoted in Lonergan, 1-2.

Chapter 2

A HISTORY OF *VIENS VERS LE PÈRE*: EUROPEAN AND CANADIAN INFLUENCES

The production of the first edition[1] of the *Viens vers le Père* catechetical series was the collaborative effort of two teams of specialists; one team dealt with primary school resources and a second with elementary. The primary team consisted of Sister Marie de la Visitation[2], Jean-Paul Bérubé, Marcel Caron and Réginald Marsolais. The elementary team changed shape even while the first editions of Grades 4, 5 and 6 were being developed. Robert Lane remained with the team only for the composition of the Grade Four programme, *Nous avons vu le Seigneur*. Alberte Beaulieu and Barry McGrory joined the team for the writing of Grades 5 and 6. Martin Jeffery and Denise St-Pierre worked with Paul Tremblay as team co-ordinator for all three grade levels. Both teams consulted widely with theologians, biblical scholars, diocesan groups and lay people. For the elementary writing team, Philippe Houyoux, a Belgian Jesuit who trained at Lumen Vitae, assumed a prominent role among the consultants.[3]

All but two of the redactors were trained in Europe at either the *Institut supérieur de pastoral catéchétique de Paris* (ISPC) or at *Lumen Vitae*; Jeffery and Bolduc availed themselves of courses in

---

1. Several editions, both translations and adaptations, of the *Viens vers le Père* series were published. Even within Quebec, more than one edition appeared over the life of the series. To avoid confusion, whenever the program is discussed, the reference will be to the original, first-edition French (unless otherwise specified). Similarly, when discussing the writing teams our attention will be limited to the members who produced the original edition.

2. Below, works attributed to Françoise Darcy, Sister Marie de la Visitation, Françoise Darcy-Bérubé and Françoise Bérubé originate in fact with the same individual. Françoise Darcy later married her erstwhile writing teammate, Jean-Paul Bérubé.

3. Paul Tremblay interviewed at Montreal, Fall 1990.

catechetics at Laval University, where such notables as Marcel van Caster and François Coudreau came to teach. Sister Marie de la Visitation was born and received her schooling in France. She brought to the writing team, in addition to her professional expertise as an educator, first hand experience of the movements which had been so prominent in the French and Belgian Churches during her formative years and early professional life. The educational background of the writing teams reflects the rich North American/European cultural exchange which marks modern Quebec society. The cultural and linguistic links between Quebec and French-speaking Europe explain why catechetical reforms in France exercised such a significant influence on the shape and content of catechetical renewal in Quebec.[4] Hence, it seems clear that little will be understood of the rapid evolution of the catechetical scene in Quebec, without a grasp of the evolution of the catechetical scene in France.

CATECHETICAL RENEWAL IN FRANCE

To retrace all the threads that led up to the very prolific period of catechetical renewal and reformation, stretching roughly from the beginning of the 1930s and continuing well into the 1970s, exceeds both our scope and purposes here. It is worth noting, however, that the Church in France dismissed the work of several of its catechetical pioneers in the early decades of this century.[5] This is hardly surprising as few movements of institutional reform spring into existence without resistance.

Founded in 1882, the organization known as the *Archiconfrérie de l'oeuvre des catéchismes* was key in promoting renewal and in rallying interest around catechetical questions. Many of the notable catechetical reformers of the 20th century passed through its ranks early in their careers.[6]

By the 1930s, progress in educational psychology and advances in the methods and techniques of secular pedagogy began to influence catechesis in France.[7] In 1912, the International Eucharistic Congress of Vienna had already adopted a three-part process for catechetical

---

4. Norbert Fournier, "Canada," *Dizionario di catechetica*, ed. Joseph Gevaert (Turin: Elle Di Ci, 1986), 97.
5. Colomb, *Service*, I, 49.
6. Fargues, *How to Teach*, 11.
7. Boyer, *Un demi siècle*, 73.

instruction which proceeded from "Presentation," to "Exposition," to "Application."[8] Other advances in the field of curriculum theory began to infiltrate catechetical thought and practice at this time. The traditional approach to catechesis was teacher-centred and assumed a passive receptivity on the part of the learner. Without exception, the new methods of the *École active*[9] sought to throw off this cumbersome patrimony. The innovative curriculum theory of the *École active* stressed the value of action, maintaining that a child learns, not only by listening, but even more by actually doing.[10] In 1928 the method presented at the Congress of Vienna, modified with an emphasis on the child's activities, was approved by the Catechetical Congress of Munich and was thereafter referred to as the "Munich Method."[11]

The theory and praxis of the *École active* implied much more than simply involving the children in activities peripheral to the central educative act. The period from 1930-1935 is generally given as the period in which the *méthodes actives* rose to prominence in religious education. Very early on, several congregations of Sisters were busy adapting these new methods for catechetical use. Most notable among these, were the Sisters of Notre Dame de Namur and the Sisters of Vorsellar.[12] A number of priests and lay women played a large role as pioneers in this exciting new field. Among the most prominent names one finds Poppe, Damez, Fargues, Boyer, Derkenne, Lubienska de Lenval, Quinet and Colomb. At this early stage, the significance and applications of the *méthodes actives* were not fully grasped by those at the periphery of the renewal. Nevertheless, the idea took hold quickly that children should no longer be expected to sit motionless in their desks as passive recipients of knowledge. The number of children in-

---

8. Luis Erdozain, "The Evolution of Catechetics: A Survey of Six International Study Weeks on Catechetics," *Lumen Vitae* 25 (1970): 9.

9. This expression is sometimes translated into English with the term "activities school". But this translation is easily misunderstood as referring to action, peripheral to the central educative act—nothing could be farther from the intentions of the principal proponents of this school, who understood the concrete, physical activities of the child as the key to his/her cognitive acquisition. As Hélène Lubienska de Lenval put it in *L'éducation de l'homme conscient* (Paris: Spes, 1956), 28: "Il s'agit de diriger l'activité musculaire, de façon à ce qu'elle devienne une auxiliaire de la pensée."

10. Rummary, 9.

11. Erdozain, 10.

12. Ranwez, *Pastorale de l'enfance*, 14-20.

volved in learning activities grew during these years, and even if the instructional goals of these activities lacked precision, the change must have been a welcome one for students.

With respect to the cognitive objectives set forth for curricula, the Munich Method greatly improved the understanding and retention of the neo-scholastic content of the catechisms. But the knowledge thus derived continued to be disjointed and disconnected and left the students with no clear picture of the overall unity of the Christian message. As late as 1950, Josef Jungmann described the situation in this way:

> Most people know all the sacraments; they know about the Person of Christ as well as about our Lady, Peter and Paul, Adam and Eve, and a good many others. They know enough about the commandments of God and of the Church. But what is lacking among the faithful is a sense of unity, seeing it as a whole, an understanding of the wonderful message of divine grace. All they retain of Christian doctrine is a string of dogmas and moral precepts, threats and promises, customs and rites, tasks and duties imposed on unfortunate Catholics, whilst the non-Catholic gets off free of them.[13]

Well before 1950, it was becoming clear to those at the forefront of catechetical practice and reflexion, that the problems of religious education were not limited to questions of methodology. This brought about yet another shift in perspective.

In *Die Frohbotschaft* (1936), Jungmann had proposed a return to the sources of Christian faith. He proposed a return to the biblical roots and to the zeal of the first Christians who responded to the primitive kerygma. In France, others were at work trying to enliven the faith experience of Christians by replacing the "God which Christian philosophers had fashioned" with a fresh image drawn from the pages of Scripture.

Before broaching the topic of biblical renewal in catechesis, it is worth remembering that the several emphases identifiable within catechetical renewal did not develop in isolation from one another. Tendencies observable in one quarter affected those at work in another, and movements at work in the Church at large affected all. The return to Patristic sources, to their treasure house of liturgical thought and practice, was taking place at the same time that a new interest in

---

13. J.A. Jungmann, "Theology and Kerymatic Renewal," *Lumen Vitae* 5 (1950): 258-259.

the Bible was taking hold in both scholarly and popular circles in the Catholic world. All this contributed to the renewal of theological thought and to the renewal of popular education within the Church.

A Return to the Bible

On the French catechetical scene, one of the earliest proponents of a return to Scripture was the priest Eugène Charles. In 1922, Bishop Landrieux published a pastoral letter, *Le premier enseignement par l'évangile*. In this letter Landrieux called for a catechesis nourished by Scripture. In what may have been a response to Landrieux's appeal, Charles published *Le catéchisme par l'évangile* in 1931. This work, which included teacher, student and parent manuals, was translated into several languages and was widely used.[14] Charles elaborated the "Gospel Method" in this catechism, a method which intended to offer a new way of initiating children to the faith. When he tried to have this catechism accepted for use throughout France, Cardinal Verdier rebuffed him with the following complaint: "C'est bien, mais c'est le catéchisme de Charles. Ce que nous voulons, c'est le catéchisme de l'Église: dogme, morale et sacrements."[15]

Joseph Colomb, a Sulpician priest who was then director of the Institute of Religious Education at Lyon, constructed a biblically-inspired programme that could withstand the critique Verdier had levelled at the work of Eugène Charles. Judging by the quality of published work, Colomb was without doubt one of the most intellectually brilliant of all those who pondered the theoretical dimensions of the catechetical renewal. In 1968, he published his massive two volume, *Le service de l'évangile* (1427 pages), which collects not only the fruit of his many years of teaching and research, but also myriad insights from colleagues at work in the fields of curriculum theory, educational psychology, theology and biblical studies. His opus magnum represents one of the most complete syntheses of the thought which led up to and shaped the catechetical renewal.

Colomb, collaborating with Marie Fargues and several others, joined early in the quest for pedagogical renewal and was particularly interested in developing a better doctrinal formation for catechesis.[16] These twin goals were in view when the first school of catechesis was

---

14. Boyer, *Un demi siècle*, 76-77.
15. As quoted in Boyer, *Un demi siècle*, 78.
16. Fargues, *How to Teach*, 45.

formed at Lyon in 1946, the same year as the *Centre National*, the central office of catechetics for France, was founded. The following year a Licentiate programme in religious education was in place at Lyon.[17] Shortly after taking over the principalship there, Colomb submitted a report to Cardinal Gerlier calling for changes in the catechism. He concluded with four points:[18]

1. While retaining the instructional aspects of catechesis, the programme ought to focus on providing an education of the student's personal religious life;

2. Catechesis should be offered throughout the entirety of the child's schooling;

3. Catechesis should be given according to a method adapted to the child, i.e., as active and individualized as possible.

4. Catechesis ought to be progressive and adapted to the profound interests of each age group.

The implementation of these points would, of course, mean the disappearance of the old manual and the need to formulate something new in its stead. In order to effect these changes, a programme for educating catechists would need to be established. Thus in the years immediately following these recommendations, Colomb published *Aux sources du catéchisme* (3 vols.), which was meant to provide the basis for the education of catechists.

Colomb was the first French catechist to promote the use of both Old and New Testaments as the basis for a catechism. As a consequence of the biblical movement, texts dealing with biblical history, or sacred history as it was most often called, were being used side by side with the catechism.[19] The OT was used extensively and was appropriated in a salvation history hermeneutic. This was a very different emphasis from that found in the gospel-centred catechism of E. Charles. The divisions of Colomb's *Aux sources du catéchisme* followed a plan based on the liturgical year and salvation history: Vol. I—*Au temps de l'avent: la Promesse* (1946); Vol. II—*De Noël à Pâques: la vie de*

---

17. Colomb, *Service*, I, 50.
18. Colomb as reported in Boyer, *Un demi siècle*, 236.
19. For an extensive list of texts dealing with biblical history, in use at the time, see Ranwez, *Pastorale de l'enfance*, 238-276.

Jésus, (1947); Vol. III—*De Pâques à l'Avent: le Christ glorieux et l'histoire de l'Église* (1948).

Prior to the biblical movement, the Bible had been virtually unknown to most lay Catholics, apart from the lectionary readings at Mass. Use of the Bible, and more particularly of the OT, in religious education had become associated with Protestant styles of catechesis. Therefore its use in Catholic circles required a note of explanation. In the preface to the first volume, Colomb compares his use of the OT to that of the resurrected Jesus, when he accompanied his disciples on the road to Emmaus (Luke 24:13-25).[20] Colomb's rationale for his use of Scripture rejoins the emphasis of the kerygmatic school at Innsbruck.[21] That Colomb was aware of Jungmann's work by this date is unclear, since he makes no mention of *Die Frohbotschaft* in either his text or notes. This absence, however, could easily be explained by the fact that he is writing a pastoral work for a French-speaking audience. For reference works in "biblical studies" Colomb directs his readers to the treatment of sacred history by Riciotti, Daniel-Rops and Bouvet.[22]

In the years that followed, Colomb continued to stand at the forefront of the drive to educate catechists. In 1950, he published a catechism that corresponded to the criteria he had originally laid down in Lyon. His *Catéchisme progressif*, appeared in three volumes that year with three corresponding teacher guides. He followed in 1953-1954 with *La doctrine de vie au Catéchisme*, another three-volume work, intended to serve as a general reference work for catechists, especially teachers of Volume III of his *Catéchisme progressif*.

When reform in catechesis seemed to be going nowhere, Colomb published a book warning of the crisis in religious education. The alert he sounded in *Plaie ouverte au flanc de l'église* (1954) echoed, in catechetical terms, the acclaimed work of Godin and Daniel,[23] which had warned of a crisis in the life of the Church in France. During his career, Colomb published numerous articles in virtually all the French language catechetical journals and his views became available in translation through his many articles in *Lumen Vitae*. He later taught

---

20. Joseph Colomb, *Aux sources du catéchisme: Au temps de l'Avent: la Promesse* (Paris: Desclée, 1946), 2.
21. Cf. Jungmann's *Good News*, 5.
22. Colomb, *Aux Sources*, I, 36.
23. Henri Godin, Y. Daniel, *La France, pays de mission?* (Paris: Éditions du Cerf, 1943).

at the *Institut supérieur de pastorale catéchétique*, and gave courses from time to time at the catechetical centre at Lumen Vitae. After a public rejection of many of his catechetical innovations by church authorities in Paris, Colomb moved to Strasbourg to teach.

Colomb was not alone in making a connection between liturgy and catechesis. Françoise Derkenne had already championed this emphasis within the field, and Colomb was quick to refer his reader to her work, as well as to that of Countess Hélène Lubienska de Lenval.[24] Along with the use of Scripture, the liturgy was to become an important element in the new catechisms. *Viens vers le Père* reflects both these emphases.

Liturgy as a Source of Catechesis

The liturgical approach to catechesis took shape alongside the Gospel method of E. Charles. Françoise Derkenne was the initiator and great promoter of this approach in France. Employing the methods of the *École active*, Derkenne used the liturgical year as the framework of her catechism. Her christocentric method treated the great feasts of the liturgical year in terms of the scriptural record of sacred history underlying these memorials. Her goal was to make the Mass, the central act of Catholic life, come alive for the children who followed her classes. In 1935 and 1939, Derkenne published *La vie et la joie au catéchisme: Introduction pédagogique* (2 vols.). She wanted to put the children in contact with Jesus as he may be found in the Gospel, in the liturgy and in their souls.[25]

This emphasis on interiority linked her to Hélène Lubienska de Lenval, another catechetical bright light, who was interested in the links between liturgy and catechesis. Lubienska came to the catechetical renewal somewhat later than Colomb, Fargues and Derkenne, but merits attention, as Françoise Darcy-Bérubé (Sister Marie de la Visitation) cited her as one of the key influences on her own catechetical thought and as a major influence in the shape of years one, two and three of the *Viens vers le Père* series.[26] In fact her name appears twice in a very brief list of twelve references for teachers in the guide to year

---

24. Colomb, *Aux sources*, I, 12.
25. Françoise Derkenne, *La vie et la joie au catéchisme. Introduction pédagogique*, I (Lyon: Éditions de l'Abeille, 1935), 4.
26. Françoise Darcy-Bérubé, interview by author, St. Lambert (P.Q.) 7 March 1991.

one of the *Viens vers le Père* series.[27]

Lubienska considered the Mass to be the *méthode active* par excellence for the faith education of children. An ardent promoter of the idea that children possess a capacity for interiority—for a rich spiritual and imaginative life—Lubienska asserted that the perception of things spiritual is a capacity educable in a child. She believed that before one can speak of God to a child, one needs to help that child recognize his/her spiritual experiences or indeed provide such experiences.

As we see in her *L'éducation du sens religieux*[28], Lubienska borrowed two key elements from the work of the famous Italian physician and educational theorist Maria Montessori: "walking on a line" and "exercises in silence." Both activities involve mastery of the body with the oblique goal of training the mind.[29] The new methods, with a focus on educative activities, recognized the special links between the cognitive and physical capacities of the child. This element was entirely ignored by the older programs, which tended to treat children as if they were adults suffering from a temporary intellectual deficiency. The specificity and uniqueness of the cognitive capacities and learning requirements of children were not studied or widely discussed before the 20th century.

Lubienska subscribed to the notion that long before children can articulate their knowledge, they absorb all manner of non-verbal communication, ranging from banal information to experiences of the transcendental. The young child especially has not yet the ability to abstract the content of its experiences. They are stored in the memory as impressions of physical sensations and experiences. In this sense the young child is not reflective but is rather in a stage of concrete learning, i.e., learning by way of doing. In *L'éducation du sens religieux*, she sketches the main tenets of this position :

> Lorsqu'on s'adresse à des enfants, il faut tenir compte non seulement de leur vocabulaire, mais surtout de leur tournure d'esprit. On sait que

---

27. Jean-Paul Bérubé; Marcel Caron; Réginald Marsolais; Sister Marie de la Visitation, *Viens vers le Père: Initiation chrétienne des enfants de 6-7 ans* (Montreal: Fides, 1964), 49-50.

28. Hélène Lubienska de Lenval, *L'éducation du sens religieux* (Paris: Spes, [1946] 1960).

29. For an explanation and analysis of these montessorian elements see: A Valensin, "Introduction," *L'éducation du sens religieux* (Paris: Spes, 1960), 20-24. Valensin offers an insightful introduction to the thought of Lubienska.

l'enfant au-dessous de huit ans est inapte à la pensée rationnelle et spéculative; que par contre, il est parfaitement capable de connaissance expérimentale et d'intuition poétique....

Mais, si la pensée spéculative est étrangère à l'enfant, et si, partant, son mode d'expression ne lui convient pas, les données de l'Évangile n'étant pas liées à un mode de pensée déterminé, peuvent lui devenir familières si elles lui sont présentées dans le langage qui lui est propre. Restituer à la doctrine chrétienne son aspect descriptif, qui s'adresse plus à l'intuition qu'à la pensée spéculative, tel est l'effort tenté dans ces pages....

Le point de départ fut une expérience vécue: la participation active à la messe; l'acte précède la doctrine; la vie précède les idées.[30]

Another element of Lubienska's procedure, one more properly her own and of high interest in this inquiry, is the manner in which she made use of the Bible. Valensin captures her genius aptly:

La manière dont la pédagogie de Mme Lubienska exploite, en les commentant à peine, et avec une naïveté avertie, les récits de la Bible, est peut-être un modèle du genre: l'enfant est introduit de plain-pied dans le monde de l'Histoire Sainte, invité à se mouvoir parmi ses personnages, amené à se trouver chez lui dans le voisinage de Dieu.[31]

Many of Lubienska's samples of catechetical activities involved placing children before new experiences physically, or introducing them to "new worlds" imaginatively. Unlike those inspired by the *Heils-geschichte* emphasis, Lubienska did not impose on her students an overarching hermeneutical principle for organizing the Bible. Rather she invites her children to enter the world of a text and to become part of that world. Her novel approach to Scripture integrated into her larger goal of having the children participate fully in the Mass. She led children through re-enactments of the liturgy having them perform the words and actions of the priest. These re-enactments provided the children with a means of grappling with the significance of the Mass and helped them enter into its reality. In this context she speaks of the "prayer of the body,"[32] a concept which recognizes the inability of the young child to think abstractly and which corresponds to the child's cognitive possibilities. This was a programme of practi-

---

30. Lubienska, *Sens religieux*, 31-32.
31. Valensin, 12.
32. Lubienska, *Sens religieux*, 75.

cal logic, of syllogisms acted out, allowing concepts to pass via the physical to the intellectual.[33] The discovery of the role physical experiences play in the cognitive acquisition of children profoundly changed the shape of religious education curricula. P. Ranwez cites a passage from Lubienska's *L'éducation de l'homme conscient* which he feels provides insight into her method:

> L'enfant tout jeune doit d'abord entreprendre de dominer la matière. Après de longs exercices, variés, adaptés, le corps est assoupli et discipliné. Dès le début de l'éducation de l'activité corporelle, on fait remarquer à l'enfant que son "moi," son esprit commande à ses membres qu'il meut. Après l'éducation musculaire, vient la formation de l'activité psychique, toujours au service de l'esprit. Il s'agit d'apprendre à l'enfant à dominer "le chaos des impressions et des idées," à mettre de l'ordre en soi grâce à une éducation de la pensée et de la réflexion à base sensorielle toujours. On peut ainsi organiser la leçon de silence, célèbre dans la méthode montessorienne. Silence conscient, volontaire, concentré. Silence du corps qui favorise l'activité de la pensée.[34]

The caveat mentioned above with respect to the limitations of the divisions of this historical overview bears repetition in this context. Although Lubienska has been introduced under the rubric of the rediscovery of the role of liturgy in catechesis, she patently incorporated a thoroughly renewed notion of the pedagogy of children into this emphasis. Moreover, other titles of hers demonstrate a keen interest in the role of the Bible in religious education.[35] The catechetical reformers who had recourse to the methods of the *École active* were at the forefront of innovation in their field and as such, were eager to make contact with the many sources of new intellectual stimulation, whether from new theological insights, from psychology or from ecclesial and para-ecclesial movements. Lubienska was not the first to be influenced

---

33. Valensin, 17.
34. See Ranwez, *Pastorale de l'enfance*, 210.
35. Apart from numerous scholarly articles and in addition to the works referred to above, other works by this author (prior to 1960) include: *La méthode montessori* (Paris: Spes, 1947); *Éducation biblique: les plus beaux textes de la Bible* (Paris: Éditions de l'Élan, 1949); *L'éducation du sens liturgique* (Paris: Éditions du Cerf, 1952); *L'éducation de l'homme conscient* (Paris: Spes, 1956); *L'univers biblique où nous vivons* (Paris: Casterman, 1958); *Trêve de Dieu* (Tournai: Casterman, 1959).

by the *École active* in French catechetical circles. Quinet, a precursor of the *École active* in catechetics, and Fargues, "la grande dame" of catechetical renewal, preceded her by several years.

New Methods and a New Task

In France, C. Quinet was first to develop a new method based on the conclusions of psychology. During his career he never deviated from the traditional content of catechesis and relegated psychology to an ancillary role in the catechetical process. It could provide useful tools in the communication of a pre-determined content, but could never be allowed to influence that content. Among other works, Quinet produced publications showing how to use chalk drawings on the blackboard and drawing on paper in catechesis, a catechism with pictures and colouring activities, three separate texts on sacred history and the life of Jesus, booklets on the liturgy, an illustrated mass book for children, a booklet for children's first communion and a score of wall murals for use in religious education. With A. Boyer, Quinet produced an abridged version of the advanced catechism for use with 7 to 8 year olds. Only 100 of the 429 questions in the more advanced text were used.[36]

Despite Quinet's efforts to use activities in the catechism class, Marie Fargues did not consider his work to be an authentic example of the *méthodes actives*.[37] The *École active* was much more than a source of devices to facilitate existing curriculum goals. It implied a rethinking of the entire educational process. On the basis of these new principles, theologians would eventually reform the stated goals of catechesis, its content and its intended educational outcomes. For Quinet, the content of the catechism remained inviolable and it was this conviction that prevented his work from moving toward a thorough re-thinking of the catechetical task.

It was Fargues herself who was the true pioneer of the activity methods in French catechesis and her use of psychology went far beyond the purely practical goals of Quinet. Already in 1928, Fargues presented various catechetical methods to catechists gathered at an intellectual retreat at Juilly, including those of Froebel, Montessori,

---

36. For a synopsis of these and other works by Quinet see Ranwez' annotated bibliography in *Pastorale de l'enfance*, 179.
37. Fargues, *How to Teach*, 13-14.

Cousinet, the Project Method and the method of the French kindergarten.[38] In her own recollections of the first quarter of the 20th century, this pioneer highlights the explosion of interest in childhood. Numerous discoveries in the field of educational psychology by such eminent scholars as Claparède, Piaget, Montessori, Decroly and Dewey propelled this movement internationally.[39]

Fargues followed the published work in this new field and kept abreast of developments. While teaching at the *École des Roches*, she personally had contact with several early innovators in curriculum including: Adolphe Ferrière, a Protestant, whom she called the "great animating power of the new education" in France; Roger Cousinet, who began the concept of team teaching; Dr. Simon, collaborator and successor of Alfred Binet, who used her school for some time as his field for experiment.[40] By 1934, Fargues published *Les méthodes actives dans l'enseignement religieux*, an essay in the adaptation of the activity methods of secular pedagogy to the tasks of religious education.[41] She published several volumes and numerous articles. In addition to *Les méthodes actives*, her chief works include: *Formation des enfants du peuple en milieu déchristianisé* (1935); *Introduction des enfants de 9 ans au catéchisme*, 3 vols. (1936); *Tests collectifs de catéchisme*, 2 vols. (1945 and 1951); *La foi des petits enfants* (1951); *Catéchisme pour notre temps* (1951); *Nos enfants devant le Seigneur* (1959); *D'hier à demain, le catéchisme* (1964).

Fargues began her career in catechetics around 1904-1905 and although she was several years the senior of Françoise Derkenne, the two began publishing at about the same time. Fargues and Derkenne, sometimes collaborating on projects, shared a keen interest in the work of Montessori.

In reading Fargues' historical treatment of the catechetical renewal and listening to the comments of her peers, it becomes evident that Fargues was gifted with empirical perspicacity. An incident she recalls from her early teaching days, one that she refers to as her "great dis-

---

38. Boyer, *Un demi siècle*, 75.
39. Fargues, *How to Teach*, 15. Fargues notes that Binet came to attention in France only after his fame as a scholar had already been established in America.
40. Fargues, *How to Teach*, 18.
41. Marie Fargues, *Les méthodes actives dans l'enseignement religieux* (Paris: Éditions du Cerf, 1934).

covery," demonstrates amply her curiosity and her ability to "read" her students.

> In this working class parish in Rouen where I was assigned on leaving Roches, I had to act one day as a replacement with a group of boys aged ten to twelve years, who were very intelligent and who knew their catechism very well. I do not know how it had been taught to them; not only did they know it but they understood it. They answered all my questions very well and without making a mistake. However, I felt that something was not going right. What did these children think? How did they really think?
>
> To have a clear understanding of this matter I stopped for a moment being a catechist, and with all my little people I passed over to the ground of familiar ideas, of life as it is lived, of people and things known through real contact. How did these children think? They thought as their environment thought and not as their catechism would have wished them to think, in spite of its being very well understood: every human destiny ends in a hole in the cemetery, and God is only a word.[42]

In the years that followed, Fargues searched for ways to communicate the heart of the Christian message to children, in a manner that would allow them to appropriate it as something more than pure rationality, i.e., intellectual baggage that had no effect on their lives. Catechesis, in earlier days, had been able to limit itself to the didactic task of instruction in doctrine. The teacher scarcely had to convince pupils of the truth of what she was saying since the whole social and cultural environment accepted and supported the premises of Christian faith. With the environment largely de-Christianized in France, and with a general shift towards a scientific mind-set throughout the industrialized world, the truth of propositions about the divine and the supernatural could no longer be taken for granted. If they were to be accepted, the teacher would have to persuade her class of their veracity, and do this in such a way as to address their everyday experience. Fargues' discovery had been that it was possible to conduct catechism classes, according to the accepted norms and with successful results, empirically verified by means of frequent testing, and at the same time leave the students completely indifferent to matters religious.

This conclusion resonated with the work of many other catechetical

---

42. Fargues, *How to Teach*, 22.

innovators and soon the conception of the task of catechesis expanded. No longer was its goal understood purely in terms of instruction. It was now recognized that catechism included the difficult business of persuasion. In calling students to conversion, catechesis had become a work of evangelization. The expansion of the catechetical task came as a response to new social conditions which offered challenges to the role and credibility of the Church.

Fargues never questioned the accuracy of the questions and answers provided in the traditional catechism, since they communicated sound doctrinal content in precise scholastic language. What she did question, however, was whether such a formulation of the Christian message was at all appropriate for children.

Fargues' own experience corroborated Montessori's findings regarding childhood. As a physician, Montessori took a keen interest in the links between the physical and the psychological aspects of human development. In her now famous theory about sensitive periods in childhood, Montessori built on the work of De Vries, a Dutch biologist of the 19th century. De Vries coined the term "sensitive periods" in his study of caterpillars, a study which offers a striking example of transitory aptitudes in developing organisms.[43] The first to apply the concept of sensitive periods to human development, Montessori elaborated an entire method of teaching based on respect for these windows of learning opportunity.[44] To understand Montessori's idea it will be useful to briefly describe the findings of De Vries.

The female butterfly deposits its eggs at the juncture of branch and tree trunk. Because its immature digestive system is ill-adapted for feeding on the mature leaves found near the trunk, the caterpillar must make its way to the tender leaves found at the extremities of the branches. But how does the caterpillar know that it must venture out to the limits of the tree in order to feed and survive? De Vries discovered that these larva exhibit an extreme photo-sensitivity. Light attracts them. The young caterpillars are drawn to the tips of the branches where exposure to the light is most intense and where their chances of survival are optimized. Once the caterpillar has developed sufficiently to be able to digest mature leaves, this photo-sensitivity disappears. The instinct lies extinguished once its moment of advantage to the

---

43. Maria Montessori, *L'enfant* (Geneva: Éditions Gonthier, (1936) 1968), 26.
44. Montessori, 25.

caterpillar has passed. From then on, other mechanisms of instinct assume a critical role in its development. The caterpillar, it is worth noting, has not become blind to light, but merely indifferent to it. Montessori applies the model to children with these words:

> L'enfant fait ses acquisitions pendant les périodes sensibles...C'est cette sensibilité qui permet à l'enfant de se mettre en rapport avec le monde extérieur d'une façon exceptionnellement intense; tout est facile, alors; tout est pour lui enthousiasme et vie. Chaque effort est un accroissement de puissance. Quand une de ces passions psychiques s'est éteinte, d'autres flammes s'allument, et l'enfance s'ecoule ainsi, de conquête en conquête, dans une vibration incessante, reconnue par tout le monde, et que l'on traite de joie enfantine.[45]

This author uses the ease with which children acquire a second language as an example of the achievements possible during a sensitive period of development.[46]

In contrast to the montessorian schools, most teaching of the early 20th century imposed not only a rigid content on students, but also an inflexible conduit of traditional methodology, replete with abstraction and endless memorization, i.e., the means by which that content would be delivered. It is inevitable that the ultimate goals of schooling be determined in relation to the needs and values prevalent in the society which educates. But which means are the most appropriate to ensure that the young of a society appropriate the wisdom and insights of their forebears in a way which allows them to make their own contribution to the world? In the field of catechesis, Marie Fargues offered an illuminating answer to this question and it involved more than handing on a "deposit" of accumulated knowledge, pre-fabricated and ready for consumption. Rather than impose questions from the world of grown-ups on children, Fargues wondered:

> What if we catechists would take up this role? What if we would lead the child first to become aware of his own questions and then to put

---

45. Montessori, 27.
46. The noted neurologist and second language theorist, Wilder Penfield demonstrated decades later, that the capacity to acquire a second language without a detectable accent or grammatical interference from the mother tongue diminishes after puberty when the child's brain function undergoes change. See W.F. Penfield, "The uncommitted cortex: the child's changing brain," *Atlantic Monthly* 214 (1964): 77-81.

them to us? Then it would be the doctrine of the Church that would answer him, that would give him the materials for his interior construction. This would then be coherent and solid, a Christian construction.[47]

Fargues generalized about the notion of sensitive periods, when she said that she had enough experience with nine to eleven year olds to know that this is the fundamental age for each of them to acquire a system of ideas.[48] The order in which she wished to present doctrine corresponded not to adult logic but to the needs of the child's development such as they are felt. It is this concept which made an attentive observation of perceptible periods a necessity for Fargues.[49] Her method meant to lead the child, but the leadership she intended held a novel twist:

> We shall establish then a contact between the doctrine of the Church and her ignorant disciple in listening to the questions that arise; the child's own questions. Ours are not important. It is at *his* time that we must help him to ask them; not at *our* time. As all of this must be done with moderation and clarity, and as through inexperience and thoughtlessness children do not always distinguish their true questions from their vain ones and their deep interests from their superficial ones, it is for us, the catechists, to guess, to foresee, and to arouse. I said just now that we must *follow*...this must be understood. We must precede the child, but only on a road that he can follow.[50]

The idea of learning by discovery, of developing one's own questions from the situations of one's life (or from skilfully contrived situations of the pedagogue's construction) is found in the thought of the noted American educational theorist, John Dewey. Dewey, in several of his works, but especially in *Education and Experience*, sets out a theory by which children might be lead to discover not only definitions of such complex abstracts as "government," "law" etc., but also an understanding of the conditions which gave rise to the need for such institutions.[51] It was hoped that a process which guided students

---

47. Fargues, *How to Teach*, 23.
48. Fargues, *How to Teach*, 23.
49. Fargues, *How to Teach*, 25.
50. Fargues, *How to Teach*, 25-26.
51. For examples of learning based on the everyday experiences of children see John Dewey, *Experience and Education* (New York: Collier Books, (1938) 1963), 94-107.

through learning situations, designed to allow them to discern the need for and function of many of the structures of their world, would produce critical thinkers who would not be stifled in their creativity by their education. This emphasis in educational theory encouraged thought over memorization. It tended toward intellectual autonomy and away from a sedulous, cognitive dependency.

It was just this kind of appropriation of the curriculum content which Marie Fargues was trying to establish in her corner of the pedagogical world. She came to believe that catechism did not have to be disconnected from the everyday experiences of life. She concluded that one could occupy oneself with God and things divine without ceasing to be human, i.e., without ignoring one's humanity in the consideration of these matters.

Needless to say, her attempts to reform the pedagogy of a catechism so deeply ensconced in the popular and ecclesial consciousness did not proceed without controversy. In recalling the decade of the forties, Fargues reflected:

> Even those who repudiated the word as equivocal (méthodes actives) were in agreement on the thing, and perhaps they never really contested the idea that a child could be educated without his personal participation. But they had not realized to what extent it was important to know psychology to put into action his personal activity, and many theologians, not the least influential of them, regarded with distrust this importance given to the subject.[52]

Through her work, Fargues discovered a fundamental canon which also forms the organizational matrix of Joseph Colomb's *Le service de l'evangile*.

Theology traditionally dealt with revelation from its transcendental aspect, from a perspective of immanent Trinitarianism. Hence, theological discussions remained largely a-historical and ananthropic. If revelation implied an encounter between the divine and the human, the human had been all but forgotten in the conversation. Revelation appeared more monologue than dialogue in this model. In Christology, this view surfaced in the emphasis on the divinity of the glorified, heavenly Christ to the neglect of the humanity of the earthly, historical Jesus.

At about the same time scientific investigation of the human subject was expanding with the rise of psychology, sociology and anthro-

---

52. Fargues, *How to Teach*, 46.

pology, some theologians began to show an interest in historical matters. If, as the Judeo-Christian tradition holds, God speaks to humanity, then God is logically limited to a form of communication which human persons can understand. Otherwise, one must conclude that no communication is intended or possible. As soon as the question of language is raised, it is apparent that the historical dimensions of the human person come into play. If this is the case, a theology of revelation can no longer occupy itself exclusively with the divine interlocutor.

The human dimensions of the relationship implied in revelation and in the person of Jesus Christ were largely unexplored territory. Now the emphasis shifted to an economic Trinitarianism and to the implications for human history of divine revelation. Christology began to take seriously the man Jesus and the particular, limited circumstances of his life. Of course this shift was expedited by the explosion of interest in historical criticism on the part of Catholic exegetes and theologians alike.

This shift in perspective is observable when one compares the documents emanating from the two Vatican Councils. Vatican Council I had identified revelation with the doctrine of faith, with the totality of the mysteries contained in the word of God and taught by the Magisterium of the Church. Without saying so directly, Vatican I practically identified revelation with the doctrine of faith and the truths of faith.[53] Influenced by theological developments in the first half of the 20th century, Vatican II moves beyond the concept of revelation as knowledge. Revelation is presented rather as the self-revelation of God in the history of salvation which culminates in Christ. Revelation is an event.[54] No longer a body of supernatural truths communicated by God, Vatican II presents revelation as the manifestation of God in the history of a chosen people and especially in the life, death and resurrection of Jesus Christ.

While it brought new interest in human history, a new concept of revelation could neither ignore the divine origins of revelation nor elevate humanity to the level of an interlocutor capable of conversing

---

53. H. Bouillard, "Le concept de Révélation de Vatican I à Vatican II," *Révélation de Dieu et langage des hommes* (Paris: Éditions du Cerf, 1972), 39. This article contains a succinct exposition of the changes in the theological understanding of revelation between the two Vatican Councils.

54. Bouillard, 43-44.

with God as an equal.[55] To pay attention to the cognitive and affective requirements of the human person was to put human capacities at the service of revelation. This is what Fargues had understood in and through her interest in the psychological and the spiritual development of the child. The communication of divine revelation to her pupils was hampered by a catechism which spoke a language foreign to the experience of her pupils.

A final, significant feature implied throughout Fargues' theory is the notion of individualization of instruction. To some degree, one may speak of collective experiences within a given society or group. With respect to religious faith, however, individual experience becomes the lens through which one appropriates a tradition. The new goal of catechesis, to call children to conversion, meant addressing them as individuals. The principal form of catechetical instruction, however, takes place in a group setting and so the first order of business is to discover a common element that allows the organization of instruction. "The most frequent common factor in our classrooms, sometimes the only one, is the factor of *age*; it is then from the psychology of development...that the teacher in charge will obtain the most light."[56] Attention to the traits of very young school children leads one back to the *ego*, the preoccupation with the self. This is an example of how Fargues' work combined the need for individualization and the constraints of group instruction.

While profoundly affected by developments in psychology and a general shift towards human history in intellectual circles, Fargues' presentation of doctrine, necessarily reflected a pre-Vatican II format. One has only to look at the subject headings and treatment of a variety of topics in *Nos enfants devant le Seigneur* to appreciate this fact. She remains one of the foremost innovators and pioneers of recent catechetical history.

The Intellectualist Strain

While these several reformers applied themselves assiduously to their task, producing new texts and generally affecting the scene where they lived and operated, the traditional work of the "intellectualist

---

55. In this light, one understands Colomb's emphasis on a double fidelity in the plan of *Le service de l'évangile*, fidelity to God and fidelity to human persons.

56. Fargues, *How to Teach*, 26.

strain" persevered in its presentation of a *clear* and *complete* transmission of the Christian doctrine. Traditionalists believed that their method called the memory, intelligence and will of the students into action. Their efforts continued to be reflected in the first catechism "for use in all the dioceses of France" which appeared in 1937 and was revised in 1947. While the 1947 revision lightened the presentation somewhat, adding some explanatory notes and biblical quotations, nothing basic was altered.[57]

Our treatment remains incomplete, leaving unnamed countless collaborators in the project of French catechetical renewal. Some of the most prominent thinkers have been highlighted in an effort to set the stage for subsequent developments in Canada. One figure deserving of mention, however, is François Coudreau. He played a significant role in the establishment of a centre for the training of catechists which proved most influential in the renewal process. We turn now to a consideration of this and other developments within the renewal.

SIGNS OF RENEWAL

New Institutions

François Coudreau was a Sulpician confrere of Joseph Colomb, the founding director of the catechetical institute at Lyon (1946). Paris possessed no such institute. In 1949, under the direction of Cardinal Suhard, the *Commission nationale du catéchisme* established a chair of catechetical pedagogy at the *Institut catholique* in Paris. Archbishop Feltin, who succeeded Suhard in the bishopric of Paris that same year, continued the project. Feltin invoked a motto to guide those who would implement the plan: fidelity to doctrine, fidelity to life.[58] By early 1950, a six-week course in catechetics was offered at the *Institut catholique* and by the start of the 1950-1951 school year the *Institut catéchétique* (later known as the *Institut supérieur de pastorale catéchétique* or *ISPC*) was founded. François Coudreau was responsible for planning and implementing the inaugural program offered at the institute that year. On short notice, Coudreau began an institute which has expanded and prospered enormously in its forty some years of ex-

---

57. Marlé, "A New Stage," 64.
58. Boyer, 192.

istence. Coudreau became an international figure in catechetical circles and came periodically to teach courses at the catechetical institutes at Laval University (Quebec City) and at the University of Montreal.

Apart from the foundation of catechetical institutes, P. Ranwez pointed to four signs as evidence of the durability of the renewal in catechesis which had taken shape up to the end of the Second World War:

1. The organizations established on the basis of a new orientation, which focused on the psychological needs of the child, the importance of the support of the child's social environment and the rediscovery of the Bible and liturgy as tools of religious education;

2. The growing number of handbooks written in this vein;

3. The large number of people who had become aware of the fundamental problems of catechesis;

4. The congresses and "study days" organized with the goal of improving an understanding of the questions of religious instruction.[59]

Even with the progress made up to the end of the war, Ranwez felt that the evolution of catechetics remained incomplete from two points of view: first, the progress made was centred too much on the human level, using the findings of psychology and pedagogy as the point of departure; second, the model of "instruction" had prevailed, even as the goal of catechesis had been redefined. The new goal was not merely to have the child accept knowledge, but rather to transform the child's life. Both these elements come together for Ranwez, in the notion of "initiation" into the Christian faith and the mystery of God, as opposed to mere cognitive instruction. He characterized the defect in this model as the lack of a supernatural perspective: "...they needed to be transformed by being more deeply rooted in a supernatural context and also by replacing the prevailing feature *Instruction* by the prevailing feature *Initiation*."[60]

Ranwez was a professor at Lumen Vitae. His divergence of opinion with the early work of the catechetical renewal in France with respect

---

59. Pierre Ranwez, "Typical Trends of the Contemporary Movement in Religious Training of Children," *Readings in European Catechetics*, ed. G. Delcuve, A. Godin (Brussels: Lumen Vitae Press, 1962), 15.

60. Ranwez, "Trends," 16.

to the correct starting point of catechesis, reflects the dominant theoretical option at Lumen Vitae. One's choice of a point of departure for catechesis is linked to one's idea of revelation. It is the concept of revelation which in large measure determines the biblical hermeneutic that catechetical programs adopt.

Ranwez' clear option for initiation as the defining feature of catechesis, proved prophetic, as this vital process provided a framework for a great deal of catechetical development in the decades subsequent. The concept of initiation was recovered from a study of the pastoral practices of the early Church. The mechanical rites of passage, which the sacraments had become in the modern Church, appeared foreign when compared to early practices. The incorporation of a person interested in the Christian Way often took place over a number of years, with significant stages on the journey of faith being marked by community celebrations. Christian identity was not taken as a given in this context. The new goal of catechetics, the conversion of children, also assumes a certain antipathy to the Christian message within society.

The Influence of Lumen Vitae

European influences on catechetical renewal in Quebec were not limited to France. The foundation in Belgium of the Lumen Vitae International Centre for Studies in Religious Education and its periodical of the same name, *Lumen Vitae*, marked another milestone in the renewal of catechesis internationally.

In 1937, *Où en est l'enseignement religieux?* and its Flemish counterpart, *Inleiding tot de catechetische Literatuur* were early signs of the flowering of this catechetical renaissance.[61] They appeared as responses to an international call, especially from the missions, for a centre to promote catechetical thought and education.[62] This volume was produced by the *Centre documentaire catéchétique*, a national

---

61. This book comprises annotated lists of the important catechetical resources in French, German, Spanish, Italian and Dutch in print at the time. Titles includes works on sacred history and bible teaching, pre-catechism and catechism, dogma and moral teaching, religious pedagogy and methodology, liturgy, Church history and related topics. It was the precursor of Ranwez' 1950 publication *Pastorale de l'enfance*.

62. Georges Delcuve, "Introduction," *Où en est l'enseignement religieux?* (Paris: Éditions Casterman, 1937), xiii.

body staffed by a corps of competent theologian-catechists in the famous university town of Louvain. The Jesuit priests who produced the volume were reconsidering the fate of catechesis in the Church, given new social and intellectual contexts. These scholars were aware that rationalist abstraction and individualism were under attack in a century identified with concerns for the concrete and the social.[63] Secular pedagogy, in a reaction to rationalism, had begun to place emphasis on the relationship between curriculum content and the lives of the students. The Jesuits of Lumen Vitae wondered out loud why the Church had not implemented similar advances in the field of catechetics.

By 1946 the first issue of the international review *Lumen Vitae* appeared, and in its editorial, readers were informed that the existing Catechetical Documentary Centre had changed its name to the International Centre for Studies in Religious Education. Already in the first issues of *Lumen Vitae*, the talented group of scholars who were to become so well known internationally were publishing articles. Early contributors included Georges Delcuve, Pierre Ranwez and Johannes Hofinger. Apart from an expansive new name and a change of address nothing much changed in the operation of the Centre. After a decade of service primarily to the Belgian and French catechetical communities, with a student body reflective of that fact, international enrolment suddenly shot up in 1957-1958. The catalyst for such a dramatic increase in popularity was an event that had little to do with Lumen Vitae. In fact the catalytic event did not even take place on Belgian soil.

Authorities at Rome had been viewing developments on the French catechetical scene with a critical eye and in 1957 action was taken. The new methods and many of the principal insights of the new catechists, especially those of Colomb and Derkenne, were expressly condemned as erroneous and insufficient in a "Communiqué" from the *Commission épiscopale de l'enseignement religieux*. The entire text of the Communiqué appears in the review *Catéchistes*. The following constitutes excerpts from the five areas of error outlined in the document.[64]

> On ne peut omettre, ni surtout exclure positivement, pendant les premières années, l'enseignement des vérités surnaturelles fondamentales, comme le péché originel, la divinité de Notre Seigneur Jésus-

---

63. Delcuve, xii.
64. Commission épiscopale de l'enseignement religieux, "Communiqué," *Catéchistes* 33 (January 1958): 85-86.

> Christ et sa mission de rédempteur du genre humain, le Saint-Esprit, les Commandements de Dieu et de l'Église....Pour eviter toute équivoque, on n'emploiera pas l'expression de "catéchisme progressif."
>
> La fonction spécifique et la fin prochaine du catéchisme est de transmettre le message de l'Église...Si donc le catéchiste doit se préoccuper de la formation actuelle de la conscience de l'enfant, et de l'insertion dans sa vie de l'enseignement donné, il accordera toujours la priorité à l'instruction religieuse proprement dite.
>
> Les procédés et activités catéchistiques seront jugés et admis en fonction du but surnaturel du catéchisme. Jamais ils ne resteront sur un plan purement naturel...
>
> L'experience religieuse n'est pas, par elle-même, un critère suffisant de la conscience morale....il faut expliquer que la conscience d'un chrétien est informée par l'enseignement de l'Église....
>
> L'article 256 du *Directoire pour la pastorale de la Messe* précise que les scéances d'initiation à la Messe ne dispensent pas du précepte de l'assistance à la Messe du dimanche et des fêtes d'obligation. Certains prônent des manières de faire opposées qui sont à proscrire.

In each article of reprimand, in one way or another, the commission attempted to discourage the new interest in the human subject, recalling the task of catechesis to the divine and supernatural realm and characterizing the path to God through human history as erroneous. In case there were any doubt left as to whose works were being targeted, an article by Vimont and Duperray accompanied the publication of the Communiqué and mentioned Colomb, Derkenne and a few others directly.[65] While Vimont and Duperray put the best possible face on this reprimand, insisting that certain aspects of the renewal were given the full support of Cardinal Gerlier and others, Colomb's reputation and that of the French school of catechists were sullied. In Canada, this public reprimand had the effect of making Paris suspect as a destination for priests and religious who were to train as catechists, and in that climate, Lumen Vitae offered a viable and "safe"

---

65. J. Vimont and J. Duperray, "Le sens de l'effort demandé aux catéchistes," *Catéchistes* 33 (January 1958): 87.

alternative.[66]

In Quebec, and doubtless elsewhere, catechetics was perceived as offering great promise for the renewal of Church life. At the same time, however, anything "new" in the Catholic world inspired, at the very least, great caution. In this atmosphere, it is perhaps not surprising that several of the most intellectually promising priests were first sent to Rome to obtain a licentiate or doctorate in theology before pursuing catechetical studies. This move was ostensibly to provide them with a sound doctrinal foundation before venturing into this "new" field.[67] It was at about this time that some of the program writers of *Viens vers le Père* began their training at Lumen Vitae, viz., Paul Tremblay and Jean-Paul Bérubé.

The Jesuits at Lumen Vitae moved quickly to fill the demand created by events in France. An international catechetical year was convened at Lumen Vitae for the 1957-1958 academic year, which attracted participants from Argentina, Austria, the Belgian Congo, Belgium, Brazil, Canada, Chili, Columbia, England, France, Germany, Haiti, Honduras, Ireland, Italy, Korea, Mexico, the Philippines, Portugal, Rwanda-Urundi, Spain, the United States, Uruguay and Vietnam. A report of the year's accomplishments is offered in the 1958 edition of *Lumen Vitae*.[68] What began as *one* international year of catechetical study in 1957-1958 continues to this day, as Lumen Vitae grew and prospered throughout the 1960s, declining in the 1970s with a general decline in interest in catechetics internationally.

From the earliest years of *Lumen Vitae*, articles by the most noted French catechists appeared, including Fargues, Colomb, Derkenne et al. Virtually any worthwhile piece of French scholarship on the subject was treated in *Lumen Vitae*'s review of literature. Thus the very strong emphasis on pedagogical technique and child psychology present in

---

66. J. Laforest reports that originally his bishop had planned to send him to Paris for catechetical studies. After Colomb's reprimand the decision was made to send him instead to Lumen Vitae. Source: Jacques Laforest, interview by author, Laval University (P.Q.) September 1992.

67. This was the case with both Paul Tremblay of *Viens vers le Père* and Jacques Laforest, director of the catechetical institute at Laval University. Source: Paul Tremblay, interview by author, Montreal (P.Q.) October 1990 and Jacques Laforest, Interview.

68. Georges Delcuve and Albert Drèze, "Chronique internationale: Organismes internationaux—Le centre Lumen Vitae," *Lumen Vitae* XIII (January-March 1958): 159-168.

the French school was known to the priests at the Belgian centre. For the first few years of the Centre's development, however, these important aspects of catechetical education remained underdeveloped. An example which illustrated this well is the absence of a teaching internship at Lumen Vitae. None was required there until some time after 1959, while in French circles this requirement had long been taken for granted. In part, this deficiency may be explained by a reluctance on the part of the leadership at Lumen Vitae to risk incurring ecclesiastical sanction. To have moved in the direction of pedagogical innovations which had incurred public reprimands in France may have been to invite such reprimands in Belgium. To a far greater extent, an explanation may be sought with the superior teaching experience of the women who had helped pioneer the renewal in France.

Much of what had happened in France was turned towards the child and was the fruit of decades of careful trial and error in experimental teaching carried on by Fargues, Derkenne and others. For all that, the French school was not devoid of theory. Its theory was rather simple and practical: no technique or methodology was of use in the education of a child if it did not respect both the cognitive capacities and experiences of that child.

The school at Lumen Vitae did not possess this grass-roots experience of pedagogical experimentation. Its early development at the *Centre Documentaire Catéchétique* and later in Brussels stood clearly under the influence of the kerygmatic school of theology at Innsbruck, where their fellow Jesuits were busy with an exciting project of renewal. As such, these scholars did not enter the catechetical renewal with the psychological capacities of the child as their point of departure, but were occupied rather with re-invigorating catechetical practice with an enthusiastic, recovery of the Scriptures. Soon these differences of opinion would be debated in an international forum, created in large part by the same forces which urged the foundation of Lumen Vitae itself, i.e., the foreign missions.

THE INTERNATIONAL CATECHETICAL MEETINGS

Kerygmatic Catechesis and Religious Experience

By the late 1950s, the lines of debate on catechetical issues were hardening just as the wider Church community was becoming active in the catechetical renewal. In 1959, an international meeting was convened at Nijmegen to deal with the problems of the Church in the foreign missions. The theme of the meeting, "Liturgy and the Missions," seemed to limit the gathering's agenda to the liturgical renewal.[69]

A common problem was being faced by the 200 missionaries who had assembled from all over the world: How could one adapt the Christian message, the principal vehicle of which was the liturgy, for people in non-western cultures? It was the hope of participants at this first meeting, that by promoting active participation in the liturgy the missionary apostolate would encourage the indigenous populations to assume an active role in the broader work of evangelization. It soon became obvious to those gathered that minor changes to the liturgy would not address the scope of the reforms needed.

A second international meeting, scheduled at Eichstätt for the following year under the theme "Catechetics and the Missions," considered catechesis within the larger mission of the Church. The scholars of Lumen Vitae had opted for a biblically-based model of catechesis, built on a "federal theology" which united Old and New Testaments. At Nijmegen and Eichstätt, they held the day. This first phase of renewal is commonly referred to as the Kerygmatic Stage.

In 1955, after a decade of effort, the dioceses of Germany published their catechetical manual for 9 to 12 year olds. By 1958, a French translation of this text was available under the title *Catéchisme biblique*.[70] In the published proceedings of the Eichstätt conference (1960), the clash of the new catechetical schools that had developed in France and in Germany stands out.

The return to the Scriptures proved no pious or naive use of the text but rather a methodical selection and organization of scriptural content under the *Heilsgeschichte* (salvation history) hermeneutic. The *Heilsgeschichte* emphasis, known in Protestant biblical theology for over a century, was an over-arching hermeneutical principle which united Old and New Testaments in a christocentric interpretation.[71]

---

69. Erdozain, 7.
70. Réginald Marsolais, "Trois décennies de catéchèse au Québec," *Le Souffle* 49 (October 1974): 68.
71. For a nuanced treatment of the development of *Heilsgeschichte* see Hans W. Frei's treatment of Johannes Cocceius in *The Eclipse of Biblical Narrative: A Study in Eighteenth and Nineteeth Century Hermeneutics* (New Haven: Yale University Press, 1974), 46-50. We retain the original German

Two noted biblical scholars of the twentieth century, Gerhard von Rad and Oscar Cullman, refined and popularized this concept, first elaborated at Tübingen's Protestant faculty in the 19th century.[72] Biblical scholars of this stamp referred respectively to the Old and New Testaments as shadow and reality, flesh and spirit, promise and fulfilment. Everything in the Scriptures was considered from a christocentric angle. Passages were read for what they had to tell us about Christ by way of foreshadowing, forecasting, prefiguring or direct reference. Events and figures in the OT represented "types" or models that foreshadowed their "anti-types" in the NT. The only function of the OT "type" in the new dispensation was to clarify its NT counterpart.

This hermeneutic, as scholarship has made clear in the post-holocaust era, reduced the Hebrew Scriptures to a transitory step whose only religious significance lay in the fact that it formed a wonderful backdrop for the NT. OT texts were not allowed to speak for themselves as there was already a high degree of pre-interpretation imposed on their meaning.

From the point of view of historical critical scholarship this hermeneutic poses several difficulties. Today it is generally agreed in critical study of the Bible that historically-conditioned texts, drawn from widely varying epochs in the history of Israel, were not written to foretell distant historical events. Moreover, the whole Bible is forced into a unified, coherent whole, with the various theologies of its many authors being made to look curiously compatible. The *Heilsgeschichte* emphasis subsumed many individual OT texts within the plot of the larger story which presupposed the NT and a good many early Church developments.

An ancillary question arose out of this hermeneutical controversy: Is it possible to have a hermeneutic which is both christocentric and yet respectful of the religious experience of each of the authors and of each of the communities in which the texts took shape? How could Christians, who have a definite point of view about the identity of Jesus and the general course of God's story with human kind, not be reduced to making every OT text speak about Jesus, either directly or

---

term for this emphasis in biblical theology, *Heilsgeschichte*, in order to recall its scholarly setting and to avoid confusion with other, broader notions (e.g., "sacred history", "story of salvation").

72. Mary C. Boys, *Biblical Interpretation in Religious Education* (Birmingham, Alabama: Religious Education Press, 1980), 9.

indirectly? For historical critics this option stands against their methodological principles. Pre-critical scholars of the Bible had less difficulty overcoming such impasses as they admitted more senses to the text than the strictly historical sense.[73] Catholic theology has traditionally admitted readings of the text that move beyond a purely literal interpretation. Since the time of Thomas Aquinas the allegorical, moral and anagogical senses were admitted but were necessarily interpreted on the basis of the literal sense which they could not contradict.[74] Perhaps because of its dismissal of the historical underpinnings of the OT, the *Heilsgeschichte* hermeneutic exhibits a tendency to undervalue the religious experiences recorded in the Hebrew Bible. Religious experiences of OT characters were passed over if they did not fit strictly christocentric interpretative criteria. As it is our contention that catechesis should identify and elucidate religious experience, *Heilsgeschichte* makes a poor candidate for use as the basis of a religious education programme. Not only must the OT world be absorbed into the NT, so too must the history and experiences of today's readers. Instead of guiding students through a discovery of the spiritual significance of their experiences in the world, programmes based on this hermeneutic wish to lead students away from their familiar worlds into the world it understands the Bible to propose.

Catholic clergy and religious, who had been formed in the philosophically precise world of Neo-Scholasticism, seemed to have had a conversion experience in rediscovering the fresh zeal of the primitive Church which first proclaimed the kerygma. They had traded ideas for experience. An encounter with the Risen Lord of the Scriptures replaced St. Thomas, as it had replaced Luther and Calvin for a generation of Protestants. To those who had not lived through the dryness of Scholasticism, (Protestant or Catholic) the relief of kerygmatic enthusiasm made no sense; it had lost its interpretative context. Another sign that this kerygmatic zeal was not having the desired effect was its waning popularity in the missions.

The *Verkündigungstheologie* of the Innsbruck school, introduced the kerygmatic emphasis into Catholic circles in the 1930s. After dec-

---

73. As an example of other than historical readings of the Bible, see Frei's treatment of Calvin's figural interpretation. Frei, *Eclipse*, 47-48.
74. Grant and Tracy, 88-89.

ades of quiet repression, Jungmann's *Die Frohbotschaft* re-surfaced in the context of the Eichstätt meeting as a work of pivotal importance. Johannes Hofinger, a Jesuit confrere of Jungmann from the Institute for Mission Apologetics in Manilla, was chiefly responsible for bringing *Die Frohbotschaft* to the general attention of the conference participants. Hofinger had been a close collaborator of Lumen Vitae from its earliest days and his enthusiasm for the work of Jungmann shines clearly in an address he gave at Eichstätt, published under the title, "*La formation catéchétique des missionnaires prêtres.*"[75]

Jungmann's work made it clear that the problem of catechesis was not only one of methodology but also one of content. Joseph Colomb had reached this conclusion decades earlier, but few Church officials were ready to listen to him at the close of the 1950s. During this period, he had effectively been discredited. Whatever its source, this insight brought about another shift in perspective.

The views of Georges Delcuve and Marcel Van Caster informed much of the Kerygmatic Stage of the renewal. Van Caster was especially prominent in the early development of centres of catechesis in North America, where he frequently came to teach. The *Heilsgeschichte* hermeneutic was central in Van Caster's work and, in this, he was typical of the Lumen Vitae school. The divergent starting points of catechesis in the French and Belgian schools fundamentally altered their educational projects and the biblical hermeneutics implied therein, a fact which in some measure explains the incongruous fates of programmes developed on these two models. We will return to this point later in our study.

There were a total of seven international catechetical meetings and each one unfolded some new aspect of catechetical renewal. In the meetings subsequent to Eichstätt, the influence of the kerygmatic theologians declined. Whatever their shortcomings, the legacy of these first international attempts at renewed catechesis was clear. Most programs which followed in the renewal incorporated the biblical witness as one foundation of their design and most employed the insights of curriculum theory and educational psychology. From that point on, the question of content demanded as much attention as the question of

---

75. Johannes Hofinger, "La formation catéchétique des missionaires prêtres," *Renouvellement de la catéchèse: Rapports de la semaine internationale d'études d'Eichstätt sur la catéchèse dans les pays de mission*, ed. J. Hofinger (Paris: Éditions du Cerf, 1961), 414-421.

methodology. Moreover, in and through the kerygmatic renewal, there was the realization that Christianity is not a system of truths or a code of conduct, but above all a message, the Good News.[76] Nijmegen and Eichstätt disseminated what Lumen Vitae had been formulating and promulgating for most of the previous decade in the missions. Another phase was about to dawn, one that introduced a third component into the catechetical dialogue. To the questions of "How does one teach?" and "What does one teach?" was added the query, "To whom are we teaching?" There was a perceived need to address the experience of children who belonged to a new social reality. As Marlé put it, "It was no longer the God of nature or reason, deciding as if by chance to reveal himself, who presided over catechesis, but rather the God manifested in our history, in Jesus Christ, and encountered notably in the Church's liturgical life."[77] From a doctrinal point of view, catechisms had been basically theistic before the reform; they now became Trinitarian and Christological.[78]

In the setting of the missions, the move towards experience was one with the need for indigenous inculturation of a Gospel that had come wrapped in the garb of an occidental, Latin Church. Of course, the point had already been made in the work of Marie Fargues and others in France, that questions of methodology or psychology were linked to questions of sociology. Adapting to the psychological capacities of the child would do little to redress the hostility or indifference to religion in the surrounding society, just as it could do little to dissipate the cultural dissonance between native, non-occidental culture and the Christian gospel.

The Catechumenal or Anthropocentric Stage

By the third International Catechetical meeting in Bangkok (1962) a new emphasis had won over the interests of the participants. The question of the adaptation of the Word of God to the particular social and cultural setting of the listeners took on great importance. André Fossion, in his treatment of the International Catechetical Weeks depicts these first forays into the process of adaptation and inculturation as a continuation of concerns already present in the kerygmatic phase. He reminds his reader that kerygmatic catechesis had been vigilant in

---

76. Erdozain, 12.
77. Marlé, "A New Stage," 67.
78. Marlé, "A New Stage," 67.

its intention to create a space for the response of the catechized person to the word of God, maintaining that any preaching of salvation must be accompanied by a constant attention to the circumstances in which it is received.[79] This irenic reading of the evolution of thought between Eichstätt and Bangkok misses the rupture between the two phases apparent in Luis Erdozain's treatment of the subject:[80]

> The Eichstätt study week, completely immersed as it was in the kerygma, had quite properly laid emphasis on the Word of God. But in stressing the theological aspect, it had perhaps lost sight of the fact that the Word of God is, too, the Word of God given to man, and that the Revelation of God, is also man's revelation: that the history of salvation is as well a history intended for man's own good.[81]

The kerygmatic approach was not designed to help people discover God in their midst, but rather zealously delivered its audience to the God of the Scriptures. The arrival of the God of the Bible, in many circumstances must have appeared to the audience somewhat like a *Deus ex machina*. The emphasis which succeeded the kerygmatic strain directed its gaze towards the listener. It is variously referred to as the catechumenal or anthropocentric phase.[82] This model predominated at the Bangkok and Katigondo (1964) meetings.

Although the catechumenal model of catechesis was developed

---

79. André Fossion, *La catéchèse dans le champ de la communication: Ses enjeux pour l'inculturation de la foi* (Paris: Les éditions du Cerf, 1990), 200.
80. Fossion's approach has the advantage of demonstrating the connections between the various stages of development in the International Catechetical Meetings. At Eichstätt the catechumenal emphasis was vying with the then dominant kerygmatic trend for attention. At Katigondo proponents of an existential catechesis tried to be heard over the prevailing catechumenal model, and in Manilla the historico-prophetic emphasis asserted its rights as a corrective to the existential approach. In our view, Fossion does not sufficiently emphasize the fact that each successive stage represented the ascendancy of the views of different scholars and different churchmen as the process evolved.
81. Erdozain, 15.
82. Fossion uses the former term, Erdozain the latter. The use of these terms reveals their respective approaches to charting the development of thought in these international fora. Fossion's analysis focuses on the published documents of the international study weeks. Erdozain seems to refer more broadly to evidence of these tendencies observable at the grassroots level in the European and mission Churches.

primarily for an adult audience in the context of the missions and therefore often in the context of beliefs other than Christianity, it would eventually translate into childhood and adolescent catechesis. This model divided its efforts into two separate areas: 1) the precatechumenate, which further sub-divided into a stage of pre-evangelization and a stage of evangelization and 2) the catechumenate in which catechetical instruction was intended to draw out the consequences of the Word that had been preached.[83] The need for re-evangelization was already known to the Church in France, as we saw above. We recall the works by Fargues: *La formation religieuse des enfants du peuple dans le milieu déchristianisé* (1935), Godin and Daniel: *France, pays de mission?* (1943) and Colomb: *Plaie ouverte au flanc de l'église* (1954).

While the catechumenal model held all the potential for a well-rounded catechesis, in its use in the missions (and in the religious education programs that were published for adolescents in North America), it got bogged down in the stage of pre-evangelization. The anthropocentrism of catechetical programmes which incorporated this new insight, too often led in the catechetical setting to a kind of aimless exercise of examining experiences. The pendulum had now swung to the other extreme. Instead of the hegemonic imposition onto the experience of the students of an interpretation of life—extracted from the Bible by means of the artificial and extraneous *Heilsgeschichte* hermeneutic—the lived experience of the learner now became a kind of value in itself, bereft of any critical or traditional paradigm against which to measure or interpret it. The search for a balance between the human and the divine, between experience and doctrine, continued. Clearly, this anthropocentrism led nowhere.

The Anthropological Phase

With respect to the methodological point of departure for religious education, one may consider the kerygmatic approach as a thesis, the anthropocentric/catechumenal approach as its antithesis, and the anthropological approach as their synthesis. The tension between the human and the divine in the communication of revelation will never be resolved, no matter what teaching method or mode of catechesis is employed. This fact notwithstanding, methods which emphasized one

---

83. Fossion, 201.

half of this communicative equation at the expense of the other fail to do precisely what is intended—they fail to engender a dialogue. The anthropological method picks up on a theme present in the catechumenal model, that of a link between human experience and the process of coming to Christian faith.[84] The anthropocentric stage was preparing the ground for seed. One listened attentively to the social and cultural situation in order to prepare a catechesis which would adapt the Word of God to its new setting. The "Word of God" could continue to function as a deposit, as unchanged and static as the ink on the pages that represented it. As a new person came to faith, the content of revelation remained immutable. No event occurred. Revelation continued to be understood as something static and external to the believer, a reified "object" that needed only to be internalized.

The logic of incarnation implied in the anthropological model transformed this notion. The anthropological emphasis no longer limits the requirement to take human experience as the starting point for catechesis to the stage of pre-evangelization, but presents it rather as the constant preoccupation throughout the entire process of catechesis, i.e., throughout pre-evangelization, evangelization and catechesis. Fossion writes: "C'est précisément la prise en compte *systématique* et *non seulement préparatoire*, des données de l'expérience humaine qui définit la catéchèse anthropologique, dite aussi catéchèse existentielle."[85] This approach maintains that the whole of human history and the personal history of the catechumen holds the key to understanding divine revelation. Divine revelation lies locked within the experience of human persons and the Word of God meets that experience in an illuminating moment, that one may call the moment of faith, or as some have called it, the catechetical moment. Simultaneously, the course of one's life and the content of revelation are illuminated. From the perspective of the faith community, the content of revelation is illuminated through its incarnation in the life of the new believer. From the perspective of the believer, one's own particular history is illuminated and transformed by the optic of revelation. The covenanting partners, God and humanity, may not be equals in the encounter, and yet it is this condescension of the divine in the direction of the human that an incarnational catechesis portends.

The anthropological approach represents a maturation of the an-

---

84. Fossion, 204.
85. Fossion, 205.

thropocentric emphasis which came to international attention at Bangkok (1962). It was developed against the backdrop of the emerging nations of the post-colonial period in Katigondo (1964). By Manilla (1967), the anthropological approach had reached its apogee in this forum. Soon, other questions would come to the fore, questions which became visible, precisely because of the existential focus of the anthropological model of catechesis.

Summary

In 1959 after centuries of slow, and one might say, imperceptible change in catechetics, the field exploded with new ideas. Both the methods and the content were renewed, but still there were problems. The rote memorization of tersely-worded theological conclusions had been replaced with participatory curricula based on the Scriptures. Tied to these changes was a shift in the way that doctrine was used and applied in their design. The former rationalist conception of God was supplanted by an image drawn from the life of Jesus of Nazareth and complemented by Trinitarian and Christological dogmas of the Patristic era. The pressing question of the adaptation of all catechetical sources, (Bible, doctrine, liturgy) to the experiences of the target audience had been raised.

In the catechumenal phase, the catechetical process was still understood as "adaptation" and still depicted revelation as something that happened "then," "outside" the life experiences of the individual believer. The stage was set for new catechetical programs that would incorporate the theological insights of incarnational and existential approaches to catechesis. It is at this moment that *Viens vers le Père* enters the scene.

THE CATECHETICAL RENEWAL IN QUEBEC

With the exception of Newfoundland, where confessional schools exist in some parts of the province, and Ontario, where separate Catholic schools flourish, most Catholic religious education across Canada has taken place at the parish and family level. The situation which obtained in Quebec remained unique due to the position the Church occupied in the social fabric. While it is perhaps impossible to adequately deal with the remote factors which created this intertwining of Church and state interests in a brief manner, an excerpt from Gregory Baum's *The Church In Quebec* provides an excellent summary.

After the 1763 British conquest, a few years prior to the American Revolution, the British Crown wanted Quebec to be a peaceful and loyal colony. The crown was willing to guarantee the rights of the Catholic Church if the bishops promised to pacify the population. The bishops consented. They were grateful for receiving royal recognition. After the failed rebellion of 1837, the bishops again helped to pacify the colony. In the 1840s, thanks to a new, ultramontane Catholicism—aggressive, disciplined and other-worldly, promoted by a large number of priests and religious arriving from France—the Catholic Church was able to affirm itself as the spiritual and cultural force that defined, with ever-increasing intensity, the social reality of French Canada. This Catholicism was the religious cement that enabled French Canadians to resist assimilation and decline. They remained a vital people....In 1867 the bishops gave their consent, with Pope Pius IX's approval, to the new Canadian confederation. They hoped that this new political arrangement would assure the identity, vitality and freedom of *le peuple canadien*. The Church remained the soul of the people. It taught them to pray and believe in eternal life, it educated them, it made them into dedicated workers on the land and in the bush, it cared for them when they were sick and helped them when they were destitute and it shaped their religious ideology. Thanks to the Church the people understood themselves as a holy remnant in North America, the seed bed of a Catholic civilization.[86]

The British North America Act guaranteed the confessional character of the schools which existed at that time in Montreal and Quebec City.[87] This guarantee has been traditionally understood to extend to the entire educational system of the province, which developed after that period.[88] Nearly every facet of Quebec's public life was, in some measure, affected by the Church. Up to 1965, the Quebec episcopacy exercised control over Catholic schools in the province.[89] When the first stirrings of the catechetical renewal were felt after World War II, the Church had a free hand to act. All that was lacking was the

---

86. Gregory Baum, *The Church In Quebec* (Ottawa: Novalis, 1991), 16.

87. Baum, *Church in Quebec*, 43.

[88] At the moment, the educational system in Quebec remains divided into Protestant and Catholic school commissions. This will soon change as Pauline Marois, Quebec's Minister of Education, has recently announced (1997) the creation of linguistically-based school boards.

89. Fournier, "Canada," 96.

stimulus, and that was not long coming.[90]

In January of 1935 a decree of the Sacred Congregation of the Council, *Provido sane consilio* directed bishops to establish offices to oversee and promote catechesis. The decree mandated the appointment of priest-supervisors for catechetical classes in each diocese, as well as the organization of special conferences to help further the education of those at work in the field.[91] At the first synod of the diocese of Joliette in 1945, Bishop J.A. Papineau established a diocesan catechetical office. In the following year he named Gérard-Marie Coderre as its first director.[92] In 1942, Coderre had already been appointed to a commission charged with the production of a new catechism. Papineau had acted on Coderre's request to found Canada's first catechetical office.[93]

As a member of the commission for a new catechism and as director of the first catechetical office in Quebec, Coderre became wellknown to the bishops and quickly gained their respect. So it was not surprising when in 1951, he was named auxiliary bishop for the diocese of Saint-Jean-de-Québec. Coderre remembers thinking that his days in the field of catechetics were over when he received his episcopal appointment.[94] He soon discovered otherwise when, in the following year (1952), he was asked to preside at the episcopal commission on religious education.

Alongside the episcopal commission of 1942, another body was at work. A sub-commission was appointed by the *Comité catholique du*

---

90. For a succinct presentation of four distinct phases in the catechetical history of Quebec from about the turn of the 20th century on, see Robert Gaudet, "Activités catéchistiques dans le diocèse de Joliette," *Le Séminaire* XX (September 1955): 141-143. Development in Quebec followed the pattern in Europe, even if the timetable differs somewhat.
91. Sacred Congregation of the Council, "Provido sane consilio," *Acta Apostolicae Sedis* (Vatican City: 1935), 145-152.
92. Marsolais, 64.
93. Anne-Marie Ricard, "Note de recherche sur la production du catéchisme *Viens vers le Père*", *Une inconnue de l'histoire de la culture: la production des catéchismes en Amérique française*, ed. Raymond Brodeur, Jean-Paul Rouleau (Ste. Foy: Éditions Anne Sigier, 1986), 393.
94. Gérard-Marie Coderre, interview by author, LaPrairie (P.Q.) 7 January 1992.

Conseil de l'Instruction publique to develop a new religion program.[95] The purpose of such a "Programme of Studies" was to develop a master plan, which would set out the educational objectives for the first seven years of schooling. A programme of studies often precedes the development or selection of texts used to implement its objectives. Thus when the new religion program appeared in 1948, there were as yet no teacher manuals or student texts in place. In 1951, the episcopal commission published the text it had been working on since 1942 under the title *Le catéchisme catholique*. This single volume was intended only as a correction of the catechism of 1888[96], but the constant exchanges between the sub-commission of the *Comité catholique* and the episcopal commission altered this goal somewhat. Coloured illustrations appeared in the 1951 catechism and a question-answer format was retained. Unlike earlier editions, questions were now tagged for use at the various grade levels, according to the difficulty of the vocabulary and concepts used.[97] This allowed the authors to retain the full complement of doctrinal content present in the catechism of 1888, while making *marginal* concessions to the new methods.

In the final analysis, the Programme of Studies envisaged a series of catechetical resources essentially different from the single volume which appeared in 1951. In 1947, Father Lussier of the subcommission had promised separate catechetical manuals for each grade of the primary and elementary schools.[98] Neither *Le catéchisme catholique* of 1951 nor its 1954 revision made good on this promise. While *the Catéchisme catholique* of 1951 was an improvement over its 1888 predecessor, it represented no fundamental change in direction.

Teaching methods were slowly evolving in Quebec throughout this period (1940-1953). In addition to the pivotal role that priest-inspectors played in introducing pedagogical innovation, Marsolais

---

95. Raymond Brodeur, "L'enseignement religieux au Québec: Des programmes de classe!" *Les Cahiers de recherches en sciences de la religion* 9 (1988): 84.

96. *Le Catéchisme des provinces ecclésiastiques de Québec, Montréal et Ottawa* (Québec: (1888) 1976). For a discussion of the episcopal commission's intentions with respect to the correction and reworking of the 1888 manual, see J.-P. Rouleau "La Production du *Catéchisme catholique*, édition canadienne (1951)," *Une Inconnue*, 319ff.

97. For a discussion highlighting the tensions between the two religious education working groups see Rouleau, "La production."

98. Brodeur, "L'enseignement," 92.

points to three elements which favoured advances among teaching personnel:[99] 1) the repercussions of the *École active*, 2) the distribution of the *Aux Petits du Royaume* series[100], 3) the new Programme of Studies for religion published by the sub-commission of the *Comité catholique* in 1948.

As exposure to new ideas spread, expectations were raised among those at work in the field. Beginning between 1953-1955, teachers began enrolling in large numbers in courses introducing them to exegesis, the liturgy and Christian pedagogy.[101] It took some time before many of the elements known very early on to those active in religious pedagogy filtered down to the person in the street. It took even longer for the more conservative elements within the Church to accept them once they had achieved wide circulation.

In 1952, Coderre founded *l'Office catéchétique du Québec* (OCQ), the first provincial catechetical office for Quebec.[102] He was dissatisfied with the work of the 1951 and 1954 revisions of the catechism. Having become aware of the many catechetical advances taking place in France and Belgium, Coderre was convinced that reform was needed.[103] During his tenure as coadjutor of Saint-Jean-de-Québec, Coderre's influence in the Church in Quebec grew steadily. One of the chief reasons that he was able to gain the confidence of his fellow bishops may be found in his constant efforts of keep his colleagues abreast of developments in the field. Coderre kept them up to date with respect to the theological rationale behind the changes and the shape of the curriculum tools being produced. Bishop Forget of Saint-Jean-de-Quebec died in February of 1955 and Coderre succeeded him in the see.[104] Coderre's own rise through the ecclesial ranks paralleled the ascendancy of catechesis on the ecclesial agenda in Quebec. He was its key promoter and spokesperson.

In 1956, Coderre came into contact with reforms in Belgium at the

---

99. Marsolais, "Trois décennies," 66.
100. This series was published in 1939 by the Sisters of the Assumption of the Blessed Virgin at Nicolet. It offered a more concrete treatment of doctrine by evoking analogies, through the use of pictures, the blackboard and film and by providing interesting facts related to the topic under study. See Gaudet, 142.
101. Marsolais, 66.
102. Fournier, "Canada," 96.
103. Coderre, Interview.
104. Ricard, 393.

catechetical Congress of Anvers.[105] Two years later (1958), he commissioned a report from the provincial catechetical office. It appeared under the title, *Rapport général sur l'enseignement religieux donné dans la province de Québec*.[106] In 1961, the provincial catechetical office hosted the first Canadian catechetical congress at St. Jean, P.Q., with the result that the hundred or so participants in attendance unanimously called for new programmes. They specifically requested separate parent, teacher and student manuals adapted for each school grade. To ensure that this would happen as quickly as possible, the resolution stipulated that a team of competent persons be assigned to this task with all dispatch.[107] The assembly further stipulated that their intention was to implement changes which would conform to the principles established by the international congress of Eichstätt.[108]

When the conference body called for the engagement of competent personnel to carry out the task of producing new resources, its leadership knew that Canadians capable of executing the task had already been educated in Europe. There was always at least one French-Canadian in the first graduating classes of ISPC (1953-1955).[109] Numbers increased steadily for a number of years and, after 1957, Lumen Vitae began graduating priests, sisters and brothers from Quebec. Some English-speaking Canadians also began to attend Lumen Vitae during this period. With study abroad came a more general exposure to the European catechetical renewal. Homecoming graduates introduced periodicals and reviews to a Quebec teaching population eager for the insights of their European colleagues. *Lumen Vitae, Vérité et Vie*, and *Documentation Catéchistique* enjoyed the widest circulation.[110] By 1965, Canada could boast its own French-language catechetical review, *Le Souffle*. In 1954, François Coudreau, founding director of *l'Institut catéchétique* (later known as ISPC), started a long

---

105. Ricard, 393.
106. Office catéchistique provincial, *Rapport général sur l'enseignement religieux donné dans la Province de Québec*, Episcopal Offices of the diocese of Saint-Jean-de-Québec, (June 1958). A report prepared for pastoral use.
107. See *Rapport de la réunion des responsables diocésains de l'enseignement religieux*, held at Montreal, February 11, 1963.
108. Marsolais, 69.
109. Marsolais, 66.
110. Marsolais, 66.

tradition of European professors coming to teach in Quebec.[111] Many other Europeans would follow, from both ISPC and Lumen Vitae. Signs of the durability of the renewal became evident. In 1957, the bishops appointed Robert Gaudet as the first permanent secretary to the provincial catechetical office. This move engendered new dialogue between the OCQ and the various dioceses. The proof of this was the establishment of eight diocesan catechetical offices by 1960.[112] By that year, the provincial catechetical office had three permanent employees and several working groups which met periodically.[113] From this point on, there was a virtual flood of people attending classes to prepare them as catechists.

In 1961, the *Institut supérieur des sciences religieuses* in Montreal, created a Department of Catechetics where fifty or so educators followed weekend courses in a diploma program offered by Quebecois and European professors.[114] For those unable to attend weekend courses during the regular academic year, Norbert Fournier, director of the Department of Catechetics at the University of Montreal, indicated that the summer program would continue for a third year, starting in July, 1962.[115] Two levels of instruction were provided that year, one for those already possessed of a solid initiation to catechetics and religious studies, and another for neophytes.

For that summer, Marcel van Caster came from Lumen Vitae, Joseph Bournique from ISPC, Adrien Nocent from Mardesous and François Coudreau, from Paris—where he had moved from ISPC to a position as director of the adult catechumenate program in the archdiocese of Paris.[116] From Quebec, Jacques LaForest, director of the Catechetical Institute at Laval University, Jean Martucci of the *Centre de la Bible* in Montreal, Jean-Guy Myre from the seminary at Valleyfield and Bernard Coté from St. Laurent College were also involved in teaching at this summer program.[117]

---

111. Marsolais, 66.
112. Marsolais, 67.
113. For the composition of the most important of these working groups see Marsolais, 66.
114. Norbert Fournier, "Pour une meilleure formation des catéchistes," *La vie des communautés religieuses* 20 (1962): 114.
115. Fournier, 114.
116. Fournier, 115.
117. Fournier, 116.

By 1958, the evolution of the catechetical scene was already well under way in the Quebec City region where a large congregation of brothers, *Les frères des écoles chrétiennes*, had begun an institute at 1049 Route de l'Église in Ste. Foy.[118] This congregation wished to improve the teaching methods of its own brothers.[119] Vincent Ayel, a very well-known catechist from Europe, was a member of this same congregation and through his writings and work, the brothers had taken an interest in this expanding field. Oscar Contin, at that time the provincial of *Les frères des écoles chrétiennes*, founded the school at Route de l'Église and appointed Yvan Laroche as its first director.

From the first days at Route de l'Église, professors from Europe came to teach. Grégoire Lévesque, a brother who attended classes there, recalls the atmosphere of the house as being one of great intellectual stimulation. Professors such as Liégé and van Caster came to teach small classes (10-12 students) with whom they shared living accommodations. Interaction between professors and students was frequent outside class. Brother Lévesque mentioned that a great deal of informal instruction went on in this way as well.[120] Notable professors from the North American continent also taught at Route de l'Église, including Louis O'Neill, Jean-Marie Tillard, André Gignac, Aimé Hamman, Joseph Choquette and Joseph Lavoie.

The cost of running this program for such small numbers of brothers was prohibitive and, hoping to share expenses with others interested in catechetics, the congregation requested that the Faculty of Theology at Laval University establish a catechetical institute. Initially, the university refused this request, but when the brothers indicated that they would continue their efforts at Route de l'Église, and expand their school to include all the other teaching congregations and lay people who wished to attend, the Faculty acceded.[121]

Jacques Laforest was hired in January 1962 as the first director of

---

118. This period of the recent history of catechetics in Quebec has not been the subject of much research to date. What follows is a summary of the course of events, compiled largely from interviews with the principals involved, and from records held at the Faculty of Theology at Laval University.

119. Grégoire Lévesque, interview by author, Trois Rivières (P.Q.) 1 October 1992. Brother Lévesque was among the first graduates of the Route de l'Église catechetical program.

120. Grégoire Lévesque, Interview.

121. Jacques Laforest, Interview; Grégoire Lévesque, Interview.

this newly-established institute which, up to that point, existed only on paper.[122] Laforest faced essentially the same task as François Coudreau had years earlier in the foundation of the *Institut catéchétique* (ISPC), with the exception that Laforest had no centres of higher catechetical education in the North American setting from which to draw a staff for the new institute. This forced the Faculty of Theology to send Laforest, accompanied by Yvan Laroche, the former director of the Route de l'Église school, to seek out the services of their former professors in Europe for the academic year 1962-1963. The need to look to Europe for professors persisted for several years.

For the first session enrolment in the institute was around fifty students; it grew steadily until the numbers attending the *Institut de catéchèse* outweighed the enrolment of the Faculty of Theology proper. Full and part-time students in the heyday of the faculty reached nearly three hundred strong.[123] A certain rivalry developed between the *Institut de catéchèse* and the Faculty of Theology, that reflected the tension between the kerygmatic theology of the catechetical renewal and the more traditional theology of the faculty—Thomism. Moreover, the *Institut de catéchèse* was thought not to have availed itself of the intellectual resources of the Faculty of Theology.

In particular, the question of how one should use the Old Testament became a bone of contention. In a course intended to introduce future catechists to the field, Laforest developed the theme of salvation history using texts drawn from the Old and New Testaments. The principal function of this course, according to its initiator, was to provide a spiritual model for catechists-in-training.[124] Some of the theologians and exegetes of the period expressed their belief that these students ought to have an exposure to the historical-critical method as a guard against eisegetical tendencies.

The argument did not end until Laforest was urged to leave the Institute in 1971, two years after he had left the director's post to take

---

122. Marsolais, 68
123. Numbers of full-time students graduating from the programmes of Laval's catechetical institute in the 1960s are as follows: 1962-1963—43 students; 1963-1964—69 students; 1964-1965—124 students; 1965-1966—164 students; 1967-1968—169 students; 1968-1969—175 students. These figures, compiled from records at the Faculty of Theology, Laval University, do not include part-time students or auditors.
124. Laforest, Interview.

up full-time teaching of catechetics. His successor, Jean Fournier, had ideas much more in line with the expectations of the Faculty. The point proved to be moot, as the *Institut de catéchèse*, along with its European counterparts, went into a period of sharp decline in the early 1970s.

In its heyday, Quebec's catechetical movement represented one of the largest efforts at theological education in the province's history and probably in the history of Canada as a whole. Norbert Fournier wrote during the academic year of 1965-1966: "Grâce aux quelque 600 canadiens qui ont poursuivi au moins une année d'études en catéchèse et aux 4000 éducateurs...qui ont participé à des sessions d'un mois sur les principes de la catéchèse, les idées nouvelles sur la catéchèse font rapidement leur chemin et atteignent un public toujours plus grand."[125]

Alongside developments among Church "professionals," a growing voice of dissent was being raised in the public forum. Marsolais offers us some of the flavour of this unrest:

> Et parmi ces "signes du temps," il n'y a pas que les résolutions fignolées de réunions ou de congrès de catéchèse qui se tiennent ici et là (Saint-Jean, Montréal, Québec, etc.), il y a la voix de l'opinion publique qui, par des lettres aux journaux et des articles de revue, prend l'initiative de faire entendre et parfois de crier amèrement ses plaintes au sujet des déficiences du manuel de catéchisme traditionnel. Le plus percutant de ces articles paraît le 31 mai 1961 dans le no. 37 de *Cité Libre*. Il s'intitule: "L'Essentiel, est-ce le ciel?" et est signé par Marthe Henripin. L'auteur y dénonce les méfaits d'un catéchisme qui se présente comme une "prime d'assurance" mais qu'elle considère comme "engendrant le rejet de Dieu" et "assassin du mystère." S'interrogeant sur ce que les enfants devront plus tard rejeter, Marthe Henripin plaide pour un "catéchisme engendrant des espérants et non des légalistes remplis de suffisance" et pour "une réforme en profondeur."[126]

Paul-M. Lemaire, in addition to Henripin's essay, mentions a series of articles by Jean Lemoyne, distinguished by their courage and lucidity, which also appeared in *Cité Libre* and which helped to set the

---

125. Norbert Fournier, *Entre nous, catéchistes: Bulletin de liaison publié par l'Office catéchistique provincial* 12 (February 1966), as reported in Marsolais, 68.

126. Maroslais, 69.

case for change clearly before the public.[127] Lemaire draws attention to the indictment of the educational system, dramatized in a book by the husband and wife team, the Chalvins: *Comment on abrutit nos enfants* (Montreal, 1962).[128] The Chalvins brought out plenty of ammunition from the religious education programme in use at the time for their attack. Lemaire contends that without the efforts of these and other active lay men and women, many of the reform movements within the Quebec Church would have taken much longer to materialize.

It was the eve of Vatican Council II and a sense of urgency was stirring the catechetical community of Quebec. With the approval of his episcopal confreres, Bishop Coderre called together a catechetical writing team, comprised of Réginald Marsolais, Jean-Paul Bérubé and Marcel Caron.[129] Coderre charged them with the production of new catechetical resources. Each of these men was director of the catechetical office in his diocese—Marsolais at Joliette, Bérubé at Rimouski, and Caron at La Pocatière.[130]

At a meeting of diocesan directors of religious education in February 1963, Marsolais gave an account of the several significant consultations the writing team had made up to that point: Marcel van Caster from Lumen Vitae; Jean Honoré, secretary of the National Commission of Religious Education in France; Joseph Bournique from ISPC; André Brien of *Enseignement libre* in Paris; Sister Marie de la Visitation, an administrator in the Belgian religion programme for elementary schools; Norbert Fournier from the University of Montreal and Paul-M. Lemaire, secretary of the Dominican Pastoral Institute.[131]

As this committee was struck, momentous events in the Catholic Church and in Quebec society were rapidly unfolding. In the same way that Vatican Council II would soon redefine the position of the Church in the modern world, Quebec society was experiencing a radical turn towards modernization, a turn which spelled the death of the Church-

---

127. Paul-M. Lemaire, "Le nouveau catéchisme: Ses implications théologiques et pastorales," *Communauté chrétienne* 3 (May-June 1964): 184-185.
128. Lemaire, 185.
129. Ricard, 394.
130. Ricard, 394
131. *Rapport de la réunion des responsables diocésains de l'enseignement religieux* held at Montreal, 11 February 1963.

nation.[132] Maurice Duplessis died in 1959 and with him was buried the cozy relationship between Church and state. The famous "desormais" (from now on) of Paul Sauvé, Duplessis's immediate successor, presaged a new era. Jean Hamelin likens the re-awakening of the Quebec population to its identity as a people, as a nation, to the process that had taken place in many African states during de-colonization.[133]

Throwing off the yoke of colonialism, implied a rejection of the immense political and social power exercised by the Church in the public life of the province, for "Rome,"[134] as much as "Britain," was seen as the colonial overlord. The state would assume power in all the major facets of public life, which earlier had been controlled by the Church. Hospitals, social services, labour unions, orphanages and a host of other areas of public service passed from Church to state control with little public debate.[135] Handing over control of the school system to the state was a different matter. Debate erupted on all sides.

In 1960, the Jesuits asked the provincial government to pass legislation enabling them to open two new universities in Montreal. Producing clear lines of disagreement in a heated public debate, this request galvanized the action of intellectuals, who perceived it as an attempt to stifle the establishment of a secular university and the implementation of school reforms. In their view, the move was an attempt to consolidate the hold clerics had on society.[136] History and demographics were stacked against the Jesuits and in favour of school reform. Quebec was becoming increasingly pluralistic, a fact that the monolithic Catholic character of public life could not accommodate. Elementary justice demanded that a space be created for those large elements of the population, who could not identify with a vision of society, which had survived from a by-gone era; a mould cast when the social fabric of Quebec had been largely ethnically and confessionally homogeneous.

If Church leadership appeared out of touch with society, many priests, brothers and sisters were not. Of particular interest were the columns which appeared in *Le Devoir* in 1959-1960 under the nom de

---

132. Hamelin, 229ff
133. Hamelin, 229.
134. Here one thinks of the ultramontane stance of the Church in Quebec at this time, with its almost servile deference to a distant authority.
135. Hamelin, 246
136. Hamelin, 233.

plume, *Frère Untel*.[137] Dealing with questions of language, education, authority, and religious life, Pierre-Jerome Desbiens, the author's real name, represented a class of people that the traditional society of Quebec had oppressed. His pleas for a more open society and a more open Church were not falling on deaf ears.

The struggle for the schools continued for several years with proposals from the Church and counter-proposals from the government. The motor driving reform in the educational sector was the same as that which drove reform in the social services sector: the need to open the system to all citizens, without discrimination, and to produce a competent labour and managerial work force that a society on the move needs to function and develop.[138] In a period of transition, 1965-1967, the administration of the school system passed from the ecclesial to the public domain. In a last act, that may have been the swan song of the once powerful Quebec Church in the public domain, the episcopacy managed to retain the confessional identity of the public schools.[139]

The process of catechetical reform, as we have seen, predates the systemic reforms of the Lesage government in the 1960s. The episcopacy was divided on the question of the demise of Church-run schools. Some conservative bishops tried to hold on to the traditional, Catholic system of the past, while others welcomed a new arrangement in education that would give an increasingly pluralistic community a say in how its own schools were run.[140] Bishop Coderre's catechetical reforms clearly symbolized a move towards new ways of conceiving the Church, society and the relationship between the two.

Returning to the early work of the writing team, Marsolais offers several factors prompting the production of new catechisms, the most urgent of which was the need for textbooks for children six to eight years old:

> Dissatisfaction with *Le catéchisme catholique* of 1951 (1954) had become general....A large number of catechists had been trained since 1961, who could teach a new style of catechesis competently....The new programme of education for elementary schools, due to be im-

---

137. Hamelin, 239.
138. Hamelin, 249.
139. For a fuller treatment of the transition to modernization from a Church-dominated society see Hamelin, especially 229-259.
140. Baum, 42.

plemented in September 1964, planned to divide primary-elementary schools into three cycles: Cycle One being comprised of Grades 1 and 2, Cycle Two of Grades 3 and 4 and Cycle Three of Grades 5 and 6. The early plans of the committee were to produce one text for each cycle; thus, three in all for the six years of schooling.[141]

A goal of the new catechesis was to involve parents in the catechetical education of their children. The writing team thought that this goal would be more easily attained if one were to begin the process with young children.

Kindergartens were soon to be established, and catechetics needed to make connections between its insights and the very similar pedagogy of this new level of public schooling.

By March of 1963, Sister Marie de la Visitation had joined the writing team. Her experience as a teacher of young children proved an invaluable asset to the group. Through the work of Lubienska de Lenval, Marie Fargues and Françoise Derkenne, Sister Marie had become acquainted with the pioneering work of Maria Montessori in the field of childhood education. The important contribution which women had made in the development of the renewal in France (Fargues, Derkenne et al.) was repeated as the work of the renewal progressed in Canada.

As Sister Marie joined the team, the debate over when the sacraments of Penance, Eucharist and Confirmation should be administered was in full swing.[142] After polling the attitudes of teachers on the subject, no need was seen to move Penance and Eucharist preparation from Grade One, where they had been traditionally administered. Nevertheless, the decision was eventually made, on theological and psychological grounds, to move the reception of these sacraments to Grade Two.[143] By the time the second edition of Grade Two appeared in 1970, Penance was postponed another year, i.e., to Grade Three. Five reasons explaining the decision of the Canadian episcopate were

---

141. Marsolais, "Trois décennies," 6. See also *Rapport de la réunion des responsables diocésains de l'enseignement religieux*, held at Montreal, 11th February, 1963. It was later decided to provide a separate manual for each year of schooling.

142. Ricard, 395.

143. For a full presentation of the theological and psychological rationale behind this decision see Marcel Cormier and Alcide Clément, "Les sacrements en deuxième année: pourquoi?," *Communauté chrétienne* 3 (May-June 1964): 214-222.

offered in the *Introduction* of the *Guide du Maître* (Teacher's Guide).[144] By the summer of 1963, the writing team had worked out a new programme. In August of that same year, Bishop Coderre sent his episcopal confreres news that a new programme would be piloted in the province beginning that fall. Fifteen fascicles for teachers and another 15 for parents were ready for the autumn, with the remainder to follow as soon as they were completed.[145] The pilot project involved fifteen classes of youngsters distributed among the dioceses of Quebec, Montreal, Saint-Jean-de-Quebec, Chicoutimi, Sainte-Anne-de-la-Pocatière and Rimouski.

By May of 1964, Bishop Coderre announced the completed (and piloted) Grade One of the new catechism. The programme was to be introduced as an option in schools for September of that year and to become compulsory by September 1965.[146] Coderre pointed to the invaluable role that a wide variety of consultants played in the process— sociologists, theologians, catechists, parents and teachers.[147] One of the distinguishing features of the *Viens vers le Père* series was its intent to reflect the Quebec Catholic community, and later the wider Canadian Catholic Community. This publication marked the beginning of a new era: the transition from the single doctrinal code in use since 1888 (updated in 1951) to multiple catechetical resources, appropriate to the psychological development of the child.[148]

The first public announcements about the new programme's contents came from the Bishops on the first Sunday of September 1964, by way of a letter read in all the parishes of Quebec. This circular described *Viens vers le Père* as: 1) a catechism designed to favour the united efforts of home, school and parish, 2) a catechism aimed first and foremost to awaken a sense of God within the child, 3) a cate-

---

144. J-P. Bérubé, M. Caron, R. Marsolais, F. Darcy, M. Jeffery, A. Julien, R. Legentil, S. Lévesque, M. Ordway, A. Turmel and B. Vezeau, *Viens vers le Père: Initiation chrétienne des enfants de 7-8 ans* (Montreal: Pedagogia, 1970), 19. The original Grade Two programme had no booklet of introduction of its own. The authors merely reprinted the general introduction offered with the Grade One programme.

145. Ricard, 396.

146. Gérard-Marie Coderre, "Le nouveau catéchisme de première année," *Communauté chrétienne* 3 (May-June 1964): 182.

147. For a critique of the process, however, see Lemaire 185-186.

148. Marsolais, 7.

chism designed to initiate the child to prayer and to form his/her Christian moral conscience, and 4) a catechism which would place great importance on the Word of God, on the words of Jesus and the Scriptures as a whole.[149]

Norbert Fournier, several years removed from the introduction of these new catechetical resources, offers a more detailed description of key identifying features.[150] Including the key points mentioned in the bishops' letter, Fournier mentions:

1. The new catechesis was christocentric, and set against a Trinitarian background. Its aim was to initiate children into a relationship with the Triune God.

2. It proclaimed the Christian mystery in terms of relationships rather than in terms of concepts. Moreover, it was oriented towards personal and communitarian prayer.

3. This catechism was strongly inspired by the Bible as the privileged expression of the Word of God.

4. Following the tenets of an activity-based pedagogy, which invites young people to a personal engagement, it sought to bring together in the catechetical act, an education that is at once, doctrinal, liturgical and moral.

5. Since 1962, catechesis in Canada has been clearly marked by an anthropological orientation. More than simply a pedagogical approach, the import of this option was first of all theological. The ambiguity created by the two-fold source of this emphasis, however, has generated many tensions—tensions which have never fully been resolved.

6. The new catechesis insisted on being inserted into an overall pastoral project. Pastoral animation within the school, in concert with the efforts of parents and parish priests, proved especially important for childhood catechesis.

7. At least in its first ten or so years of existence, the catechetical movement depended upon a solid catechetical education of the teacher-catechists.

In the next chapter, the pedagogical factors influencing the biblical hermeneutic underpinning *Viens vers le Père* will be examined. In that context, a detailed consideration of the teaching methodology and general goals of the programme should fill the lacunæ left by this intro-

---

149. Marsolais, 7.
150. Fournier, "Canada," 97.

duction.

One grade level was published each year until the programme was completed. In 1965, *Célébrons ses merveilles* was introduced for Grade Two; in 1966, *Rassemblés dans l'amour* for Grade Three; in 1967, *Nous avons vu le Seigneur* for Grade Four; in 1968, *Préparer la terre nouvelle* for Grade Five; in 1969, *Selon ta promesse, fais-moi vivre* for Grade Six. When they appeared in English translation, the Year 1 to Year 6 programmes went under the names *Come to the Father, Celebrate God's Mighty Deeds, Gathered in Love, We Have Seen the Lord, Building the New Earth and Alive as he promised*, respectively.

In 1966, this series of catechetical resources published by the OCQ was recognized as a catechism by the Canadian Catholic Conference (CCC). The CCC, which was formed in response to the new emphasis on episcopal collegiality espoused at the Second Vatican Council, provided Canadian bishops their first on-going forum to deal with the problems common to the Church throughout the country. The CCC proposed a collaborative effort between its own office and the OCQ for all future catechetical resource production.

The fledgling CCC had no organizational equivalent to the OCQ.[151] The closest approximation of an office of religious education at the CCC was the office of the Confraternity of Christian Doctrine, (CCD). The CCD was a tightly-knit, American organization, based in Washington D.C., with anti-Protestant and anti-worldly slants as the defining features of its work. Its principal function was to disseminate information about Catholic doctrine. In rural western Canada, Bishop Carroll had some of the same problems in dealing with religious education as were present in many American dioceses. Where few Catholic schools existed, bishops needed other means to facilitate the process of exposing their youth to the fundamentals of doctrine. In an attempt to do just that, the bishops introduced the Confraternity of Christian Doctrine into the CCC offices. Gerald Fitzpatrick became its first director.

In view of the sophisticated programme of the OCQ, it must have been evident very quickly to the Bishops that the CCD would not be up to a meaningful collaboration with the OCQ. Thus in 1966, the CCC

---

151. My principal source for this early history of the CCC is Prof. Martin Jeffery, one of the first directors of NORE and a member of the original elementary writing team for *Viens vers le Père*.

created two new bodies to take on this task, the *Office national de catéchèse* (ONC), and the *National Office of Religious Education* (NORE). With this change of mandate, Fitzpatrick was sent to Lumen Vitae for a year's study in catechetics.

Despite the lack of a catechetical movement in English Canada, the efforts of the CCC and the OCQ pointed to the need to bring some English Canadians to the writing team for the elementary programme. Martin Jeffery and Robert Lane, both of whom were priests at the time were appointed. Since the resources would continue to be worked on in French, the educational background and bilingual competence which Jeffery and Lane possessed, made them ideal collaborators on the new programme. An agreement was reached providing for the English translations of all the new programmes by NORE. Martin Jeffery joined NORE with the mandate to oversee the translations and to head up what became the general catechetical renewal of the Catholic Church in English Canada.

NORE introduced the *Come to the Father* series to the United States through Paulist Press. In the U.S., the programme actually outsold Canadian distribution and stands as one of Canada's publishing successes, as cross-border traffic of text books has traditionally gone in the opposite direction. In moving from English Canada to the United States, the *Viens vers le Père* series had only begun its sojourn on the international scene. In the years immediately following its publication, the primary elementary manuals were translated into Spanish, Danish, Norwegian, Japanese, and Italian and were distributed in Belgium, Bolivia, Canada, Chili, Denmark, England, France, Italy, Japan, Norway, Paraguay, Peru, Spain, the United States and Uruguay.[152]

While the study in hand concerns itself exclusively with the primary and elementary cycles of *Viens vers le Père*, the work of the OCQ did not stop there. In 1965, a team of specialists in adolescent catechesis was formed and five programmes were published over the course of the next seven years; *Regard neuf sur un monde nouveau* (1966), *Regard neuf sur la vie* (1967), *Un sens au Voyage* (1968-1969), *La Force des rencontres* (1970-1971), *Des rues et des hommes* (1972). Year 7 and Year 8 were translated into English, but when compared to their primary-elementary counterparts, they had more limited distribution, appearing only in Canada and the U.S., and last-

---

152. Marsolais, 9.

ing only a few years even there.[153]

Despite the catechetical preparation of large numbers of teachers, despite Bishop Coderre's efforts to keep his episcopal confreres informed about the nature and goals of catechetical renewal, despite the parent booklets integrated into the new programmes, despite the calls for renewal from lay persons in the public forum, a vociferous minority of clergy, catechists, and laity mounted opposition to the reforms. Little research has been done on this question, but what is clear from interviews with the central players embroiled in the ensuing debate, is that the secondary school programmes got the brunt of the conservative backlash.

A priest from the diocese of Sherbrooke sent copies of the offending programmes to Rome with "offensive" passages highlighted. *Un sens au voyage* was singled out as particularly scandalous. Bishop Coderre in response to a request from Rome, enlisted the services of Julien Harvey, a Jesuit exegete from the University of Montreal, who was intimately involved with the catechetical renewal. Harvey travelled to Rome to respond to questions about the programmes before a committee of the *Sacred Congregation for the Clergy*. Coderre suggested that Harvey enlist the services of one of his Jesuit colleagues at Rome to help with the task. Harvey contacted Edouard Hamel and the two met with the committee on June 11, 1970. As the meeting began, the committee requested the removal from circulation of three full years of the programme and major changes to large portions of the remaining two years. By the time the Jesuits had finished their work, two pages from one year were removed and six other changes for subsequent editions of the text were agreed upon. In general, the damage had been controlled. In this same year Jacques Laforest published a critique of the manual *Un sens au voyage*,[154] and two years after that, P. Hitz launched a barthian-inspired critique of the secondary catechetical programmes in general.[155]

As the secondary programmes came under attack from such formidable quarters, the primary-elementary manuals attracted the attention of an auxiliary Bishop of the diocese of Montreal. With the collabora-

---

153. Marsolais, 9.
154. Jacques Laforest, *La catéchèse au secondaire: Etude du manuel Un sens au voyage* (Québec: Les Presses de l'Université Laval, 1970).
155. Paul Hitz, *Evangile et catéchèse: Problèmes de la catéchèse au secondaire* (Charlesbourg, Quebecc: Editions du Renouveau, 1972).

tion of two theologians and fifteen catechists, Bishop Léo Blais produced a 56 page document which was originally intended for publication. In a covering letter addressed to Cardinal Roy, Blais explained his reason for withholding this scathing critique from publication. Since the manuals for Grades One to Six had been granted episcopal approval, Blais feared:

> Mais notre monde donne à l'expression "approuvé par l'épiscopat" le sens qu'elle devrait avoir. Dans ces circonstances, ma critique eut fait tort à l'Eglise de chez-nous et diminué l'influence de l'épiscopat. Voilà pourquoi j'adresse cette étude seulement à l'épiscopat de la Province.[156]

Blais indicated that he had consulted widely with catechists, parents, and theologians in the preparation of his critique. He informed his reader that he, unlike most bishops, has read all the parent and student texts of Grades One to Six of the *Viens vers le Père* series; he noted that he had read only a portion of the teacher manuals. Ostensibly, his goal was to highlight what he and his collaborators judged best in the new programme, adding necessary correctives to its multiple deficiencies.

Blais outlined in popular terms, his ideas about revelation and faith—concepts which were pre-conciliar in outlook.

> On pourrait dire qu'il y a eu a poste émetteur céleste qui a lancé des ondes divines sur la terre des hommes. . .Pour capter les ondes divines du poste émetteur qui est Dieu, les appareils fabriqués de mains d'hommes ne sont pas assez puissants. Mais Dieu élève et dispose l'intelligence humaine pour que l'homme puisse croire en Lui, se fier à Lui, adhérer à Lui. Cette aptitude surnaturelle de notre intelligence, c'est ce qu'on nomme "vértu de Foi" ou "don de la Foi". . . .il faut la collaboration des intermédiaires qui transmettent les ondes divines, ainsi que la collaboration de chacun.[157]

The notion of revelation and faith as an overlay to human history and natural human experience informs the entirety of Blais's critique of *Viens vers le Père*. One of his major concerns had to do with doctrinal lacunæ in the new programme's content. Quoting form the *General Directory of the Congregation for the Clergy*, the bishop points

---

156. Léo Blais, "Notre Catéchèse: De la première à la sixième année inclusivement," Unpublished paper dated October 3, 1972, Montreal.
157. Blais, 4.

out that the goal of catechesis is to propose the *entire* content of Christian faith to the believer.

True to his stated goal, Blais points to a number of very positive elements in *Viens vers le Père*. He approved of the use of Scripture as an integral part of the presentation of doctrine, of the exercises with silence that lead to prayer and adoration of God and of teaching children to pray in their own words. Blais considered the identification of the resurrection as the key event for believers to be an improvement over the emphasis on the crucifixion in the past. The bishop characterized the use of imagination in teaching as reminiscent of Jesus' use of imagery and as respectful of the age of the children and the nature of the Christian message. The use of drawing was also praised.

Blais thought the new pedagogy generally superior to what had preceded it. The attractive appearance of the books with inviting illustrations and an interesting layout, the existence of teacher and parent manuals, the latter containing precious insights for the collaboration of the home—all were improvements. Despite these innovations, Blais' critique characterized the pedagogy faulty in its overall application.

> Il me semble que les moyens auxquels elle recourt, le connu, le visible, prennent trop d'importance, prennent plus d'importance que la fin à atteindre: la réalité surnaturelle dont l'enfant doit nourrir sa vie. A moins d'avoir des catéchètes très avertis, l'enfant, pris par le visible, ne passe pas à l'invisible.[158]

Blais extolled the treatment of the sacraments as theologically rich and full, and considered the liturgical celebrations to be well presented and capable of making a profound impression on the children. "Notre catéchèse, elle produit l'impression que les sacrements sont au fond, Quelqu'un. Alors les rites, gestes et paroles, signifient l'action de ce Quelqu'un; expriment une relation entre Dieu et l'homme." The insistence on the nature and meaning of baptism, Blais considered particularly helpful.[159]

On the negative side, Blais had considerably more to say. The bishop warns parents and catechists alike, that there are numerous deficiencies in the new programmes, some of which are serious. He

---

158. Blais, 12a. Here the distance Blais sees between the ordinary world of human experience and the divine world, superimposed upon it, shines through.

159. Blais, 20.

thought the horizontal dimension of the Gospel exaggerated and asked whether the love of neighbour was sufficiently linked to the love of God. He generally admits, however, that the catechism's treatment of the Christian command of love was adequate. He criticized the programme's use of memorization as inadequate, since the knowledge committed to memory was not cumulative from one year to the next. Because of this pedagogical failing, a great deal of essential doctrinal content was lost, in the bishop's view. Children could no longer answer questions such as, "What is the Trinity?," "What is the incarnation?," "What is redemption?" or "What is a sacrament?" They were no longer required to memorize the Apostle's Creed, the Commandments or the Daily Offering. On other points of pedagogy, Blais maintained that exams should be restored as a motivation and catechetical contests instituted.

In Blais' view, the ecclesiology of *Viens vers le Père* placed too much emphasis on the Church as the "people of God," thus neglecting the important roles of the Pope, the Bishops, Priests, Saints, the Laity and the Virgin Mary. The catechism should insist on the authority and mission of the hierarchy and state that the Church is assisted by the Holy Spirit. Talk of Christian unity was for Blais linked to a disobedience to the Magisterium. "Depuis une dizaine d'années, d'une part on ne (sic) n'a jamais tant parlé d'unité entre les chrétiens; d'autre part, on n'a jamais tant désobéi au Magistère de l'Eglise."[160]

Bishop Blais characterizes the treatment of sin, as defective in *Viens vers le Père*. The new catechism omits a mention of original sin, a major fault in the presentation of doctrine. The important distinction between mortal and venial sins disappears, except in the first edition of the Year Two teacher's manual. On these grounds, Blais roundly condemns the work: "Une catéchèse qui ne parle presque pas du peché n'est pas dans l'esprit du Christ."[161]

Other important omissions Blais notes are: (1) the notion of controlling one's body and of serving God through the renunciation of self; (2) a discussion of demons and angels; (3) the notion of sacrifice in the Mass and the concept of transubstantiation; (4) a discussion of the sacraments of Holy Orders, Extreme Unction and Marriage; (5) a reference to Hell; (6) an adequate treatment of the 4th, 5th, 7th, and 8th commandments and even a mention of the 6th and 9th; (7) a summary

---

160. Blais, 19.
161. Blais, 29.

of OT history.

The criticism's which Blais voiced regarding the *Viens vers le Père* series reflected the complaints of the more traditional Catholics of his day. It is worth noting that he read only a portion of the teacher manuals, since both the theological and pedagogical rationales for so many of the points of his critique are clearly laid out therein. The deficiencies Bishop Blais roots out, were not haphazard oversights on the part of the writing team, but rather deliberate, pedagogical and theological choices, based on the principles of the catechetical renewal.

The public furore created over the introduction of the new catechetical programmes in Quebec reached astounding proportions. The September 1973 edition of the well-known Jesuit review, *Relations*, aptly captures this upheaval in its title, "La guerre des catéchismes." As the cover of that issue suggests, it was denounced by the fringe as the gospel of Satan, the death of Christianity and a word of death, and hailed by the majority as a sign of a springtime in the Church. In Quebec, where the catechetical renewal made rapid inroads through the education of clergy and catechists, this reactionary stance proved finally to be the exception rather than the rule. In English Canada, the results were not always so felicitous. Priests often found themselves estranged from these new catechetical instruments unable to integrate their significance.

Eventually a major revision of Years 5 and 6 was published in Quebec but was not translated into English, as the close links between OCQ and NORE dissolved in a rising tide of nationalist sentiment in the Quebec Church. More problematic yet was the thorny dispute about whether NORE or OCQ should reap the financial benefits of the lucrative American distribution rights. The Grades 5 and 6 revisions appeared in Quebec in 1975 and 1980 and were called *Quand souffle l'Esprit* and *Avec Dieu sur nos chemins*, respectively. In Quebec, *Viens vers le Père*, was eventually replaced by new programmes developed through the provincial Ministry of Education. In English Canada, the *Come to the Father* series, remained in use until the expiration of the publishing contract with Paulist Press. The Canadian Conference of Catholic Bishops, the new name of the CCC, established a publishing company of its own, *Concacan*, under the direction of NORE and began a process of renewal of the *Come to the Father* series that was completed in 1990. The new *Born of the Spirit* series continues many of the pedagogical insights of its predecessor, building on its strengths and trying to remedy weaknesses identified by educators who had used the resource for many years.

An historical treatment of *Viens vers le Père* will prove helpful in untangling the several threads which get easily confused, as catechetics brings together insights from so many quarters. We have had an opportunity to consider the pioneering pedagogical actors on this stage, who relied on prompters reading from scripts of psychology and curriculum theory. We have seen successive theologians take their parts as the story line unfolded. Punctuating the entire production, a clamouring chorus, peopled with ecclesiastical and secular players, poured forth the atmosphere and set the parameters of the play. The review of the action which follows, will focus on the contributions of these various players and the effect they have on the interpretation of the Bible, in the six acts of the production. We begin with the effect which the pedagogical options have exercised on the selection and interpretation of Scripture.

CHAPTER 3

PEDAGOGY AND HERMENEUTICS IN *VIENS VERS LE PERE*

Catechetics emerges at the confluence of several related disciplines and embodies assumptions from each. As a result of this synthesis, the "purist" demands of subsidiary specialities undergo inevitable modification and adaptation. Thus, for example, theological requirements for a complete and coherent presentation of doctrine are qualified by the psychological possibilities of a young audience, and a response to the evolving patterns of childhood socialization tempers a rigid view of education as cognitive acquisition, unsullied by affect. A balance must be struck between such competing interests as educational psychology, sociology, theology, and biblical studies—an elusive equilibrium at best.

Our goal is to explore the extent to which the pedagogical options of *Viens vers le Père* influenced its reading of the Bible and its use of biblical scholarship. We will analyze the chief pedagogical underpinnings of the series and present the redactors' self-confessed understanding of their task. To bring the pedagogical innovations of this series into relief, we will occasionally compare *Viens vers le Père* to its catechetical predecessor(s).

This chapter is divided into two parts; the first largely descriptive and expository in function, the second more analytical and critical.

We begin Part One of our study with a description of the scope and sequence of the programme, leading up to a discussion of *Viens vers le Père*'s three principal centres of interest. An exposition of the series' methodology and content follows. Against this backdrop, we examine the way in which educational psychology has shaped this catechism, demonstrating that a respect for the social and intellectual development of children influences the use of Scripture in the programme. The catechism's choice of doctrine as an organizing principle is also examined with respect to its influence on scriptural interpretation. The concept of a "progressive revelation," an important element in the programme's organization, also influences its hermeneutics. Part Two begins with a challenge to the programme's catechetical point of departure, as we situate the series in the context of the philosophy of education. Two broad philosophical approaches, one centred on the legacy of human knowledge and the other on the connections between life-experiences and learning, provide a backdrop for our analysis. An integrated approach which combines elements of both the *heritage* and *experience* curriculum models is then outlined.

PART ONE

THE SCOPE AND SEQUENCE OF *VIENS VERS LE PERE* (VVLP)

Creedal formulæ organize the doctrinal content and provide a basic structure for this series. The programme writers identify the Trinitarian perspective as one of their foundational options.[1] Like ripples expanding from a stone dropped in water, each subsequent year widens the implications of the core of doctrine already presented *in nuce* in Grade One. Three principles inspired the choice of themes: 1) Catechesis should be limited to essentials but be vigilant in maintaining a doctrinal balance; 2) Catechesis should be doctrinally precise; 3) Catechesis should present each truth within the living "today" of the salvation event.[2]

The Primary Years

The primary years aim at giving a panoramic view of Christianity, bringing the children into relationship with the three divine Persons

---

[1]. OCQ—Équipe, "Bilan d'une enquête sur l'utilisation du nouveau catéchisme *Viens vers le Père* dans les diocèses du Québec," *Catéchèse* 7 (1967): 103, note 3.

[2]. OCQ—Équipe, Viens vers le Père, Guide du maitre, 17-18.

and making them aware of the basic attitudes of the Christian life.[3] The articles of the Creed provide the doctrinal framework to be developed:

I believe in God the Father, maker of heaven and earth.
I believe in Jesus Christ, his only Son, our Lord.
I believe in the Holy Spirit, the holy catholic Church.
I believe in the resurrection...life everlasting.

Grade One, *Viens vers le Père* (*Come to the Father*) seeks to initiate 6-7 year olds into the "fundamental movement of the Christian life: to go to the Father through Christ in the Spirit."[4] This objective is sustained throughout the entire six years. This first year seeks to capitalize on the natural sense of wonder of the 6 year old in order to initiate him/her into the sense of God, beginning chiefly from the signs of God in creation, in home life and in the liturgy. The authors created an instrument which hopes to awaken a sense of God in the child's life, nurturing the child's prayer-life and allowing him/her to grow in the awareness of God's call to share his love.[5] Thus, the focus of the first year is on God the Father, the maker of heaven and earth. The visible world stands as the principal sign of God.

Grade Two, *Célébrons ses merveilles* (*Celebrate God's Mighty Deeds*), focuses on the sacramental initiation of 7-8 year olds, often using Gospel stories and liturgical signs as the points of departure.[6] Children were taught, that through baptism Christians become children of the Father and enter into an intimate relationship with God—Father, Son and Spirit.[7] This is also the year in which children complete sacramental initiation into the Christian community. Eucharist, Confirmation and Penance are presented as encounters with the Risen Lord and related back to the child's baptism as the pivotal event in the

---

[3]. Collaboration: OCQ-NORE, *We Have Seen the Lord: Teacher's Manual* (Toronto: Paulist Press, 1968), 8.
[4]. Collaboration: OCQ—NORE, *Come to the Father: Teacher's Manual* (Toronto: Paulist Press, 1966), 9.
[5]. *Come to the Father, Teacher's Manual*, 9.
[6]. OCQ—Équipe, *Viens vers le Père*: The New Catechism for the Province of Quebec," *Lumen Vitae* 20 (1965): 246.
[7]. OCQ—Équipe, *Célébrons ses merveilles: Initiation chrétienne des enfants de 7-8 ans, Livre de l'enfant* (Québec: Éditions Pedagogia, 1965), Chapters 6-9.

initiation process. This new-found appreciation of baptism sets the program apart from its predecessors in which baptism, by comparison, held only minor interest. Still marked by the debates of the Reformation era, the Tridentine style catechisms were preoccupied with fine distinctions about the nature of Christ's presence in the Eucharist and similarly contentious issues. For the Grade Two child, the Risen Lord is shown to continue the *mirabilia Dei*, saving people of our time as once God had done in the history of salvation.[8]

Grade Three, *Rassemblés dans l'amour* (*Gathered in Love*), finishes the first stage of religious formation by helping 8-9 year olds assimilate and reflect more authentically in their daily comportment the basic Christian doctrine received in Grades One and Two.[9] The writers were well aware that not everything taught in the first two years would be absorbed by the children. The goal was to give children a vital learning experience. Kierkegaard's statement—"I know a truth only when it has become a part of my life"—captures for the authors, that "vital" quality critical to understanding.[10] Grade Three does not provide much additional religious knowledge but aims at guiding its young audience to a clearer initiation into the mystery of the Church. Doctrine is integrated into daily living by means of an appeal to the child's life experiences.

The Elementary Years

Grades 4, 5, and 6 proffer a refinement and a sharpening of the focus of content presented in Grades 1, 2, 3. In these years the children learn to read the "signs" or "mediations" through which the Christian mystery is revealed for themselves. The Catholic principle of sacramentality informs this movement. The humanity of Jesus himself is the first and greatest of the "signs" or "mediations."

> In him converge all other signs that reveal his presence and activity, namely, the signs of the liturgy, Christian life and created reality. The three years of the second cycle will therefore be centred on the mystery of the Lord Jesus discovered mainly: i) in its historical manifesta-

---

[8]. OCQ—Équipe, *Célébrons ses merveilles: Initiation chrétienne des enfants de 7-8 ans, Guide du maitre* (Québec: Éditions pedagogia, 1965), 6-7.

[9]. OCQ—Équipe, *Rassemblés dans l'amour: Catéchisme des enfants de 8-9 ans, Guide du maitre* (Québec: L'action sociale, 1966), 17.

[10]. *Rassemblés dans l'amour, Guide du Maître*, 32.

tion in Palestine (*We Have Seen the Lord*); ii) in the liturgical life (*Building the New Earth*); iii) in the human spiritual experience of the children (*Alive, as he promised*).[11]

Each year in the elementary cycle is marked by a dominant emphasis: Evangelical—Year 4; Liturgical—Year 5; Existential/moral—Year 6. These three grades investigate the Gospel, the Liturgy and the Christian life, respectively.

Grade Four, *Nous avons vu le Seigneur (We Have Seen the Lord)*, catechizes 9-10 year olds through a series of ten "approaches" to Jesus, i.e., the children walk the roads of Palestine and discover Jesus of Nazareth along with those Gospel figures who reportedly encountered him—John the Baptist, the people of Galilee, Matthew, Peter, Mary et al. With the Gospel witness they learn his "secret" and hear of his "mission." In Grade Four children receive a copy of the New Testament in a ceremony that identifies it as the Book of the Good News, which the Church hands on from generation to generation. This year ends with the image of the first Christians living in peace and confidence, strengthened by the promise of the Risen Lord, "Behold, I am with you always." (Mt. 28:20)

Grade Five, *Préparer la terre nouvelle* (*Building the New Earth*), focuses its catechesis of 10-11 year olds on the liturgy. It continues the "rediscovery" of the mystery of Jesus begun in Grade Four. In its consideration of signs manifesting the presence of the Risen Lord in the world, it offers many examples of human progress—scientific advances, milestones in ecumenical understanding, peace work, the civil rights struggle and so forth. The greatest sign which reveals the Risen Lord is the faith of the Christians of the whole world, and this despite their sinfulness and weakness.[12] In line with this, Grade 5 presents the liturgy as the most explicit sign of the active presence of the Lord Jesus in the world.

Grade Six, *Selon ta promesse, Fais-moi Vivre* (*Alive as He Promised*), concentrates its catechesis of 11-12 year olds on fundamental attitudes that the Spirit of the Lord awakens in the Christian's heart. Its goal was to explore and deepen the true significance of Christian

---

[11]. *We Have Seen the Lord, Teacher's Manual*, 8.
[12]. Collaboration: OCQ—NORE, *Préparer la terre nouvelle: Catéchisme des enfants de 10-11 ans, Guide du maitre* (Montreal: Centre éducatif et culturel, 1968), 16a.

living.[13] In this regard, the programme maintains that:

> A Christian is not defined solely by his submission to divine and Church law; he is determined, first and foremost, by his relationship to the Lord Jesus. To become a Christian is to transform one's life progressively through faith in Jesus Christ, Son of God and Saviour.[14]

People from the history of the Church whose lives were transformed in this way become models for the students of Grade 6: Paul of Tarsus, Augustine of Hippo, Maria Montessori, Tom Dooley, Francis of Assisi, Catherine of Sienna, Mary (the mother of Jesus), Joseph Cardijn and many others.

THREE CENTRES OF INTEREST IN VVLP

Three centres of interest attract our attention in *Viens vers le Père*'s catechesis: 1) The Word of God, expressed in Scripture and Tradition; 2) The student; 3) The relationship between the two. Either "the Word of God" or "the Student" may serve as the axis for the catechetical process.

The notion of the Word of God informing the catechetical renewal was profoundly influenced by popular biblical and liturgical movements.[15] Within the catechetical renewal in France and Belgium, God's revelation was depicted as having been communicated in three languages: 1) the language of events which gives rise to biblical catechesis; 2) the language of symbolic gestures which gives rise to liturgical catechesis and 3) the sapiential and notional language of formulæ which gives rise to doctrinal catechesis.[16] This three-tiered conception of revelation especially marks Grades One to Four of the *Viens vers le Père* series.

The emphasis on revelation, as it is expressed in the Scriptures proclaimed by the Church and in doctrine, pervades the entire six years. Liturgical practice, scriptural interpretation and doctrinal content harmonize in this series.

---

[13]. Collaboration: OCQ—NORE, *Alive as He Promised: Teacher's Manual* (Toronto: Paulist Press, 1970), vii.
[14]. *Alive as He Promised, Teacher's Manual*, xix.
[15]. Regarding these movements, see Chapters 1 and 2 above.
[16]. Marcel van Caster, *Catéchèse et dialogue* (Bruxelles: Éditions de Lumen Vitae, 1966), 13.

Since the goal of the work in hand is to critique the interpretation and use of Scripture in *Viens vers le Père*, it will be essential to dissociate specifically biblical concerns from related doctrinal and liturgical matters. In order to sketch a role peculiar to the Bible within this programme, an introduction to its methodology seems essential. Following the resources themselves and the several pieces of documentation which appeared in various catechetical reviews around the time of its publication, we will begin our description by noting some of the innovations which appeared in the series.[17]

Before moving on, it is worth noting that, just as the "Word of God" proves to be a complex notion in the catechetical renewal, so too do the ideas of the "student" and the "relationship between the student and Word." No student arrives as a *tabula rasa* to the learning process. All come with a host of experiences and a profile of intellectual abilities which define their interaction with the curriculum. Pedagogical research since the turn of the century has consisted largely in describing the student in terms of psychology, sociology and biology.

A consideration of the relationship which obtains between the axes of "student" and "Word" constitutes the principle object of inquiry in this book.

METHODOLOGY AND CONTENT

When compared with its predecessor, one of the most striking characteristics of this new catechetical series is its multiplicity of texts. The old catechism consisted of a single text for use at all levels of education. *Viens vers le Père* not only introduced age-appropriate student texts for each year of schooling but also provided extensive teacher manuals, complete with theological and psycho-pedagogical justifications for course content. The student texts included *parent pages* designed to draw households into the catechetical process and *theme sheets* designed to help priests and others responsible for classroom celebrations.[18] The move to re-situate the catechetical task both within the setting of the family and the Christian community revives the an-

---

[17]. What we have in mind here are innovations relative to the earlier catechisms in use in Canada. *Viens vers le Père* brought together many of the best insights from a number of French and Belgian catechisms in use at the time.

[18]. OCQ—Équipe, "Bilan d'une enquête sur l'utilisation du nouveau catéchisme *Viens vers le Père* dans les diocèses du Québec," *Catéchèse* 7 (1967): 104.

cient catechetical practice of the Church.[19] Moreover, it corresponds to the best insights available within the behavioural sciences of the period.

Hervé Carrier published research in the 1960s supportive of the view that parental involvement is a critical factor in the religious education of children.[20] As cultural transmission is intimately related to the early education a child receives in the home,[21] a child's religious habits and belief system depend largely upon family structures and religious practices.[22] Carrier concluded that the child, by the fact that he/she enjoys the security and protection of the family group, learns to esteem and to revere what his/her parents revere.[23] Françoise Derkenne concurred with these findings when she observed that young children are captivated by the Christian conduct of their parents and adults in general.[24]

Sparked by the insights of Fargues, Derkenne, Colomb et al., *Viens vers le Père* seeks not only to transmit doctrinal content, but hopes also to lead to the conversion of the child, to metanoia. The lines between teaching and preaching blur in this model, as cognitive and affective goals supplement one another and intellectual aims complement spiritual ones. When introducing Grade One of the new series, the writing team offered four principal aims for the programme:[25]

1. To help the child to have relations with the three divine persons.
2. To transmit to the child, God's living Word which the Church utters for us today.
3. To start from the children's experience so as to help them dis-

---

[19]. For a treatment of the role of the family and Christian community in catechetical formation in the early Church see Carter, 56ff.

[20]. Hervé Carrier, *Psycho-sociologie de l'appartenance religieuse*, Third edition (Rome: Les presses de L'Univeristé Grégorienne, 1966), Chapter 5.

[21]. T.W. Newcomb, *Social Psychology* (New York: Holt and Co., (1950) 1958), 448.

[22]. J.H.S. Bossard, *The Sociology of Child Development*, Second edition (New York: Harper, 1954), Chapter 14.

[23]. Carrier, 117.

[24]. Françoise Derkenne, *Vive le Seigneur, Livre des catéchistes* (Paris: Fayard-Mame, 1966), 12.

[25]. L'Équipe catéchétique, "*Viens vers le Père*: The New Catechism for the Province of Quebec," *Lumen Vitae* 20 (1965): 247-248.

cover the signs of God in their lives.
  4. To provide at school a first experience of life "in the Church."

The hope of initiating children into a relationship with the Trinity goes hand in hand with the intention of initiating them into the Church. The goal of the former is to open the child to an experience of faith, while the latter aims at providing an environment where that nascent faith might be nurtured. The writers acknowledge the divine origins and cause of faith and see the project as co-operation with the work of the Spirit.[26] In this new model, more is demanded of the teacher than the simple purveyance of cognitive data. The teacher must witness to the faith of the community and be truly convinced of the child's readiness, both psychologically and spiritually, to respond to that witness.[27]

In an effort to dispose the child for a faith experience, four emphases are explored. Throughout all six years of the programme, *doctrine*, *Scripture*, the *experiences of the learner* and the *liturgy* are variously combined. Scripture is present as a significant element in every theme of the entire catechetical series. Week One of the Grade One Programme will serve as an illustration:

> 1. *Invariably, a point of doctrine is to be communicated*: Week One—"God the Father all-powerful made heaven and earth."

> 2. *The child's concrete experience is evoked*: Week One—The child's experience of nature is central. A "nature walk," a "Talk" about experiences of the outdoors and a colourful illustration of a natural scene (trees, flowers, grass and water bathed in sunshine) are the means of bringing the child into contact with the natural world. This experience serves to clarify the doctrinal point.

> 3. *A scriptural excerpt appears*: Week One—A paraphrase of Genesis 1 provides the scriptural basis of the doctrine. While higher criticism is acknowledged throughout the programme, it is most often a point of departure for determining the sense of a passage. Hence, Genesis 1 is not taken as an historical or scientific account of creation that requires explanation, but is used to show that its authors understood God to be the author of creation. In the Grade Two Teacher's Guide, the first

---

[26]. *Viens vers le Père, Guide du Maître*, 8.
[27]. *Viens vers le Père, Guide du Maître*, 9.

creation account of Genesis is characterized as a "Poem."[28]

4. *A liturgically-inspired response to the scriptural passage follows:* The organization of the programme—both the structure of individual lessons and the plan for a whole year of catechesis—follows a liturgical pattern. Strongly influenced by the work of H. Lubienska de Lenval, all six years of the programme respect the major movements of the liturgical year such as the Advent-Christmas and Lent-Easter cycles. Less important feasts are also worked into various themes. Each year includes a theme in traditional honour of Mary, the mother of Jesus. Grade One (Week 8) incorporates a reference to All Saints Day and so forth. In addition, the primary programme organizes each theme in such a way that the introduction of the biblical passage follows the pattern found in the Mass: the proclamation of the Word is followed by a psalm of response. Week One—Genesis 1 is the Word Proclaimed and the children respond with paraphrases of Psalms 101 and 113.

Whether the concrete reference for a lesson is situated in a story from the Bible, in a liturgical rite or in the experience of the child, the path always leads to the same destination—*doctrinal content*. The distance between the scriptural source and the doctrinal content all but collapses in this model of catechesis, as Scripture echoes doctrinal themes or expresses verbatim the point of doctrine to be learned. While one may verify the degree to which the doctrinal, biblical and liturgical content, have been assimilated by the children, the other goal of the programme remains elusive. Faith cannot be empirically verified.[29] Experience, doctrine, liturgy and Scripture are the constants of this programme—a basic characteristic of Catholic religious education curricula under the influence of the European catechetical renewal.

Hence, a defining feature of the *Viens vers le Père* series is its intention to communicate Catholic doctrine, and its belief that such doctrine could be communicated to 6-12 year olds in a way that would allow them to apprehend it with something more than verbal knowledge, *scientia nominis*.[30] Moreover, and this is of great interest with regard to the reading of the Bible proposed in this series, the redactors

---

[28]. *Célébrons ses merveilles, Guide du Maître*, 65.

[29]. Although see Chapter 4 below re: the possibility of knowing that grace is at work within a person.

[30]. This concept will be developed at length in Part Two of this chapter.

believed that in every case the doctrinal content they cite can either be found directly in Scripture or is at least consonant with the witness of Scripture. On both these points this programme situates itself squarely within Catholic Tradition.

In order to ensure that the approach of the programme would not contradict the "surer" findings of critical biblical scholarship, the finished fascicles were submitted to a biblical scholar at the University of Montreal, Jean-Louis d'Aragon S.J. Later, another Jesuit exegete, Julien Harvey, carried out a review of these programmes when they came under attack. The positive results of these evaluations testifies to the considerable expertise of the writing team in theological and scriptural matters.[31]

In their attempt to produce a series which would represent a reform of the Roman Catholic catechetical institution and in their anticipation of several doctrinal developments which would follow in the wake of Vatican Council II, the redactors of this programme may be said to have critically appropriated Catholic Tradition.[32]

CHILD PSYCHOLOGY AND SCRIPTURE

In the teacher manuals for all six grade levels there stands a section entitled "What psychology teaches us." If the old catechism levelled the audience by its methodology, *Viens vers le Père* raised the psychological and social peculiarities of 6-12 year olds to a determinative factor in its curriculum. Virtually every aspect of its construction rests upon insights gained from the behavioural sciences: 1) the coloured illustrations, 2) the length of text and difficulty of vocabulary, 3) the emphasis on an active pedagogy in which children learn by "doing," 4) small group work, 5) research assignments. All these choices and myriad others correspond to the evolving capacities, interests and sociability of the child.

The psycho-social evolution of the child over this period, i.e., between 6 and 12 years of age, is striking. Typically, children arrive in Grade 1 unable to read or write and incapable of moving from cause to effect, and leave in Grade 6 with literacy skills and a developed capacity to reason. In the Introduction to Grade One, the writing team ex-

---

[31]. See Jean-Louis d'Aragon, "Marx ou Satan?" *Relations* 385 (September 1973) and in the same issue, Julien Harvey, "Nos manuels de catéchèse: expérience et message."

[32]. These doctrinal points will be taken up in Chapter 4.

plains that unreflected action, i.e., gross and fine motor activity, predominates in the life of a six year old and hence becomes a key factor in the curriculum design. As the child matures, more place is given in catechesis to reflection and higher order mental processes.

The series moves towards the four overall goals identified earlier, by introducing one theme each week, intended to be assimilated through a variety of means:

1. the *talk* announcing the Word of God and revealing the doctrine;
2. the *activities* that permit assimilation and encourage personal reactions in the child;
3. the *celebration* that repeats the theme in the framework of community prayer and initiates into the liturgical life;
4. *singing* and *memorization*;
5. *audio-visual materials*: pictures, records etc.[33]

Each of these elements aims at respecting the needs of the student.

Since it may not be immediately evident how these five elements correspond to the learning needs of primary and elementary school children, let's take an example of a psychological profile of one of the age groups targeted by this series. We will proceed with a synopsis of the psychological profile of 6-7 year olds. From this example, we will try to indicate how respect for the developing child's capacities conditions the appropriation of Scripture within the programme. The authors make no pretence of the applicability of their statements to each individual child—children mature at different rates. They intend their profiles to be a general guide which corresponds to the great majority of children within an age group. Examples of psycho-social factors influencing the series' pedagogy from other grades will follow.

Profile of the Six to Seven Year Old Child

The Swiss psychologist, Jean Piaget, described stages in cognitive development from concrete operational to abstract operational. Grade One children fall within the former category. To use the words of the grade one teacher's manual, the paths to knowledge for the 6-7 year old child are three: 1) action; 2) sensory experience; 3) personal relationships.[34] Borrowing a term from the psychologist Gesell, the authors characterize the psychological state of the 6-7 year old by the

---

[33]. *Come to the Father, Student Text*, 25.
[34]. *Come to the Father, Teacher's Manual*, 11.

word *dispersion.* The term aptly captures the states of affairs which results when the child's untried energy and superabundant vitality encounter a multiplicity of new experiences.[35] The Grade One child is described as simultaneously 1) hyperactive, and therefore eager for a variety of activities, 2) imaginative-contemplative, and so capable of an interior life, 3) emotionally responsive, and thus eager for warm relationships.

Colomb, citing as his sources the works in child psychology of G. Collin, J. Piaget, R. Hubert, and E. de Greeff, offers an excellent summary which corresponds in great detail to the picture offered in the Grade One teacher's manual.

> ...chez le tout-petit, la pensée est très subjective; elle ne sait pas analyser; elle est syncrétique et pointilliste, animiste et tournée d'ailleurs plus particulièrement vers les relations personnelles. La pensée est aussi très liée à l'action présente; elle se réalise plus facilement encore par le geste que par la parole, bien que de plus en plus penser consiste à nommer. Enfin cette pensée est très affective, et nous savons que l'affectivité du tout-petit est essentiellement commandée par le besoin de "grandir"; elle lui permet de s'identifier à des êtres même éloignés ou inexistants, et de comprendre par la confiance qu'il porte à ses éducateurs.[36]

The tendency to personify and animate the world, the desire to grow up and the strong links between cognitive acquisition and affective disposition, taken together, guided the primary writing team.

The programme capitalizes on yet another characteristic of these young learners. In adopting a pedagogy of religious awakening centred on the child's capacity for wonderment, the writing team depends principally on the work of Pierre Ranwez. In discussing the religious experience of young children, Ranwez had this to say:

> Dès que son âme s'est ouverte à un premier sentiment d'admiration ou d'amour, l'élan qui jaillit des sources profondes de son être dépasse la réalité immédiatement offerte à son regard ou à son étreinte. Il cherche Dieu sans le savoir. Il est temps de le lui nommer.[37]

This series realizes that religion cannot be *explained* to the six year

---

[35]. *Come to the Father, Teacher's Manual*, 10.
[36]. Colomb, *Service*, II, 273.
[37]. Pierre Ranwez, "Le discernement de l'expérience religieuse chez l'enfant," *Lumen Vitae* 19 (1965): 228.

old since this child can not yet handle the rational abstraction which such an explanation requires. Rather, it aims at presenting the essential realities of the faith, in an atmosphere of contemplation, wonder and awe, which the authors hope will allow the child to enter into relationship with the divine Persons, whose loving purpose gives meaning to the whole universe.[38] This does not mean that the child is incapable of cognitive acquisition, but rather that this cognition must be anchored in concrete realities within the experience of the child. In the introduction to *Come to the Father* (*Viens vers le Père*) we read:

> Any idea, which is not based on concrete experience or which the child cannot interpret and re-express in personal activity, is not accessible to his mind; it can reach him only on the superficial and often misleading level of verbal knowledge.
>
> For the child, the process of assimilation is slow. To grasp a truth, he must encounter it several times and under different forms. But the end result of his personal search will leave him happy and proud in the security that flows from *personal* accomplishment in grasping a truth. It is not unusual, then, for him to be able to transmit this truth to others with surprising precision.[39]

In this excerpt, one recognizes: 1) the need for many opportunities for children to assimilate content proposed for cognitive acquisition coupled with a pictorial dimension to understanding: "he must encounter it several times and under different *forms*"; 2) the personal nature of understanding; 3) the primordial character of experience and of a "doing" in the process of assimilation; 4) a caveat regarding that superficial level of knowledge referred to above as *scientia nominis*.

Taking a page directly from the work of M. Montessori (likely via Lubienska de Lenval), the Grade One programme begins its year not with doctrine, but with the physical (corporeal) preparation of the child. The preparatory week focuses on self-mastery through "Walking

---

[38]. *Viens vers le Père, Guide du maitre*, 8-9.

[39]. *Come to the Father, Teacher's Manual*, 11-12. Given that the book in hand is addressed to an English-speaking audience, the English Version of *Viens vers le Père* will be quoted, where it is a verbatim translation of the original French. Martin Jeffery, having collaborated on the original French Version of Years 4, 5, and 6, directed the translations into English of all six years. According to Jeffery, the original translation involved only minor adaptations.

on a Line" and "Exercises in Silence."[40] These exercises in self mastery try to bring the child to an inner quiet, allowing him/her to become aware of the life of the mind, the power of the imagination and the human capacity to contemplate. Similar exercises resurface regularly throughout the programme. Week Six of Grade One bears the title, "God our Father gives me life, he makes me able to think."[41] Following the insight of Lubienska, this programme believes in the child's capacity for interiority from the very first year of primary schooling.

Respecting the attention span of the six year old child, the *Talk*—a pedagogically important technique—is not to exceed 10 minutes. An exception is made in the case of a Bible story as children are able to attend to a narrative for a longer period.[42]

The *Activities* proposed for the programme, have a pivotal function. Their aim is expressed with the following description:

> To really understand, the child must re-live in his own way the message that has been transmitted to him. For this reason, after the talk, the catechist suggests an "activity." This activity will permit the child to assimilate the message received and to re-express it in his own way. For example, after the talk on the Word of God we might say to the child:

> "Draw the Book of the Word of God, and draw children around it happy to be listening to the words of the Lord Jesus."[43]

Drawing serves as the principle activity for young children and it should always be linked to the goal of the lesson; it is usually an illustration of what has been heard.[44] Other activities include modelling in clay, dramatization, miming, outings and celebrations.

As for the social characteristics of this age group, the 6 year old remains highly egocentric.[45] Despite this egocentric quality, from about their fourth year of life, children spontaneously seek out the company of friends in informal work and play groups and display an active concern for others—a fact which leads Colomb to conclude that

---

[40]. *Viens vers le Père, Guide du Maître*, 53-62.
[41]. *Come to the Father, Student Text*, 24.
[42]. *Viens vers le Père, Guide du Maître*, 26.
[43]. *Come to the Father, Teacher's Manual*, 30.
[44]. *Viens vers le Père, Guide du Maître*, 27.
[45]. Colomb, *Service*, II, 275.

self giving seems to be as primitive as egocentrism.[46]

Six Year Olds Reading Scripture

Studying the Grade One programme, *Viens vers le Père*, against the backdrop of this psycho-social profile, provides a unique explanatory perspective for many of its pedagogical options.

Respecting a Grade One reading ability, the amount of print in the student's book is kept to a minimum (usually between twenty five and seventy five words per theme) and increases gradually throughout the primary grades, always respecting the child's general vocabulary and taking care to explain new words. Scripture passages invariably occupy the lion's share of the text. Statements of doctrine take up, at most, one or two lines per theme. This adaptation to the reading ability and rational capacity of the grade one audience explains the willingness of the writing team to radically simplify biblical excerpts. In this sense the reading of Scripture is made to conform to the requirements of the six year old. The fact that many of the passages from Scripture, including the psalms of response, are intended to be committed to memory, provides yet another reason for maintaining brevity.[47] In first grade, the points of doctrine to be committed to memory are limited to five and the prayers to be learned by heart are kept to a strict minimum, two or three.[48]

The child's innate sense of wonder before nature is capitalized upon; wonder before nature becomes wonder before the maker of nature, God the Father. The titles of the first three themes reveal this link: *Week One*—"God the Father All Powerful Made Heaven and Earth"; *Week Two*—"We Praise God for Our Beautiful World"; *Week Three*—"God the Father is Very Holy, Heaven and Earth are Filled with His Glory." In the third week, the scriptural selection (Exodus 3: Moses before the burning bush) evokes the child's sense of wonder by inviting the child into the experience of Moses who bows to hide his face before the Lord. The child's natural sense of wonder unites with Moses' reverence before God to give a content to the biblically inspired doctrine: "God the Father is holy, heaven and earth are filled with his glory." Again the biblical excerpt is loosely adapted and kept

---

[46]. Colomb, *Service*, II, 275.
[47]. *Viens vers le Père, Guide du Maître*, 32.
[48]. *Viens vers le Père, Guide du Maître*, 32.

to a few words—"C'est moi, Dieu, ton Dieu, qui est là."
Not only does the child's sense of wonder determine which Scripture to include, it also suggests uses that should be avoided. The personal teaching experience of Sister Marie de la Visitation seems to have been translated into the programme design:

> Personnellement, l'expérience nous incline à penser qu'à cet âge il est préférable de faire une plus grande place aux paroles de l'Ecriture qu'aux récits. Ceci pour un motif pédagogique: l'enfant de 6-7 ans est friand d'histoires, mais il ne distingue pas encore clairement le merveilleux du surnaturel.…C'est pourquoi il nous semble préférable de ne pas trop multiplier les récits, ni même d'évoquer trop souvent les personnages bibliques, pour axer plutôt la catéchèse sur les personnes divines elles-mêmes et sur les paroles du Seigneur. Le petit nombre des récits permet de mieux les différencier du merveilleux et d'en exploiter davantage le contenu spirituel.[49]

One of the basic assumptions regarding the interpretation of Scripture in this programme is suggested in these words of Sister Marie de la Visitation, viz., Scripture is read for its spiritual content. By spiritual content, Sister Marie is not referring to one of the five senses of Scripture developed in the scholastic period (see Grant and Tracy, Chapter 9), but rather to the Bible as a record of religious experiences.

Links between cognitive acquisition and affective disposition are strongly evidenced in the programme design. The role of the family emerges as pivotal in subsequent themes. The affection that a child knows within the home will be a powerful educative tool, if the doctrinal content can be linked to it. *Weeks Five and Seven*, "God my Father is your Father, too" and "God our Father looks upon us with love; we belong to him," begin with the child's experience of their own father and family life respectively. The illustrations depict a loving father (Week 5) and a two-parent, two-child, smiling family gathered together in a collective embrace (Week 7). The teacher is warned of the possibility that some children may lack paternal affection at home and so she should not press reticent children to participate in a discussion. Rightly so—the negative experience of the child could not serve as a source for an analogy of divine love. Scripture passages,

---

[49]. Sr. Marie de la Visitation, "Le Dieu de Jésus-Christ présenté aux enfants de 6-7 ans," *Communauté chrétienne* 2 (July-August 1963): 273. Cf. *Viens vers le Père, Guide du maître*, 26.

chosen as the source and illustration of these themes include the *Our Father* from Matthew 6:9; a paraphrase of John 20:17, "God my Father is your Father, too"; a paraphrase of Isaiah 54:8, 10, "I love you with an everlasting love. I will always love you"; a paraphrase of Isaiah 43:1, "I have called you by your name, you are mine."

The adjacent themes similarly connect experiences of interiority and loneliness to scriptural passages. Week 6 contains a paraphrase of Isaiah 45:12, "I, your God, made the earth. I made all men who live on it. I, your God, made the heavens and put the stars in their place." Week 8 contains a paraphrase of John 14:2-3, "I am preparing a place for you in my Father's home, because I want you, too, to be where I am." Week 9 contains a paraphrase Isaiah 41:10, "Do not be afraid, I am with you." Week 10 relates the child's experience of silence to the experience of the boy Samuel who awoke to a voice that no one else could hear (1 Samuel 3).[50]

The choice of all these themes flows from an informed view of the psychological and social traits of the grade one child. As an example, we saw the capacity for wonder dictate the shape of the theme and determine also the selection and use of Scripture. Respecting the child's predisposition to sensorial learning, the programme for the primary grades uses many texts that calls one or more of the senses into play. Abstraction, an empty category for the young child, is avoided.

Other Examples. By Grade Two, the 7-8 year old typically enters a period of calm after the hyperactivity of the 6 year old child. The seven year old experiences a period of interiorization and reflexion which brings with it the joy of understanding, of comprehending a reality.[51] This new stage is accompanied by an awakening of a moral sense in the child and the programme seeks to develop it. Scripture provides texts which encourage children to consider moral choices and to contemplate Christian norms of morality. Week 25 of *Célébrons ses merveilles* provides a typical example of the way in which the moral awakening of the 7-8 year old dictates both thematic choice and use of scripture. It presents the Love Commandment in Matthew 22:37, 39: "You shall love the Lord your God with all your heart. You shall love your neighbour as yourself."

---

[50]. Cf. the goal of the exercises in control.
[51]. *Célébrons ses merveilles, Guide du Maître*, 8.

Moving on to the Grade Four programme, *Nous avons vu le Seigneur*, psychology points to the principle of causality as the great discovery of the 9-10 year old. The writers quote a lucid description from Deconchy:

> Until now, the child moved from one idea to another, connecting them by *and*. Now words like *since, for* and *so that* begin to appear. For an 8-10 year old child the principle of causality is still a passive one. He can see that one thing causes another. But this knowledge is not yet active—that is, he cannot yet utilize the principle of causality to foresee a future situation as emerging from a present situation.[52]

The 9-10 year old has a liking for adventure and exploration and is beginning to acquire notions of time and space, but still finds a sense of history difficult.[53] Translated into the design of the Grade Four programme, these characteristics call for a presentation of its message through concrete facts and gestures, following the example of God's revelation in the Bible. The writers speak of an existential approach which appeals to the curiosity of this age group.[54] The children discover for the first time many facts related to the Bible in a "Documents" section which has been added to respond to the growing, fact-finding curiosity of the 9-10 year old. A map of Israel, reports about the Dead Sea Scrolls, pictures of the settings where Jesus exercised his ministry, information about the climate and terrain of Palestine—all have a bearing on the child's appreciation of the many narratives which form the nexus of the Grade Four Programme dealing with Jesus, the Christ.

In Grade Six, *Selon ta promesse, Fais-moi vivre* (*Alive as He Promised*), one of the social characteristics of the 11-12 year old has an interesting effect on programme design. The child of this age lives an intense experience of being part of groups; groups which assume a certain social stability among children 10 -12 years old.[55] At this age, one understands oneself less in individual terms than in relation to others. At the same time as group life exercises such a significant role in their social lives, these young people become interested in the world

---

[52]. J.P. Deconchy, *Le développement psychologique*, as cited in *We Have Seen the Lord, Teacher's Manual*, 9.
[53]. *Nous avons vu le Seigneur, Guide du Maître*, 10.
[54]. *Nous avons vu le Seigneur, Guide du Maître*, 10.
[55]. *Selon ta promesse, Fais-moi vivre, Guide du Maître*, 15a.

of adults, whom they wish to emulate.[56] Heroes past and present appear in the programme as models to inspire the children. Paul of Tarsus stands as an obvious Christian hero and major events from his ministry are tracked through his own epistles and the Acts of the Apostles in the Grade Six curriculum. Scripture provides models for the children using this programme, as it has for generation upon generation of Christians.

DOCTRINE AND THE READING OF SCRIPTURE

The Primary Years

Throughout the primary grades, the choice of a Trinitarian catechesis carries with it pedagogical implications for the selection and use of Scripture. Already, Christian use of the word "God" occasions a certain confusion in the mind of the child, a confusion which J. Moltmann contends does not abate with the onset of adulthood.[57] Is one referring to the three persons of the Trinity or to one in particular. The confusion arises because we have come to use the word "God" to refer to both the divine nature and the persons who share that nature. "Whether we like it or not, *the word God for children*—especially those aged 6-7—*suggests a person, not a nature*."[58] In order to avoid this confusion the divine persons were referred to as God the Father, God the Son, God the Holy Spirit. The writing team presents a clear explanation for this approach to the question of the Trinity, calling upon the erudition of J. Vagaggini:

> Historically, there were two ways of speaking of the Trinity: the first started from the distinct persons to arrive at the oneness of nature; this is found in the New Testament, nearly all the Greek Fathers, and the most ancient Latin ones; the second way began from the unity of nature and reached the plurality of Persons; this method prevailed with St. Augustine, St. Anselm and especially St. Thomas and all the scholastics of the XIII century. The second way was derived from the

---

[56]. *Selon ta promesse, Fais-moi vivre, Guide du Maître*, 15a.

[57]. Jürgen Moltmann, *The Crucified God: the cross of Christ as the foundation and criticism of Christian theology*, trans. R.A. Wilson and John Bowden (New York: Harper and Row, 1974), 236.

[58]. OCQ—Équipe, "*Viens vers le Père*: The New Catechism for the Province of Quebec," *Lumen Vitae* 20 (1965): 253.

first, and has been used chiefly with apologetical intent to defend the faith against Arian heresy. Later on this method of presenting the Trinity became set in the same perspective.[59]

The authors rightly maintained that, in the context of ancient polytheism, it was likely imperative to insist on the unity of God, whereas the most prevalent modern threat to the faith is from atheism. "Children are less likely to believe in several Gods, but God may remain for them a mere abstraction, an invention of man's mind with no living link to the Real."[60]

Psychologically also, children can pass more easily from a plurality of persons to a spiritual intuition of their unity in love, than from the notion of unity to a multiplicity of persons.[61] The writing team offers an excellent analogy of the difficulty young children have in understanding abstract notions such as the divine nature.

> If a child can grasp some idea of nature, it is only when loosely connected with the concrete. For example (with apologies for the comparison!) to the question: "Is a cat, a dog, an animal?," the child will answer correctly because he has often seen dogs and cats, and been told that they are animals. He might not be sure if asked the same question about a butterfly, a swallow or a fish; the idea of an animal is often only extended to quadrupeds.[62]

Now all of this is in keeping with the choice of the writing team to adopt an inductive, experiential and historicized methodology for the course. Scriptural passages are selected for the way in which they demonstrate the action of one of the divine persons specified in the text. Throughout Grade One, children hear of "God the Father," of the "Lord Jesus," and of the "Holy Spirit."

True to the learning capacities of the child, the *Viens vers le Père* series speaks of the conversion process in terms of the child's getting to know or entering into a relationship with the three divine persons. As we saw, this is the principal aim of Year One and the series as a whole. The key way of getting to know God the Father, God the Son and God the Holy Spirit is through Scripture. Children are encouraged

---

[59]. J. Vagaggini, *Il senso teologico della Liturgia*, as cited in "*Viens vers le Père:* The New Catechism for the Province of Quebec," 256.
[60]. "*Viens vers le Père*: The New Catechism," 256.
[61]. "*Viens vers le Père*: The New Catechism," 256.
[62]. "*Viens vers le Père*: The New Catechism," 258.

to commit to memory the small scriptural excerpts of their themes. The memory work is not intended to be an intellectual endurance trial but rather an invitation to the children to "treasure it in their hearts," where the Holy Spirit will gradually bring it to fruitfulness.[63] With the goal of fostering the conversion of the students, the authors call upon three kinds of scriptural passages throughout their work:

> 1) words that reveal an aspect of the mystery of God such as "God so loved the world that he gave his only Son," Jn 3:16—Week 13;
>
> 2) words that convey a call or command of the Lord and function as a source of knowledge about the mystery of God: "You will love the Lord your God with your whole heart," Mk 12:30—Week 10;
>
> 3) words that respond to a revelation or call of the Lord such as "Lord, how great and wonderful you are!" Ps 104—Week 1 or "Here I am, Father. I have come to do your will," Heb 10:7—Week 21.[64]

By nurturing interiority and a prayer life, the writing team hoped to have the children "approach" the Trinity through the Scriptures, through life in the Church and through their own experiences. In this catechetical series, Scripture does not serve the function of mere support for doctrines formulated in a non-biblical language—it becomes, rather, the expression of doctrine itself. Indeed the point of doctrine and the scriptural quotation are often identical or nearly so.[65] Even where the wording differs, the doctrinal point is often a generalization extrapolated from the scriptural passage. The old catechisms formulated the point of doctrine in Scholastic language and cited the Bible only in passing. The connection between Scripture and doctrine—while it may never have been entirely absent in the Tridentine-style catechisms—was not considered pivotal since the Magisterium greatly emphasized the guidance of the Holy Spirit in the formulation of the Church's faith.

Stated in general terms, one might say that the Bible stands at once as the source and illustration of doctrine. This tendency to view the Bible through the optic of Tradition differentiates Catholic curricula

---

[63]. *Viens vers le Père, Guide du Maître*, 11.
[64]. *Come to the Father, Teacher's Manual*, 16.
[65]. For examples see *Come to the Father*, Weeks 4, 5, 8, 9, 21 et al.

from American Protestant models developed at about the same time. Iris V. Cully reviewed several American Protestant programmes which began with the Bible or human experience as the point of departure, intending to lead either to an "intelligent" reading of the Bible or an illumination of human experience.[66] Not surprisingly, none of the programmes she reviewed included an explicit interpretative key comparable to the corpus of Catholic doctrine, since the Reformation sought specifically to exclude such mediation between the believer and the Word of God. This said, it would be surprising if many popular Protestant Sunday school treatments of Scripture did not also include a Trinitarian perspective and other early doctrinal developments in their hermeneutic.

The Elementary Years

The Grade Four programme, *Nous avons vu le Seigneur* (*We Have Seen the Lord*) deserves special attention in an investigation of *Viens vers le Père*'s biblical hermeneutics. Unlike the other years of the series, Grade Four used the NT as its pedagogical point of departure and clearly wished to have children enter its narrative world. The goal of Grade Four is to discover the Gospel, beginning not with references to the children's lives as in the three previous years, but with an encounter of Jesus and the first disciples.[67] With respect to its ultimate epistemological object, Grade Four holds the same object in view as the primary grades. There, doctrine was most often presented in the words of Scripture and formed the true object of understanding and reflexion. The child's experiences furnished the pedagogical means to the attainment of the doctrinal end. This view is echoed clearly in the statement from the elementary writing team:

> The children's experiences which we use are chosen because they are calculated to help them participate more fully in the experience of the evangelical witness. By proceeding in this manner, we believe that the children themselves will establish close connections between faith in the Lord Jesus and their daily life.[68]

If Grade Four is to be understood as a continuation of the creedal

---

[66]. Iris V. Cully, "Problems of Bible Instruction in American Catechetical Literature," *Concilium* 53 (1970): 128-139.

[67]. *We Have Seen the Lord, Teacher's Manual*, 18.

[68]. *We Have Seen the Lord, Teacher's Manual*, 18.

structure laid out in Grade One, then the purpose of this entire year could be expressed as an attempt to understand the doctrine of the incarnation. Constructed around narratives drawn from the NT, the catechesis of *Nous avons vu le Seigneur* appears more affected by the organization and structures of the NT than do the other years of the programme.

An inductive approach is applied to the incarnational theme. The title, *Nous avons vu le Seigneur*, implies that the Gospel witness presented in Grade Four begins from a post-resurrection awareness of the identity and mission of Jesus.[69] But for children with little experience of the Gospels, the affirmation that Jesus Christ is Risen might not hold great significance, as the authors were aware. The series' authors retrace the experiences of the disciples in order to help children discover Jesus.

This approach is grounded in a low christology and is well suited to the catechesis of young children. One problem with the use of high christologies with children is that they tend to admit Jesus' divinity so easily that they are inclined to neglect his humanity.[70] Students are invited to accompany the disciples and to share in their experiences of meeting Jesus and learning his "secret" and his "mission."[71] While William Wrede's famous work concerning the messianic secret may have been part of the theological education of several of the authors,[72] the existential approach to reading the text is more likely due to the influence of Lubienska de Lenval (via F. Bérubé). This technique of inviting children into the world of the story, allowing the text's narrative world to become their world, corresponds closely to the approach of Lubienska. The authors further explain their intent:

---

[69]. That the Gospels were written from a post-resurrection perspective is perhaps obvious, once one has begun to inquire into the process of their composition. Christological titles at the beginning of Mark and Matthew assume this, and the foreshadowing of the resurrection in various miracle accounts also supports this view. For an example of these themes in a modern work introducing the Gospels see Jean Delorme, *Lecture de l'évangile selon saint Marc* (Paris: Éditions du Cerf, 1972), 51-52.

[70]. *We Have Seen the Lord, Teacher's Manual*, 18.

[71]. *We Have Seen the Lord, Teacher's Manual*, 13.

[72]. William Wrede, *Das Messiasgeheimnis in den Evangelien* (Göttingen: Vandenhoeck und Ruprecht, [1901] 1963).

Our effort will be not so much to initiate the children to the reading of a Gospel text as to help them enter into the world of the Gospel, the world of the Good News and of evangelical values. There we shall meet real people with their feelings, their desires, their illnesses, their sins, their divisions...[73]

The ten Gospel encounters of Jesus in Grade Four provide an unhurried and progressive unfolding of his identity. These encounters allow the children to discover Jesus as the narrative players meet him, to observe the drama of the various situations from within the narrative world and not as outsiders.[74] The children move with *Mark* towards the disclosure of the secret that Jesus of Nazareth is the Christ, the promised one of Israel. Grade Four provides several individual and group study projects to support this inductive approach.

This is done so that the pupils may discover for themselves Jesus speaking to the crowds, gathering his disciples together, curing a sick man, confronting his adversaries, seeing the people abandon him, condemned to die for saying he was the Son of God, eating and drinking with his disciples after his resurrection and "living" in the midst of the first Christian community[75]

Many details are provided about the historical setting of Jesus, a fact which enriches the reader's experience of the narrative world.

Children are obviously not ready for an introduction to the synoptic problem.[76] Grade Four students may, however, come to a simplistic understanding of the differences in the Synoptics by "reliving" an event which has been described in several different accounts. The programme contrives an opportunity to do this.

In a preparatory lesson, a ceremony takes place in which a copy of the New Testament is handed out to each student by the parish priest. Guests are invited to the ceremony, such as parents, grand-parents, friends, the school principal, and so forth. Songs are sung and the priest addresses the children. Pictures are taken of this significant catechetical event. Later the children write an account of their celebration, using the pictures to jog their memory. Although all were present at the party, each one noticed something different and recorded

---

[73]. *We Have Seen the Lord, Teacher's Manual*, 16.
[74]. *We Have Seen the Lord, Teacher's Manual*, 18.
[75]. *We Have Seen the Lord, Teacher's Manual*, 19.
[76]. The synoptic problem is a complex argument about literary dependency in the gospels of Mt, Mk and Lk.

events in a slightly different way. Attention is drawn to the fact that no two accounts are identical and that some students record conversations to which not all were privy. This is meant to give children an idea of how multiple versions of the same event are possible and is applied in general terms to the multiple witnesses of the Gospels. The principal goal of this exercise is to demonstrate that *point of view* changes one's perspective on events, both in narratives and in observation of real events.

The use of Scripture in *Nous avons vu le Seigneur* is not truncated as in the primary grades. Longer narrative passages appear and even though the length of time required to cover an encounter with Jesus limits the total number of pericopes, no attempt has been made to avoid the unpleasant confrontations and suffering which were so much a part of the life of Jesus; the epic character of the saga precludes such a trivialization of the events of the Gospel's protagonist.

Although the goal of this series proves to be the elucidation of doctrine, a constant tension may be felt. The authors struggled to respect the experience of children but were torn, as respect for the Word of God took precedence. *Nous avons vu le Seigneur* embodies that tension, probably because its choice of Jesus of Nazareth as subject demanded fidelity to the wording of the text. In the teacher's manual of Grade Four one discovers perhaps the clearest statement—applicable to the series as a whole—about the nature and function of experience.

> By an "experience of the child" we mean certain situations, feelings, desires or values to which a child is subject in his life at home, in school or in his free time with his friends. By way of illustration, some of the approaches in the program are based on the following experiences: the desire and the joy of sharing a discovery; the desire of being better known and of getting to know certain persons more intimately; participating in the faith of parents; belonging to a given parish community; the desire to grow up and belong to youth groups; budding friendships; family ties. These experiences obviously may be either religious or secular. They may even be brought about in an actual classroom situation, like the "vacation book" made during the introductory lessons.
>
> Such real-life experiences of the child may serve as the starting points for our catechesis...These experiences will be utilized in various ways. Most of them will provide psychological preparation for the catechesis

to be given....

It should be clear, therefore, that these references to the children's experiences are much more than "comparisons" to help them understand, more than illustrations or examples. They permit the children to make the connection between faith and the life situations in which the Lord comes.[77]

The last paragraph of this excerpt notwithstanding, children's experiences remain a means to an end. Given the programme's methodological assumptions, "natural" human experiences can serve as no more than analogies or comparisons for revelation. The program always treats experience as if it is someone else's experience or the experience common to a certain class of people. The personal element, which constitutes experience, is largely missing.

The tension created by trying to do justice to both heritage and experience eventually forces one to give priority to one or the other. Clearly, the fundamental option of this series is to throw light on Tradition, rather than to use Tradition as a means of throwing light on the experiences of the child. In the remaining two years of the elementary cycle, this basic schema remains unchanged, even though the theological vocabulary of Vatican Council II marks these years. The change in Grades Five and Six consists in the range of experience that is called into play in the analogical process. In keeping with the psycho-social capacities of the children, heroes from the past and present could be called upon to illustrate the text as could the many signs of the Risen Lord at work in the modern world. This marks a change in the view of the world, even as compared with the first four years of the programme; we will discuss these elements in the following chapter. Nevertheless, with respect to the goals of teaching and preaching, these years offer nothing new. Consistently, the pedagogical point of arrival remains doctrinal content.

PROGRESSIVE REVELATION

As we have seen, throughout Grades One, Two and Three, the selection principle for the choice of childhood experiences related directly to the point of doctrine in question. With this type of catechesis, the possibility of presenting the entirety of Catholic doctrine in each

---

[77]. *We Have Seen the Lord, Teacher's Manual*, 16-17.

year of schooling, in the style of the old catechisms, was precluded from the outset. The choice of which doctrines (and how much doctrine) to include in any given year depended on the learning capacities of the children in question; the programme demanded uncompromising respect for the psycho-social development of the child. Young children are not ready to integrate—in a single year of schooling—a complete picture of the doctrinal content of the Catholic heritage. Some elements were therefore deliberately postponed to later years in the primary-elementary cycle. Hell, demons and serious sin were not felt to be appropriate themes for the impressionable minds of Grade One children. When the theme of Hell enters in the Grade Three programme, its presentation is marked by the pedagogical principles which govern the programme as a whole. In studying the educational outcomes of the new catechesis in 1970, F. Darcy and J.-M. Beniskos had this to say about the treatment of this theme:

> Si nous avons inséré ce dernier thème, c'est que l'enfer est justement un des points de l'enseignement eschatologique de l'Eglise sur lequel les programmes nouveaux essaient de réaliser une catéchèse corrective, modifiant les représentations anthropomorphiques courantes pour acheminer les enfants vers une conception plus théologique, plus intérieure et symbolique, de ce thème.[78]

The scriptural passage which serves as the key reference for Week 25 of Grade Three in which the theme of hell comes up is Mark 12:30-31, "You will love the Lord your God with all your heart, with all your soul and with all your strength and your neighbour as yourself." The theme deals with God's unceasing call to conversion, with humanity's ability to refuse and with the consequences of that refusal; God respects our choice to be alone, but to be without God is hell. The figure of the devil and the fiery consequences of sin are downplayed in this section on conversion and liberty.

There is a temptation to look at one grade level apart from the others. This led J. Harvey, among others, to question whether this might not lead teachers to treat deferred material as eliminated material, if they were not sufficiently aware of the antecedent and subsequent

---

[78]. Françoise Darcy and Jean-Marie Beniskos, "Il y en a qui disent...," *Lumen Vitae* 26:2 (June 1971): 259.

content of the programme.[79] Despite some argument about the doctrinal approach, which he characterizes as linear and not concentric, Harvey judged the programme to have taken pains to ensure the integrity of the transmission of the faith.[80] The transmission of doctrine represents, after all, the raîson d'être for the entire series—its pedagogy attests to this fact. It is evident that if passages dealing with demons and hell are left out of the doctrinal exposé, they will also be lacking in the Scripture called upon.

In this model, however, the child's prior experience was not essential in itself. The main goal was to respect the psychological development of the young child, which demands that an idea—in order to be accessible to the young mind—be based on a concrete experience or be re-expressed in personal activity. Thus in *Célébrons ses merveilles* teaching about the sacraments could start either with the sacramental rite itself, or with a biblical passage.

> Les deux (démarches) semblent également adaptées à l'enfant car ce qui importe pour lui, c'est que la démarche pédagogique prenne appui sur le concret. Or un récit biblique peut, aussi bien qu'un rite sacramentaire, servir de point d'appui concret.[81]

Thus in Week Three the movement of the theme goes from the biblical narrative of the man born blind (Jn 9.1-38) to the sacramental rite of baptism, and in the twentieth Week the movement is from the sacramental rite of the Eucharist to the Bread of Life discourse (Jn 6).

---

[79]. Julien Harvey, "Mémoire sur les Manuels de Catéchèse de l'OCQ: Grandes options des manuels," Unpublished paper, 18 pages, October 1973, 12.
[80]. Harvey, "Mémoire," 12.
[81]. *Célébrons ses merveilles, Guide du Maître*, 18.

PART TWO

Education, i.e., teaching and learning, has been conceived of either as a process of transmission or as a process of intellectual midwifery. The relationships obtaining between learner experiences and curriculum content are at odds with one another in these two instances.

Conceived of as transmission, education is the communication of a content which is in the possession of the teacher but is foreign to the learner. The knowledge which the teacher possesses has been judged valuable and worthy of preservation by society and pre-exists the educational process. On this view, curriculum content remains virtually unchanged even as it is addressed to various audiences; it has value independent of the audience's evaluation of it.

Conceived of as maieutic process, education rejects the possibility of a transfer of knowledge and understands teaching to be an exercise in intellectual midwifery. On this view, the ideas and understandings which result from education are the intellectual children of the learner, who has given birth to them. The teacher does not transfer knowledge but rather serves as a facilitator for intellectual activity proper to the learner. The teacher's role consists chiefly in helping the learner to organize ideas already in his/her possession in such a way that a new insight presents itself. Understanding remains personal and relative to the learner's intellectual history, which in turn is tied to the learner's experiences in the world. In this model each act of knowing relates directly to the learner's life and helps throw light upon his/her existence. In this way the experiences of the learner possess a value in and of themselves.

These two concepts of education disagree as to what constitutes the subject of education, i.e., what it is ultimately about. The transmission model understands the subject of education to be *humanity's accumulated wisdom and knowledge*. The model of intellectual midwifery understands the *learner* to be the subject of education.

We will continue our examination of the educational options of this series by trying to identify the role assigned to human experience in its catechesis. Our working hypothesis is that the role assigned experience in the programme's pedagogy will likely reflect the role experience plays in its concept of revelation. In the next chapter, we will attempt to demonstrate the determinative role the concept of revelation (and related theological options) plays in this catechism's hermeneutical choices. For now, we turn to a consideration of *Viens vers le Père*'s pedagogical method, paying particular attention to its point of departure and the goals it pursues.

THE ROLE OF EXPERIENCE IN VVLP

Pedagogically, one of the most significant elements in the programme is the *Talk* which begins each lesson. Variously described as a "salvation event," a "spiritual journey" and a "meeting with God," the *Talk* occupies a leading role in the programme.[82] The *Talk* proclaims the Word of God and affirms the doctrine to be taught.[83] The teacher initiates this chat, using an experience of the child (e.g., the experience of relationships with parents, of family life, of early perceptions of the Church) as an *Anknüpfungspunkt* for doctrine. These primary experiences offer a means of communicating the proposed content. For example, a relationship with one's father serves as an analogy for a relationship with God; the home becomes a sign of the Church, and the Church in turn is a sign of the Father's heavenly home. The *Talk* continues with a doctrinal affirmation, which whenever possible, is presented as a proclamation of the word of God, i.e., in a manner similar to the reading of the Scriptures at the liturgy. A moment of contemplation of the "Word proclaimed" is followed by a response of the group—a hymn or psalm, a gesture or vocal prayer. Finally, an activity allows the child to interiorize the Word by reliving it in art work or some other activity.

This procedure begins in the child's experience but leads elsewhere. The intent is not, first and foremost, to clarify the child's experience, but rather to clarify the point of doctrine, or the biblical passage in question. "If each of the catecheses forming this work genuinely relies on an experience of the child, the entire catechism, for its part, is based on a predetermined doctrinal structure."[84] The pedagogically verifiable aim for each of the lessons is its doctrinal content. In other words, as the authors confirm, the cognitive content to be evalu-

---

[82]. *Viens vers le Père, Guide du Maître*, 23-24.
[83]. *Viens vers le Père, Guide du Maître*, 21.
[84]. Louis Racine, "The Child's Psychological Experience and his Evangelization: A Ground Yet to be Covered," *Lumen Vitae* 22 (1967): 479.

ated (tested), the true goal of the lesson, is doctrinal: "Chaque thème comporte un contenu doctrinal précis, exprimé en termes d'actions et de relations."[85] In order to make the content understood, the authors draw analogies from the child's experience as a means of assimilating the doctrinal point into the life of the child. The importance of the psycho-social development of the child as a determinative factor in this schema becomes evident. The more familiar one becomes with the typical experiences of one's audience, the more fully that experience may be exploited in the communication process. Unlike the Socratic method, the "truth" which the child receives in this schema is not a dormant intuition already unconsciously present within the child's intellect, awaiting only a maieutic process to bring it to birth in the mind. In *Viens vers le Père*, salvation comes to the child, foreign to his/her own experiences, but is presented to the child's understanding by means of those very experiences.

One of the chief principles of this catechesis is to: "Present each Truth within the living 'today' of the salvation-event."[86] *Viens vers le Père* builds its pedagogical methodology on an understanding of the psychology of the child. In each stage of psycho-social development, analogies drawn from a general picture of the child's everyday experiences serve as the vehicles of doctrinal communication. The true point of departure is doctrine, whether that doctrine is presented in creedal formulas, biblical passages, or Church decrees.

Louis Racine, a Quebecois theologian, has identified a shortcoming of this procedure and addresses the *Viens vers le Père* series as an example of a doctrinally-centred catechetical methodology. When doctrine serves as the point of departure for catechesis, the elucidation of experience is truncated. Undoubtedly in reaction to its conservative predecessors, the liberal theology underpinning *Viens vers le Père* de-emphasizes both the concept and the reality of sin. Evil in the world appears distant, not menacing or foreboding, and the human situation looks generally optimistic. Given its theological emphasis, *Viens vers le Père* appears "too exclusively confined to the analogical procedure

---

[85]. Sr. Marie de la Visitation, Jean-Paul Bérubé, Marcel Caron, Réginald Marsolais, "Présentation du nouveau catéchisme," *Communauté chrétienne* 3 (May-June 1964): 196.
[86]. *Come to the Father, Teacher's Manual*, 22. Truth here should be read as "doctrine."

which selects only the 'rosy' situations from the child's experience..."[87] Racine understands the point of catechesis to be the evangelization of the child's experiences. On this point he writes:

> a) We believe, moreover, that not only does it (the analogical procedure) select a particular experience, which is in any case necessary, but that very often it arbitrarily *isolates*, within the experience, segments or aspects of the latter according to a pedagogical process which, in relation to maturity, might seem debatable. Negative experiences, for instance, in particular the experience of aggressiveness, of destructiveness, of frustration, or simply of imperfections, will be relegated to a special compartment ("Evil in the world"); in this way, they will lose a great deal of their vibrating power to situate God's redemptive action in the right perspective, and—a further point to be considered—they will do disservice to the essential aim of the catechesis, which is the *evangelization* of the child's experiences such as they are in an imperfect world, while awaiting a redemption that comes from within him (and not from something external to him) through divine action....
>
> b) In elaborating a truly anthropological catechetical procedure, we must always remember that experience should not illuminate the message but that the message should illuminate experience....
>
> c) Could we not conceive another kind of procedure which, taking the contrary direction, would no longer attempt to descend towards life merely to draw analogies from it, but would try to descend downwards towards it in the true sense by bringing out the Christian significance of the listener's human experiences?[88]

Continuing his critique of this catechism, Racine goes on in the article to offer useful examples of how one might, when starting with human experience, avail oneself of even negative experiences as opportunities to discuss the Christ event. Detractors of an experience-based pedagogy[89] point out that this methodology would likely result in doctrinal lacunæ, as the curriculum seeks to respond to the student's questions rather than follow the dictates of Tradition. Racine anticipates this charge. His response is that catechesis does not consist pri-

---

[87]. Racine, 475-476.
[88]. Racine, a)477-478, b) 481, c) 478.
[89]. Racine does not consider this *Viens vers le Père* to be an experienced-based pedagogy.

marily in adducing the whole of Christian doctrine, but in evangelizing to the best of its ability, the whole life of the person it addresses.[90] Despite this uncompromising critique, Racine praised the programme as an interesting attempt at anthropological catechesis, but suggested that a great deal of research needed still to be carried out before a thoroughgoing existentially-based programme would be feasible. Although this article appeared in *Lumen Vitae* in 1967, it was written some time earlier, when only the first year or two of the programme were in circulation.[91]

Bernard Grom, concentrating on Grades One and Two, *Viens vers le Père* and *Célébrons ses merveilles*, proffers a more positive evaluation:

> Dès le départ, donc, nous sommes en présence d'un programme précis et cohérent: le Dieu bon et saint est révélé. Révélé au niveau *affectif et intuitif* tout comme à celui des concepts; révélé *à partir de l'expérience naturelle et spontanée de l'enfant* et aussi *à partir de l'Ecriture*, qui purifie et approfondie l'expérience.[92]

Grom refers to the way in which the programme's writers capitalize on the child's capacity for wonder, a typical characteristic of the 6-7 year old, in order to unfold for the child the marvels of the world which surround him/her.[93] This method of proceeding puts the child in contact through a natural sense of curiosity and wonder with their own environment. Only after this focusing of the child's attention does the association between the point of doctrine and the child's experience become clarified: God the Father is the maker of heaven and earth. Grom continues:

> Cette introduction générale est ensuite développée (étapes suivantes) en liaison avec l'année liturgique et en rapport avec les réalités les plus importantes dans la vie de l'enfant: beauté de la nature, croissance de sa propre force, mystère de la famille, relation avec les parents et les camarades—comme lieux où l'Esprit de Jésus se manifes-

---

[90]. Racine, 485.
[91]. L. Racine, interview by author, 15 December 1992.
[92]. Bernhard Grom, "Regard de l'étranger," *Relations* 385 (Sept. 1973): 253.
[93]. Grom, 253.

tera par ses "fruits."[94]

Large elements of Grom's description of the programme correspond to Racine's reading, while his overall appraisal betrays no awareness of the critique which the latter levels at it. Grom is aware that experience in the *Viens vers le Père* model is a vehicle and not the object the programme seeks to understand. In the list of experiences to which he alludes as primordial in the life of the child, Grom, like the *Viens vers le Père* series, leaves out one which is of paramount importance for young children, viz., the initiation into school life, with its attendant insecurities, fears and misunderstandings.[95] This omission of a rather fundamental experience is not the only important reality of the child's life to slip by Grom. He fails to remark the penury of negative experiences dealt with in the life of the child. He fails to notice that the treatment of the child's experience remains incomplete.

Many of the problems raised in this debate are better left to the following chapters in which a discussion of the theological underpinnings of the programme and the hermeneutical implications of these choices will be discussed. For now, let us observe, that the choice of doctrine as the pedagogical starting point has certain implications for the manner in which the experience of the young person has been dealt with and may also affect the use of Scripture.

EDUCATION AS LEGACY

> We are like dwarfs sitting on the shoulders of giants; we see more things and more far off ones, than they did, not because our sight is better, nor because we are taller than they were, but because they raise us up and add to our height by their gigantic loftiness.[96]

These images express in elegant simplicity the great debt successive generations of humanity owe their forbears for all that is held as valuable—our intellectual and cultural legacy. Over time, a positive consensus forms around the achievements of certain charismatic or brilliant figures, and their contributions to human progress are conserved for posterity. The great classics of literature and music, founda-

---

[94]. Grom, 253.
[95]. See Racine, 253.
[96]. Quoted in Etienne Gilson, *History of Christian Philosophy in the Middle Ages* (New York: Random House, 1955), 619. These words are attributed to Bernard of Chartres.

tional texts of religious and political movements, works of scientific and technical genius, all become fixtures in our intellectual and cultural worlds. And we pass these gems of civilization on through our systems of education. Frederick Crowe, in discussing the notion of education as heritage, evokes the image of a child's personal museum of art, literature, and music, his/her own private store of treasures.[97] This tendency to conserve that which is of value from the past pervades the entire educational enterprise. As William Torrey Harris suggested in the 19th century, education provides an economic and systematic means of making the accumulated wisdom of the human race available.[98] Language, the very substratum of education, constitutes a prime example of a set of historically-evolved conventions which successive generations have conserved and built upon. Hence, education becomes feasible only because of this intellectual tendency to conserve the achievements of earlier generations; and mercifully we are not condemned to endlessly "re-invent the wheel."

Can a view of education as conservation foster creativity and progress in human knowledge? Is conservation enough? John Dewey, an early critic of this conservative concept of education critiqued its main features in these words:

> The traditional scheme is, in essence, one of imposition from above and from outside. It imposes adult standards, subject-matter, and methods upon those who are only growing slowly toward maturity. The gap is so great that the required subject matter, the methods of learning and of behaving are foreign to the existing capacities of the young. They are beyond the reach of the experience the young learners already possess. Consequently, they must be imposed; even though good teachers will use devices of art to cover up the imposition so as to relieve it of obviously brutal features....
>
> Learning here means the acquisition of what is already incorporated in

---

[97]. Frederick E. Crowe, *Old Things and New: Strategy for Education* (Atlanta: Scholar's Press, 1985), 70.

[98]. Cited in Lawrence E. Cremin, "Curriculum Making in the United States," *Curriculum Theorizing: The Reconceptualists*, ed. William Pinar (Berkeley: McCutchan, 1975), 28.

books and in the heads of the elders.[99]

Here, education might properly be characterized as the consumption of intellectual products. The conclusion, the theorem, the axiom, the definition are presented as givens, not derived. Once the universal principle had been provided, the student tests its veracity (as if the truth value of such givens ever lay in doubt!) in several particular instances. This deductive approach characterized not only mathematics and the sciences, but virtually every course in the school's syllabus.

A quick illustration may help. In much the same way as physicians-in-training would approach a cadaver, traditional methods often saw teachers and text books exploring poetry as an exercise in dissection. Meter could be separated from feet, alliteration from assonance, simile from metaphor until the unfortunate literary victim lay in pieces. A poem became a means to understand poetic devices. But anyone who has had the pleasure of a good teacher, knows that more is required in the appreciation of poetry than methodical analysis. The pedagogue able to unlock poetry for students is one able to forge imaginative links between the listener's sphere of experiences and those evoked by the text; one able to help students become aware of their world in a new way, allowing them to reclaim "lost" experiences, enter "lost" worlds and compare them with their own. As readers, the students become in their turn, the creators of new worlds, sharing in a process that helps create the "event" which is the poem. They are not simply invited to consume an intellectual product, sliced into bite-size portions, but rather to enter into a poietic process, to become in their turn poets. A creative complicity obtains between author and audience and the quality of the poetic event depends on both, even if unequally.

While new methods do not necessarily good teachers make, and while good teachers have always managed to edify the intellect of their young charges (little matter what system they struggled under), on the whole, the revolution in pedagogical theory and practice this century, may be understood to have had positive results for education. An insight into the creative process has assumed new importance in the understanding of how children learn. In theory at least, knowing "how" has become as important as knowing "what." Clearly, educational practice precludes extreme positions of the all-or-nothing variety, but a

---

[99]. John Dewey, *Experience and Education* (New York: Collier Books, (1938) 1963), 4-5.

major shift to an inductive, historicized approach characterizes the dominant pedagogical theory afoot today. The pioneers at the forefront of the new curriculum theory, were not rejecting the value of our western heritage, but were rather seeking ways for students to appropriate that heritage as a response to their own vital forces, calling into play their own ingenuity as they sought to understand the circumstances of their own lives. In this view, the "educational moment," which begins and ends in the experience of the learner, simultaneously illuminates both that experience and the experiences recovered through the text. This "existential" interpretative key would allow students to do more than understand texts and heritage; it would prepare them to add to that heritage, even as they gain insight into their worlds and their lives.

In addition to the existential impertinence of a curriculum which intends chiefly to elucidate humanity's cultural and intellectual legacy, recent critics underline the passivity of students and the paucity of critical thinking skills in this set-up. Radical developments in the field of curriculum theory contend that all pedagogical options proceed from certain political, economic and social assumptions, whether these are conscious or not, whether they are made explicit or not.[100] This critical epistemology sets about to uncover the presuppositions informing the assembly and transmission of knowledge within the context of schooling; it is aware of the social construction of knowledge. Surveyed from varying angles, the dominant intellectual heritage represented in the curriculum of modern societies has been shown to be deeply coloured with sexist and racist tendencies.[101] Feminist, black, environmentalist, and neo-marxist activists attack the notion of educa-

---

[100]. For examples of this critical pedagogy see *The Reconceptualists,* ed. Wm. Pinar.

[101]. Paulo Freire critiqued that heritage as the institutionalization of an inequitable economic arrangement, used to systematically oppress a socioeconomic underclass. Freire developed a curriculum for illiterate peasants in northern Brazil aimed at raising their consciousness to the arbitrary nature of the social and political assumptions which defined their world. To gain critical awareness of and therefore distance from that formerly all-enveloping and seemingly inevitable *Weltanschauung* was to realize that another social, political and economic vision might emerge, if enough of the oppressed stood in solidarity in its construction. See Paulo Freire, *Pedagogy of the Oppressed* (New York: Seabury, 1970).

tion as heritage by attacking curriculum content. In general, these groups share a desire to raise the critical awareness of students through the curriculum. They wish to transform the mode of the learner from passive receptivity to active critique.

As for the catechetical renewal, those at its forefront understood Christian faith as anything but a dead letter. Catechetical reformers characterized the magisterial approach of the question and answer catechisms, ubiquitous before the renewal, as dry and lifeless. Understanding faith as assent to a body of revealed truths, expressed in the doctrine of the Church, reduced the requirement of faith to its intellectual component. In a cultural context that gave support to the Church and Christian doctrine without much questioning, this method got by. The social context changed, however, and these assumptions are no longer valid. Just as definitions of simile and metaphor became more important than the poems from which they were extracted, within catechetics the structures which mediated knowledge of the faith assumed more importance than a living experience of the faith. In the old catechisms, the product of someone else's reflection, someone else's insights, supplanted that process of "seeing" it for oneself; a process essential to coming to faith. A kind of idolatry of the structures prevailed. Again, the faith "event" became subordinate to its vehicles, all of which exist expressly to foster such an event. Pedagogical action in catechesis has the goal of ensuring a meeting between the Word of God, which is God's revelatory initiative, and the possibilities, expectations and requirements of the human person.[102]

The pedagogy of *Viens vers le Père* may be situated squarely in this overall thrust for renewal which crossed all disciplines and spanned the globe. Its organizing principle remained, nevertheless, the *content* of Catholic heritage and tradition.

EDUCATION AS ACHIEVEMENT

There is no pretence within the model of "education as achievement" which we present below, that a student holds within his/her individual experiences all that is required for a full and rich education. Clearly also, there is no rejection, holus-bolus, of our intellectual heritage. What one could argue, however, is that if a student learns to trust his/her experiences and his/her understandings, they may come to

---

[102]. Colomb, *Service*, I, 48.

have, to paraphrase Kant, *the courage to make use of their own understanding.*[103] If education begins as an attempt to clarify one's experience, not everything within one's intellectual and cultural heritage will exercise equal claim on one's attention. Here the experience of the human person becomes the point of departure for an educational process which may enlist any number of resources as it moves towards its goal. This whole process then, has an inherent ability to foster critique which has relevance to the learner's experience. As an example, feminists, who have critically reflected upon their own experiences and those of their fellow women, have become very critical of a *patrimony*, that even in its very nomenclature excludes them.

Seen as achievement, education proceeds from experience to understanding, to reflection, and finally to values.[104] Values differ from knowledge in that the term implies a normative element, a judgment that things, activities, persons or experiences of individuals or groups are good, worthwhile.[105]

Experience provides raw data that is stored in memory, possibly to be recalled later and to be subjected to higher level mental processes. Language is the essential tool which allows the data of experience to be stored and retrieved. At an early stage in language development, children learn to associate symbols with objects. The first stage of the symbol-object association amounts to little more than labelling. Babies can be taught to mouth a given word when certain objects are produced, long before they possess any apparent understanding of what defines that object. In scholastic terms, this ability to name things was referred to as the *scientia nominis*, whereas a grasp of the essential reality indicated by that name, fell under the category of *scientia rei*, i.e., a knowledge of the object's cause.[106]

Understanding follows upon experience. Nothing will be correctly understood, nothing will become part of a person's intellectual prop-

---

[103]. Referred to in Hans Georg Gadamer, "The Elevation of the Historicality of Understanding to the Status of Hermeneutical Principle," *Critical Theory Since 1965*, ed. Hazard Adams, Leroy Searle (Tallahassee: Florida State University Press, 1986), 843. (Hereafter cited as *CTSN*.)

[104]. Crowe, 32. Here we follow Crowe, Chapters 3.

[105]. J.L. Elias, *Encyclopedia of Religious Education*, ed. I. V. Cully, K.B. Cully (San Francisco: Harper & Row, 1990), 678.

[106]. Crowe, 34.

erty, if the words used to describe and communicate it, have no referents in the experience of that person. To understand by analogy means simply to proceed from the clear in order to clarify the obscure, to proceed from that which has a referent in one's experiences to that which, as yet, has not. The intellectual pathways, i.e., the associations made, the analogies evoked, that lead to understanding, differ from individual to individual and are shaped by one's experiences. Hence, the act of understanding cannot be communicated since it is a "wholly interior event, immanently generated, personal to the individual pupil."[107] To gain intelligence of a reality, to have an insight with respect to it, consists in more than a cumulative compilation of data: "reaching the solution is not the mere apprehension of any clue, not the mere memory of all, but a quite distinct activity of organizing intelligence that places the full set of clues in a unique explanatory perspective."[108]

If teachers are to help students understand, it will be by helping them to question and re-question their experiences in new ways, prodding them to see their own world, of intellectual construction, from a different perspective. Crowe, following in the steps of Lonergan, contends that humans possess a built-in drive toward understanding which acts spontaneously. It is our sense of wonder, a wonder which marries awe with curiosity and is seen most readily in the child's exuberant and continual 'Why?'[109] Crowe, with Lonergan, characterizes a freely roaming imagination as a key to the process of understanding.

Paul Ricoeur concurs in his treatment of cognition as imagination.[110] For Ricoeur, cognition or understanding, does not resemble the operation of a computer which encodes and decodes so many bits of information, respecting the precise rules of logic. An image-forging process which allows the mind to "see" what it is apprehending characterizes the unique action of the intellect in its mode of understanding. Interpretation involves the production of mental images, i.e., psychological phenomena which allow the simultaneous contemplation of two juxtaposed images at once; something akin to being able to bring

---

[107]. Crowe, 39.

[108]. Bernard J. F. Lonergan, *Insight: a study of human understanding* (New York: Harper and Row, 1978), ix.

[109]. Crowe, 41.

[110]. See Paul Ricoeur, "The Metaphorical Process as Cognition, Imagination and Feeling," *CTSN*, 424-434.

two holograms in close proximity to one another so that the similarities between the images might be contemplated. In Ricoeur's presentation, one may speak of *seeing* the truth of a proposition—in other words understanding has a pictorial dimension, an imaginative element.

The next step toward the development of one's own intellectual options is *judgment*. To a great extent judgment is at the mercy of understanding. If one has misunderstood, then judgment cannot be but faulty. Here again, Crowe speaks of a human dynamism at work in the operation of judgment: "Before data, the dynamism expressed itself in wonder: what can this be? Now it expresses itself in *reflection*: is my idea of what this might be, the correct idea?"[111] But in order to be able to reflect, to wonder about the correctness of one's idea, other possibilities must be available from which to choose. Thus the background of the reflective process, the process of judgment, is a set of ideas consisting of images and data. To judge is to discriminate among a variety of ideas.

Finally the fourth level, that of *values* formation brings the student to ask the questions "Should I or should I not?"[112] The whole educative process seeks the autonomy of the learner—it seeks to allow the person to "think" for themselves, i.e., to experience, to understand those experiences, reflect upon those understandings and reach a decision. Each of the subsequent steps in this path, is conditioned and qualified by the previous steps in the operation. A narrow set of experiences restricts the sorts of ideas that one develops and similarly qualifies the judgments one may make.

Our outline of both the heritage and achievement models of education follows closely the work of F. Crowe. It should be noted, however, that even as Crowe develops a model of education as achievement, he confesses his preference for a heritage-centred model. Despite the fact that experience is presented as the point of departure for the educational process, it does not constitute the object of understanding of that process. Experience becomes a vehicle, a source of analogies, wherein the data of the intellectual deposit may be understood. Applied to religious education, the goal for this educative process could not be chiefly the understanding of experiences, not even of religious experiences,

---

[111]. Crowe, 47.
[112]. Crowe, 54.

but rather the understanding of tradition. To make the lives of believers more meaningful to them, their experiences comprehensible to them, is this not a central aim of authentic religion?

THE INTEGRATED APPROACH OF VVLP

In the context of schools, it must be conceded that learning involves both the assimilation of an intellectual heritage and a synthesis of thought which is the new creation of the learner. But this irenic admission does nothing to clarify the point of departure for the educational process. What is the relative weight one should assign to either the experiences of the learner or to humanity's intellectual legacy in the development of a curriculum? Louis Racine's critique revolved around the role of experience in the curriculum. The problem might also be examined from the point of view of the role of texts, since the practice of *curriculum as content* (the heritage-centred model) or *curriculum as process* (the learner-centred model) is ineluctably bound up with a variety of texts, such as the Bible, texts of literature, of arithmetic and mathematics, of science and so forth. Are the texts proposed for the curriculum, ends in themselves? Is the Bible an end in itself? Must the curriculum be structured so that these monuments are imposed upon the experience and intellectual formation of the student; the former, arrogating by their very grandeur, priority in the educational process?

Marie Fargues, among others, conceived of a curriculum emerging from the world of experiences of the student, where the questions pursued in the course of studies, are the questions of the students and not those of the teacher, or the text, or society. Classic texts, in this model, serve as a timeless resource, a store of experiences through which one contemplates one's questions.

The Bible, and the corpus of Catholic doctrine along with it, need not be idolized as sacrosanct fixtures possessing absolute truth claims prior to and superior to the experiences of humanity in the 20th century, or in any century for that matter. These elements of Tradition have value precisely because of their ability to illuminate contemporary experience, allowing today's people to gain insight into the questions which life stirs up; questions in which cognitive and affective concerns exist in symbiosis. Classic texts, religious or otherwise, address more than the "head"; they also capture the "heart" of the learner. It is precisely because of the classic's power to enlighten human experience, through what David Tracy refers to as an "excess of meaning" that successive generations value it.[113] A goal for the educational process would be to help learners identify their questions and guide their search for answers. Along the way they may discover, as did their intellectual forebears, that some texts are immensely more helpful than others, some veritable treasure houses of experience, which do much to illuminate one's own experiences. Alfred Shutz speaks of a "stock of experience" (Erfahrung in the original German) that is handed on.[114]

With experience as the focus of the educational process, the trials of learning do not disappear. The treasures held within texts are transmitted through a system of symbolic representations which the reader must learn to interpret, if the reader is to enter into these experiences? Reading requires more than an ability to decode sound-symbol correlations. Many other levels of literacy allow for a more thorough exploration and appreciation of texts. These are the myriad literary devices and specialized languages of the various disciplines that should serve the reading process. In the case of scientific texts, for example, the results of experimentation are conserved in precise technical jargon, which will exclude the uninitiated. Experience, held within the text, waits to be recovered, looking once again to be resurrected. But the élan which spurs the recovery of these experiences, conserved *in potentia*, is not located within the text itself but within the experience of the reader. Hence, subject matter remains, to some extent, audience-specific, since all do not possess the same scope of experience nor the same levels of literacy. Of course the psychological development of children plays a determinative role in deciding which texts may be effectively used with which age group. Many works of literature would be altogether unsuitable for young readers, even though they might possess the mechanical lexical skills to read them. So also, Aristotle thought it impractical to teach ethics to the young. Experiences of reading unfold against the backdrop of the experiences of life.

An inductive, student-centred method pervades Canadian curricula

---

[113]. David Tracy (Robert M. Grant) *A Short History of the Interpretation of the Bible* (Philadelphia: Fortress Press, 1984), 157.

[114]. Alfred Schutz, *The Phenomenology of the Social World* (Evanston: Northwestern University Press, 1967), 80ff.

today. It has been appropriated even in the study of mathematics, which was once taught largely as the manipulation of abstract formulæ but proceeds now, through a carefully-constructed, "historicized" approach, which guides students through a "rediscovery" of the logical sequence of steps through which a formula or theorem was originally derived. Moreover, mathematics begins in an inductive approach applied to a problem drawn from the world of the student's experiences. Existential pertinence and affect are thus linked and teachers of mathematics strain to hear the questions which occur to students as they struggle with the problems identified. Similarly, young children no longer simply memorize addition tables, but also work with *manipulables* (wooden blocks, marbles etc.) in order to gain a concrete experience of addition. Alas, the drudgery of memorizing addition and multiplication tables seems unavoidable, lest one become a slave to the hand-held calculator! This historicized, inductive approach to arithmetic and mathematics, which involves a poiesis on the part of the student is captured in the title of C. Kamii's, *Young Children Reinvent Arithmetic* (N.Y.: 1985).

Bernard Grom' *Botschaft oder Erfahrung* (Zurich, 1975), which looked at the confrontation between the kerygmatic catechesis of the German school and the existential emphasis of the French, catches this distinction well in its title. When the debates of these catechetical schools are considered against this philosophical backdrop, the focus is sharpened to a choice between *education as message* or *education as experience*. In the former model, the curriculum content has been predetermined and judged as valuable apart from the learner's reception of it, while in the latter, the learner must discover at least some of its value in a personal process, seeking insights beginning with the problems or questions which arise in his/her own existence. Scripture and Tradition are valued in both models but are used very differently.

Viens vers le Père was consciously elaborated in the Catholic tradition and patently accepts the model of education as heritage. Nevertheless, it affirms this heritage as vital. In its attempt to educate its young audience within an ancient tradition, its goal is clearly to allow the tradition to be apprehended in and through the experiences of that audience. Its methodology intends to get children to adopt the values of the Catholic heritage. This programme brings together heritage and experience and does so in a manner which subordinates learner experiences to the content of the heritage to be communicated. The integration of experience and intellectual heritage in the *Viens vers le*

Père series resembles closely the position set forth by F. Crowe. While the four steps of experience, understanding, judgment, and decision appear as the natural progression in the educative process, Crowe concurs with Lonergan that "human development from above downward is the prior and more fundamental way of forming the child."[115] Crowe has this to say about the shape of the process as it is applied to the maturing person.

> This development follows the child's advance in years (at first, there is lots of experience, little understanding, and almost no judgment), so we will not expect mature deliberation from the child, and the values held will be those received from family and community as heritage...[116]

And so in the case of children, Crowe would start with inherited values, incorporating the experiences of the child as a means to illustrate effectively the point to be taught. He asks: "How then can the pupil's experience, developing in life with siblings, parents, schoolmates, neighbours, the village community, how can it be *used*..." in the educational process?[117] In this model, experience serves as a tool in the process of assimilation of pre-determined values. It does not constitute the object of epistemological inquiry.

CONCLUSIONS:

Our goal in this chapter has been to suggest a perspective from which to view the several elements comprising these six years of catechetical instruction; a pedagogical perspective which allows readers to organize their contents and grasp their methodology. Our immediate goal has been to investigate the way in which pedagogical options influence the interpretation of the Bible.

The *Viens vers le Père* series ushered in a new era of religious education in Canada. It proffered a complex model for catechesis and used a variety of textbooks adapted to the psychological development of children. Its intent was to involve home, school and Church in the religious education of the child. In pursuing their goals, the authors of this series published a catechism which combined the *doctrinal* and

---

[115]. Crowe, 55.
[116]. Crowe, 53.
[117]. Crowe, 57. Italics mine.

the *cognitive* with the *spiritual* and the *affective*. The goal of *Viens vers le Père* was to have children appropriate the Church's rich doctrinal heritage by appealing to their concrete experiences. Most often, doctrine was formulated directly in the words of the Bible, but the Apostle's Creed and other major points of doctrine provided a means of organizing the programme. Each of these features influenced the pedagogy and consequently influenced the use of Scripture and its interpretation.

Grounded in the philosophy of education, our critique suggests that much of the content of the educational process necessarily arises from our intellectual and cultural heritage. On the other hand, it seems clear that if education is to have durable effects which contribute to the edification of the person, it must find existentially pertinent ways of presenting that intellectual heritage. The heritage model offers little room for critique and even less for dissent; a problem which feminist, black and socialist critics have brought to light. In the worst scenario, a tradition-centred model may lead some students to doubt themselves, their own experiences and intuitions, e.g. females, students of colour and the economically disadvantaged.

We have demonstrated that this catechetical series exhibits a content-centred orientation and intends to inculcate in students, by means of doctrine, the values embodied in the Tradition of the Catholic Church. Scripture plays a critical role in the presentation of doctrine, as doctrine is most often communicated via scriptural quotations. This choice contrasts sharply with the theological formulæ of the Tridentine style catechisms.

We further discovered that much of the use and interpretation of Scripture was determined by the psycho-social limits of the intended audience. *Viens vers le Père* tries to strike a balance between respect for the integrity of Tradition and respect for the evolving psychological profile of the child. It adopts a tradition-centred pedagogy but presses it to its utmost as it enlists the experience of the student as a means to effectively assimilate the intended values.

As we saw, the findings of educational psychology indicate that children develop a capacity to think in abstract terms relatively late in childhood. Since certain points of Christian doctrine normally require the use of abstraction in their presentation, they are often better left to the latter years of elementary schooling. *Viens vers le Père* adopted a progressive presentation of Christian doctrine which respected this characteristic of the learner. Scriptural passages were chosen on the basis of their appropriateness for use with 6-12 year olds. Since Scripture followed doctrine, it too was selected and adapted to meet the learning capacities of the young audience; whether this meant paraphrasing scriptural excerpts so as to respect the average reading level of a grade or (as in the case of young children) selecting passages for their "concrete" appeal to the five senses. Therefore, this basic design option conditioned the selection and use of Scripture.

Viens vers le Père adapts the content of Catholic Tradition to the psychological requirements of its audience. This constitutes a first and essential step in any curriculum which would be child-centred. What becomes equally clear in this context, however, is that respecting children as a general class (for example, 6-7 year olds or 10-11 years olds) does not move far enough in the direction of the child to make such a programme truly child-centred. Individualization of educational programmes is called for; a notion already discussed by Marie Fargues several decades ago. Education ought to respond to the requirements of individuals and be relevant to their existence. Since it will not be in the interests of the student to send him/her into society ill-prepared to meet life's basic needs, large portions of the curriculum may not appear immediately relevant from the perspective of the learner. Nevertheless, methods of teaching, which are historicized and inductive, do much to dispel learner apathy and allow students to gain insight into their own questions or questions which have become their own. The child-centred curriculum should be designed in such a way as to listen to the student's questions, probing for opportunities to communicate curriculum content as a response to these questions. *Viens vers le Père*, in our opinion, does not sufficiently attend to the questions of its audience to be classified as a thoroughly child-centred curriculum.

We further established that the programme uses doctrine (the articles of the Creed and other important points) as its criterion of selection for Scripture. Scripture was selected to reveal a particular aspect of the mystery of God or to call the student to conversion. Given its intended use, this series did not discuss the literary and historical background of the texts it used. This, however, does not imply that a "spiritual" or pastoral use of Scripture is contradicted by the findings of literary and historical scholarship. The completed series was reviewed on two separate occasions by competent exegetes and not found wanting on this score.

In the Grade Four programme, *Nous avons vu le Seigneur*, the use of longer narrative passages allows for greater contextualization. The use of the NT is central and forms the real basis of the curriculum for that year. It is in this year of the programme that the positive attitude toward the findings of critical scholarship becomes most evident. Scholarly works are alluded to and historical data about the life in ancient Palestine is provided. In general, the treatment of the Gospels suggests a degree of sophistication in biblical interpretation among the members of the writing team.

Liturgical concerns were a second major factor influencing the selection and presentation of Scripture. Esteem for the great movements in the liturgical calendar, the proclamation-response format of the Liturgy of the Word during Mass, and (likely) the salvation history recounted in Catholic Eucharistic Prayers have heavily influenced the reading of the biblical text in this programme.

In *Viens vers le Père*, the Bible serves as a faith document which contains God's self-disclosure and offers basic attitudes before the divine, exemplified in the experiences of the biblical characters. Hence, many of the texts used present role models for the children—they contemplate the attitude of the psalmist or the values and insights expressed by characters in a narrative. The biblical texts are re-actualized in the sphere of the student's experiences. In Grade One, the student considers Moses' awe before the Lord (Week 3). In Grade Two, 1 Cor 6:4[118] is meant to become the expression of the student's hope in the resurrection (Week 28). In Grade Three, the paraphrase of Acts 1:8 [119] stands as an invitation to the children to become those witnesses of the Risen Lord (Week 29).

Both Testaments are called upon throughout the series to provide the wording of doctrine. Typically, and unremarkably given the Catholic context, the interpretation of Scripture takes place in the context of salvation history. The use of the OT is considerable and we have seen that the programme finds there the expression of fundamental religious and spiritual values, (we recall the use of Exodus 3 and 1 Samuel 3). This respect for the witness of the OT notwithstanding, the notion of a progressive revelation seems integral to the authors' understanding of the Bible; the roots of such an interpretation are already

---

[118]. "God our Father who has raised up the Lord Jesus will raise us up, too, by this power."

[119]. "You will soon receive the power of the Holy Spirit. You will be then my witnesses to the ends of the earth."

traceable in Paul and Luke.[120] The relationship one may infer from the use of the Old and New Testaments in the programme, is one in which NT figures stand in continuity with the religious experiences of their OT counterparts. The religious experiences of the people of Israel are appropriated from the OT in a variety of contexts.

Apart from these brief notations describing the attitude towards the findings of critical scholarship,[121] we have cited the work of L. Racine who identifies the point of departure for the pedagogy of this series as standing in contradiction to the goals of catechesis in general. Racine holds that the goal of catechesis is to illuminate the lives of believers and not simply to illuminate Tradition? It is our contention that both the lives of believers and Tradition can be illuminated in the same act of catechesis when Tradition is put at the service of life.

The use of the learner's experiences as a means to a pedagogical end, parallels, it would seem, the use of Scripture as a source of doctrine. If one regards the experience of the learner as a means and not an end, then one might be tempted to reduce the "experiences" captured within Scripture to a similar status. Texts contain expressions of life fixed in writing.[122] By pressing Scripture into the role of doctrinal support, the danger is that one may truncate the experiences it mediates.

The selection principle which has led to the choice of what Racine calls the "rosy" experiences from the life of the child has worked a similar stifling effect on the selection of the kinds of experiences taken from Scripture. But what are the origins of this selection principle? It is our contention that its origins are theological. Moreover it appears tied to the question as to whether or not human experience can form the legitimate object of theological inquiry.

A child cannot be educated without his/her participation. Education requires a certain poiesis, a creating and a doing. It involves more

---

[120]. For a discussion of the way in which a number of prominent biblical scholars have dealt with salvation history as the basis for a NT theology see Boys, *Biblical Interpretation*, Chapter 1.

[121]. We return to these questions in Chapter 5.

[122]. Paul Ricoeur cites this in a passage from W. Dilthey. See Paul Ricoeur, "Preface to Bultmann," *The Conflict of Interpretations: Essays in Hermeneutics*, ed. Don Ihde (Evanston: Northwestern University Press, 1974), 382.

than simply receiving. The entire venture of education bears the personal stamp of the learner and without it a learner may be induced to parrot great quantities of data, but nothing will be appropriated in a manner that truly edifies the intellect and the whole person. *Viens vers le Père* valiantly attempts to bring together the experiences of biblical characters and those of its audience but most often those of the former overshadow the latter.

To educate in matters religious, as in all education, means to help the learner to question. This sort of critical questioning is only likely to arise when the child's experience becomes, in its entirety, the intended object of educational inquiry. To educate means to imbue the person with faith in themselves and their own questions. We contend that this catechetical series does not go far enough in this direction.

To choose child-centred education in no way implies a reduced role for Tradition and heritage. Rather it means that the impossible goal of assimilating the full scope of one's Tradition is abandoned, in favour of as rich an appropriation of it as the circumstances of one's life allows and requires.

CHAPTER 4

THEOLOGY AND HERMENEUTICS IN *VIENS VERS LE PERE*

Any attempt to establish an aetiology for the methodology of the *Viens vers le Père* series must weigh the relative influences exerted by theology and educational psychology in its creation. Even though the influence of Lumen Vitae's kerygmatic catechesis may be seen in *Viens vers le Père*, the principal inspiration of the series is to be found in the pedagogical innovations of the catechetical movement in France. At the cross-roads of disciplines, this series was unable to remain theologically neutral. It remains to be seen which theological options informed its work. Perhaps because this catechism's élan is pedagogical in origin, the theological inspiration guiding its development may appear somewhat eclectic. Nevertheless, as we will see, certain broad traits of a theology are identifiable and its theological choices clearly influence its interpretation of Scripture. The role which the Bible played in neo-scholastic catechisms was transformed in *Viens vers le Père*, largely because the authors of this renewed catechesis conceived the connection between the Bible, theology and doctrine differently than did their predecessors. In contrast to *Le catéchisme canadien* (1951), *Viens vers le Père* gave Scripture a central role in its catechesis, emphasizing biblical themes which had previously been considered peripheral and dropping others it thought inappropriate.

Undeniably, the *Viens vers le Père* series with its emphasis on the psycho-social dimensions of the catechetical process, reflects the turn towards historicality and the human subject which began in the thought world of the 19th century and was translated into the praxis of the 20th century. Theology and pedagogy were profoundly affected by this shift in thought. Philosophy too, embarked on an existentialist project. A preoccupation with the *hic et nunc* surfaced in the work of such notable thinkers as Martin Heidegger and Jean-Paul Sartre, among others. But if this catechism manifests a keen interest in the child of the 20th century, its methodology precludes the elucidation of that child's experience as its chief end, as we have endeavoured to demonstrate above. This catechism was reluctant to focus on experience as the locus of God's gracious activity, even though the intent of its writers *was* to bring doctrinal content into contact with the lives of the children.[1] One is left wondering why a catechetical programme, which ostensively wishes to address the experiences of its audience, relegates these experiences to a secondary role in its design. Two possible explanations for the authors' reluctance to focus on experience are discernible in the history of the catechetical renewal, but a third and more ancient suspicion of the value of experience within Catholic Tradition may be at the root of this reticence.

First, the team of redactors were aware of the perils of anthropocentric catechesis. They affirmed that the goal of catechesis is to ensure a meeting between the Word of God and the human person, but knew that anthropocentric catechesis had allowed the conversation to degenerate into a human monologue. To allow the elucidation of experience to stand as the primary objective in catechesis may have appeared to diminish the role of the Word of God. The writers may have feared that the life of the individual might never be placed in that unique explanatory perspective which is offered by the Gospel as proclaimed and received. Doctrine and Scripture might simply have appeared as afterthoughts. This would plainly run counter to the goals of the renewal from which this catechism issued, a renewal which sought to retrieve a prominent place for Scripture in catechesis.

Already aware of some unhappy experiments in anthropocentric catechesis in the 1960s, J. Colomb criticized catechisms which sought to abandon their doctrinal heritage. He urged catechists to balance the need to present the intellectual structures of the faith against the duty to educate with a personal and lively faith:

> Nous croyons que nous continuons actuellement d'être emportés par une réaction anti-intellectualiste qui devait fatalement suivre une caté-

---

[1]. For the intentions of both writing teams in this regard see *Viens vers le Père, Guide du Maître*, 11 and *Nous avons vu le Seigneur, Guide du Maître*, 17-18.

chèse abstraite, laquelle fut étrangement coupée de ses sources et de sa finalité pratique. On pense que la connaissance rationelle, conceptuelle, comme telle nous éloigne du concret alors qu'elle est pour notre nature d'êtres raisonnables une manière de la pénétrer. On a certes bien raison de penser qu'il ne suffit pas de transmettre une doctrine mais qu'il faut annoncer un message de salut qui rejoigne l'expérience et les besoins des auditeurs et qui concerne leur existence. Mais parfois on risque d'oublier la nécessité de donner un contenu précis.[2]

In short, Colomb and the writers of the *Viens vers le Père* series were striving to develop a catechism which coupled the enthusiasm of kerygmatic catechesis with the intellectual clarity of notional catechesis, all the while respecting the psychological development of the child. It would seem that the writing team understood the word *experience* to refer primarily to those critical, formative events, taking place in the child's family life and immediate social environment, which are a part of "normal" psychological development.[3] By *experience* they intended those events from the lives of the learners which can easily be exploited in a catechesis whose *point d'arrivée* is doctrine. The concern Colomb expresses for a clear doctrinal content mirrors a major preoccupation of the *Viens vers le Père* series.

A second, more proximate factor influencing programme design was the immediate context of the Church in Quebec. Years of work on catechetical renewal had resulted in *Le catéchisme catholique* of 1951, a paltry result for such concerted effort. In this context, the move to the progressive presentation of doctrine represented in the *Viens vers le Père* series registered a profound shift in emphasis. Since, from the decade previous, the intransigence of higher Church authorities still lay fresh in the collective ecclesial memory, the attempt to develop a catechism which understood doctrine as *vehicle* rather than as *terminus*, while simultaneously introducing the principle of a progressive presentation of revelation, may have seemed (and indeed may have been) more than was feasible.

A third and more fundamental ground for the objection to a catechesis thoroughly centred on an elucidation of experience may be found in the traditional Catholic opposition to subjectivism, with a concomitant mistrust of experience.

In this Chapter, we will examine the dominant theological trends

---

[2]. Colomb, *Service*, I, xii.
[3]. See *Nous avons vu le Seigneur, Guide du Maître*, 17-18.

of the catechetical renewal in France, particularly as they are represented in the work of Joseph Colomb. It is our contention that this theology has exerted the greatest influence on the *Viens vers le Père* series, in particular on the role it gave to biblical interpretation. Colomb's magnum opus, *Le service de l'évangile* incorporates the contributions of the best achievements of his colleagues at work in the field. The implications of this theology for the use and interpretation of Scripture will hold our attention. A second, crucial theme for our critique will be the role of experience in the life of faith as seen in the debates of 20th century Catholicism.

The interpretation of Scripture is intimately linked with the question of theological options in catechetics. If the theology which informs catechetics is understood primarily as a dogmatic theology, with reference to its object, if not also to its methodology, a tradition-centred catechesis is inevitable. If one conceives of a theology whose primary goal is to elucidate experience, new possibilities manifest themselves. The theology of Karl Rahner represents one of the most successful attempts to accomplish this task in the 20th century, and we will have occasion to examine themes within his work in our attempt to clarify the theological vision of the *Viens vers le Père* series.

Since in Catholic thought the sources of revelation are two, Scripture and Tradition (*Dei Verbum*, para. 9), investigating the relationship between experience and doctrine may simultaneously provide insight into the relationship between experience and the interpretation of Scripture. Both the Bible and doctrine are accorded a prominent status in the *Viens vers le Père* series. Given that the transmission of doctrine is the *telos* of this series, it is not surprising that both the modern-day experiences of children and the ancient experiences recounted in Scripture should be exploited in the elucidation of doctrine.

We begin with a brief account of the theological climate immediately prior to the reform of Catholic theology at Vatican Council II. A presentation of the catechetics of Joseph Colomb will follow, placing particular emphasis on the role Colomb assigns to the "Word of God." Next, our attention will turn to a description of the evolution of the concept and function of experience in contemporary Catholic theology using the work of Henri de Lubac and Karl Rahner as our points of reference. We will conclude with a description of the way in which the theology underlying this series governs its understanding and use of Scripture.

A SITUATION CALLING FOR REFORM

In his description of the Church between the two World Wars, Herbert Vorgrimler sketches the profile of an authoritarian institution, characterized by unrelenting rigidity in matters of doctrine and an orthodoxy frozen in arcane language since the scholastic period—an orthodoxy meant to prescribe even the thoughts one might entertain:

> ...the terms once found in Scholastic theology and philosophy, in Thomas and before him in Aristotle, were to be the only permissible terms, the only correct terms for all cultural circles, to bring the message of Christianity, the content of its faith and its ethical instructions to people of all times. There was a prohibition against questions and experiences which went beyond this stereotyped framework of thought and language. Control was supervised from Rome with the help of a system of clerical informers and willing denouncers...The local bishops, who in any case could only become bishops after following a fixed pattern of ordinariness, adaptability and obedience, had to proceed against rebellious theologians with harsh measures; books had to be withdrawn from book shops, teachers were not allowed to teach but were removed from theological faculties, sometimes banished to monasteries. In Rome there was the 'Index of forbidden books'...[4]

Vorgrimler argues that these oppressive measures were intended to stem the spirit of the European Enlightenment and to combat heretical tendencies found in various national settings. In German Catholicism there were the influences of the Reformation, while in England and France, Modernism was the perceived threat. Subjectivism was very often the charge levelled at theologians who moved away from the neo-scholastic model.

Already in the 19th century, the German theologians, Georg Hermes and Anton Günther were laying the groundwork for the inclusion of subjective elements in theology. They had sought to lay out a starting point for theology which included the Cartesian principle of

---

[4]. Herbert Vorgrimler, *Understanding Karl Rahner: An Introduction to His Life and Thought*, trans. John Bowden (New York: Crossroad, 1986), 52.

doubt.[5] Later, theologians of the Catholic Tübingen school, in critical dialogue with German Idealism, sought to develop a theology which would relate the content and history of faith to human subjectivity.[6] At the turn of the 20th century, modernist theologians were attacked most vehemently for their tendency to set individual experience above the dogmas of the Church. The Modernists, who viewed religious experience as more basic than doctrine, considered doctrine to be merely the linguistic expressions of religious experience and thus to be open to reformulation.[7] The Magisterium was joined in its rejection of this expressive concept of language by philosophers interested in the constitutive (or formative) role which language plays with respect to our experiences.

As the battle heated up between the Church and the modern world, the Popes came to see themselves primarily as the preservers and possessors of the *depositum fidei*; Catholic theology, especially Patristics, exegesis and Church History, came to a virtual standstill. Theologians had no other role than to use their learning in defence of the teaching of the Church, Vorgrimler recollects. Although for a time, curial authorities effectively stemmed the flow of free thought *intra muros*, the dikes erected were eventually breached by the titanic swell of modernity, as Catholics—both theologians and lay people alike—were touched by the spirit of the age.

Church authority shifted focus and the anti-modernist polemic waned just about the time that historical studies began to flourish. In Patristics, the production of critical editions of early Church writings (complete with translations and critical commentaries) recovered new riches which reinvigorated theology from about the 1930s on. Biblical scholars were also working quietly on critical, historical research which contributed to the burgeoning biblical movement.

Neo-Scholasticism, or Neo-Thomism as it was often called, was the weapon of choice used in the defence of the "Pian monolith." Karl

---

[5]. Francis Schüssler Fiorenza, "Systematic Theology: Tasks and Methods," *Systematic Theology: Roman Catholic Perspectives*, I (Minneapolis: Fortress Press, 1991), 36.

[6]. Fiorenza, 36.

[7]. Fiornenza, 43.

Rahner coined this term as a description for the dominant image of the Church which took hold following the papacy of Pius IX and which reached its apogee under Pius XII; it was the image of the Church as an absolute monarchy.[8] A sharp separation of nature and grace in neo-scholastic theology granted Rome a certain distance from modern experience, allowing the Church to operate in the supra-mundane and a-historical sphere of the supernatural. In creating this rift between nature and grace and in expanding the *praeambula fidei* into a full blown natural theology, Neo-Thomism drove a wedge between natural human experience and the encounter with God.[9] One result of this distance from the dominant trends of society was the critique that the Church was able to direct against the inhumanity of *laisser-faire* economics, which was characterized by a rationalized efficiency designed to serve capital but not people, (cf. *Rerum Novarum*, 1891). In almost every other way, this rift produced a growing, tension which alienated Catholics from the modern world in which they lived.

The theologians, who were to prove most influential at Vatican Council II, rejected the separation of nature and grace as un-Thomistic. It was these same men who brought the thinking of Thomas Aquinas into contact with modern philosophy. Their efforts produced re-interpretations of Aquinas and led to a plurality of re-interpretations of Catholic Tradition as a whole. A dialogue between Catholic theology and modern philosophy opened up. Francis Schüssler Fiorenza provides a concise summary of the most salient examples of these early forays outside the bounds of Neo-Scholasticism:

> Karl Rahner's study of the epistemology of Aquinas incorporates both Kantian and Heideggerian categories. Bernard Lonergan's two dissertations...relate Thomas to modern cognitional theory. Edward Schillebeeckx's dissertation on Thomas' understanding of the sacraments relates the sacraments to a phenomenology of encounter. Both Henri Bouillard's study on the relation between grace and nature and Henri de Lubac's historical studies on the development of the notion of the supernatural show the importance of Augustinian elements—which Neo-Thomism had neglected—in Thomas's theology. Even the following generation of theologians (most notably, Johann Baptist Metz, Max Seckler, and Otto Pesch) continued this dialogue with Thomas

---

[8]. Vorgrimler, 54.
[9]. Fiorenza, 36.

Aquinas.[10]

These men advanced the progress of Catholic theology through their careful scholarship and soon the results of their achievements were being felt in many quarters. Joseph Colomb was a contemporary of these intellectuals and his scholarship developed against the same backdrop of rigidity and myopia. It was in this context that he began wrestling with the questions of catechesis. We turn to him now as a key representative of the renewal in France, which so heavily influenced the form and content of the *Viens vers le Père* series.

VVLP: MAJOR THEOLOGICAL INFLUENCES

JOSEPH COLOMB

Joseph Colomb proved himself an adept of both pedagogy and theology. As a priest in the Sulpician order—an order with a long pedigree in catechetical instruction—Colomb had received a solid theological education. His pedagogical expertise was sharpened through associations with numerous colleagues at work in the field of curriculum theory and experimentation.

Colomb the educator, understood the significance of the advances in educational psychology. No matter how exalted the course content, its communication remained subject to the psycho-social development of the audience. The strides forward in education, examined in Chapters 2 and 3 above, were the fruit of years of teaching experimentation based on the careful observation of children. Traditional catechisms were simply ignorant of these requirements and the catechetical renewal wished to fill these lacunæ. Colomb grasped the need to translate the progress made in the understanding of psychology to the field of catechetics.[11]

Colomb the cleric, having personally suffered public castigation at the hands of ecclesial authorities in 1957, was anxious to avoid controversy. Aware of the hardships visited upon the Modernists some

---

[10]. Fiorenza, 37.
[11]. Colomb, *Service*, I, xv.

decades earlier, he attempted a nuanced approach to the values which modernity embodies. He attacked the un-Christian values which appear in modernity[12] but identified and praised other developments he considered to be positive.[13] Colomb's modus operandi is a study in restraint and prudence—his reader appreciates that he is well aware of the Magisterium's suspicion of experience in questions of faith. *Le service de l'évangile* confirms his unequivocal assent to the primacy of the "Word of God" as it has found expression both in the Scriptures and the Tradition of the Roman Catholic Church. The structure of this two-volume work reveals his intention to allay concerns about anthropocentrism and/or modernist tendencies. After an introduction to the purpose of the work and a brief history of catechesis, the author devotes 133 pages to the topic of *Fidelity to God* in the catechetical process.

Throughout this work, Colomb sets about building bridges between the two intellectual worlds he inhabits by demonstrating their complementary character. On the one hand, scientific, "religious" psychology studies the material structures of the faith, and, on the other, catechesis seeks meaning guided by philosophical and theological reflexion. Without the first, Colomb concludes, the second often risks making assertions which do not correspond to the needs or intellectual possibilities of the audience; without the second, the first has no spiritual depth and cannot connect with the ultimate questions of human existence.[14] The existential pertinence of catechesis was imperative for Colomb. He explains:

> Quand nous étions en chrétienté, un système purement objectif de propositions doctrinales pouvait sembler efficace, étant soutenu par une communauté unanime; dans une société pluraliste les vérités abstraites paraissent vides, si elles ne se rattachent pas clairement à une existence concrètement vécue à laquelle elles donnent sens, lumière et force. L'homme croyant...sera celui qui aura fait une expérience personnelle du christianisme et que la Parole de Dieu ramène sans cesse

---

[12]. Particularly objectionable to Colomb was the tendency within modernity to view humanity as "the prime mover of the universe."
[13]. Within rationalizing thought, he considered the growing sensitivity to the symbolic and the existential as a positive sign. See Colomb, *Service*, II, 493.
[14]. Colomb, *Service*, I, xi.

à cette expérience pour la creuser plus profondément.[15]

Despite his awareness of the need to respond to a subjective element in the life of faith, Colomb takes great pains to affirm the objective, historical character of revelation. He observed that the modern person is capable of being interested in the past to the degree in which it helps make sense of the present. His eloquent description of the Word of God at once underlines its objective, historical character and the incarnational structure of its communication:

> Pour l'Écriture, la Parole de Dieu ne se situe pas sur le seul plan de la connaissance. Elle est à la fois puissance et illumination. Prise en son sens total, elle est Dieu même réalisant son acte sauveur... La Parole de Dieu est *créatrice* d'êtres et d'événements; elle est historique du salut: Ancien Testament, Christ et Église. Mais parce qu'elle est créatrice d'êtres conscients, qui doivent connaître ce qu'ils sont et le vouloir librement, la Parole de Dieu se fait, en eux, *révélatrice* de ce qu'elle opère. Ainsi la Parole révélée signifie, exprime toujours un événement, un être, et par-delà Dieu lui-même, créateur et sauveur. Au-delà de la Parole illuminatrice, de la Parole-langage, il y a les êtres que cette Parole dit et il y a Dieu qui crée ces êtres...Cette Parole révélée peut être écrite: c'est l'Écriture Sainte.[16]

Scripture is the record of the experiences of God's revelation and it is also the source one returns to in order to plumb the depths of one's own experience of God. For Colomb, religious experience offers one of the keys to the interpretation of the profound significance of Scripture. This is not to suggest that Colomb did not inscribe this general approach within a sophisticated and critical understanding of biblical interpretation. He exhibited particular interest in Bultmann's programme of demythologization as a means of communicating to moderns the significance of the Christian message for their lives.[17]

In the second part of his work, entitled *Fidelity to the Catechized*, Colomb begins his reflexions by stating that fidelity to the catechized person implies fidelity to the Word of God, since the Word was spoken

---

[15]. Colomb, *Service*, I, xiii.
[16]. Colomb, *Service*, I, 16.
[17]. See Colomb, *Service*, I, 580-589.

to be heard.[18] In his view, catechetical discourse does not consist, first and foremost, of a body of knowledge or doctrine but is rather a message which gives meaning to existence and transforms life. All specific catechesis, is only an element in this 'response to the mystery of our life.'[19]

As the basis of his catechesis, Colomb relies on a christocentric theology, the ultimate aim of which is to reveal the Trinity: "Le Christ est le centre de notre catéchèse dont la Trinité est la fin."[20] These interrelated elements assume crucial importance in the shaping of *Viens vers le Père*. Colomb weaves a tight connection between his understanding of Christology and the nature of scriptural revelation. For him, both are linked by an incarnational theme. When Colomb contends that the Word exists only as incarnate, he means at once the written word of God's revelation in the Bible and the most important instance of God's Word to humanity, Christ himself.

> Le message du Père à l'homme c'est le Christ même. L'homme tout entier est atteint, convoqué, par l'Incarnation. La Parole de Dieu est d'emblée humaine. C'est l'homme avec ses ressources et ses faiblesses, ses mentalités, ses dimensions, ses désirs, ses projets et ses refus qui est appelé....C'est pourquoi la catéchèse implique non seulement une théologie, mais une anthropologie; mieux elle implique une théologie qui est anthropologie.[21]

In this context, Colomb goes on to say that the Word of God is already radically humanized in Christ and that it falls to the catechist—and one might add "to every Christian"—to continue the incarnation of this Word within his/her own life situation.

Even if revelation assumes an incarnational structure for Joseph Colomb, he clearly understands its content to be something foreign to the experience of the believer. Colomb's idea of revelation fits the general category which Maurice Blondel, a Catholic theologian of the turn of the 20th century, referred to as *extrinsicism*.[22] Blondel believed that in the official apologetics of the Church there were ideas about God and revelation which were in direct conflict with modern experi-

---

[18]. Colomb, *Service*, I, 193.
[19]. Colomb, *Service*, I, xiii.
[20]. Colomb, *Service*, I, xiv.
[21]. Colomb, *Service*, I, xv.
[22]. For a lucid explanation of Blondel's position see Gregory Baum, *Man Becoming* (New York: Seabury, 1970), Chapter One, "The Blondelian Shift."

ence. In Blondel's view, these ideas made it virtually impossible for intelligent and critical people to adhere to the Christian faith.[23] One of the ideas about revelation which Blondel rejected was the (then widely accepted) concept that the supernatural is an addition to human nature, an addition which is at once arbitrary and extrinsic to human nature. For Blondel, the supernatural

> ...n'est pas un surcroît arbitraire, une forme extrinsèque à l'homme... C'est une adoption, une assimilation, une incorportaion, un *consortium*, une transformation qui assure à la fois l'union et la distinction des deux incommensurables par le lien de la charité.[24]

Later, Blondel adds further precision, maintaining that the supernatual is not—

> ...une sorte d'être distinct ou un réceptacle destiné à nous aspirer en nous faisant sortir de notre nature humaine; il est au contraire fait pour être en nous, *in nobis*, sans être jamais pour cela issu de nous, venu de nous, *ex nobis*.[25]

Gregory Baum provides insight into the theological context in which Blondel wrote:

> According to the official apologetics (of the period), God is a divine being facing man from beyond history, and divine revelation is the communication of heavenly truths to men caught in their own limited, earthly knowledge. Blondel called this approach "extrinsicism." Against the extrinsicist trend of Catholic theology, Blondel insisted that the only message that modern man can accept is a truth that answers men's questions or corresponds in some way to their experience of reality. A message that comes to man wholly from outside, without an inner relationship to his life, must appear to him as irrelevant, unworthy of attention, and unassimilable by the mind....During the nineteenth century, wrestling with the issues raised by rationalism and

---

[23]. Baum, *Man Becoming*, 3.
[24]. Maurice Blondel, *Exigences philosophiques du christianisme* (Paris: Presses universitaires de France, 1950), 162.
[25]. Blondel, *Exigences,* 58.

fideism and resisting the extremes of both, Catholic theologians had introduced a radical distinction between faith and its rational credibility. They acknowledged with the entire Christian tradition that faith is a free gift of God and hence essentially indemonstrable. Yet what can be demonstrated, they added, is the divine origin of the message believed by faith. What can be proven, ultimately by reference to miracles, is that the message preached by the Church is not of human making; it is a divine message and hence, however startling, it is worthy of belief or is credible...[26]

Catholic theologians paid a high price for the solution of separating faith and credibility. That price was the exclusion of God's revelation from the spiritual process by which a person comes to know what is important and true. In the Church's official theology of the 19th century, the inner continuity between the rational discernment of the credibility of faith and the Spirit-created acknowledgement of the divine Word was obscured. "In other words, the credibility of faith remained totally extrinsic to faith itself."[27]

Colomb's own words demonstrate that he worked from an extrinsicist concept of revelation:

> On ne saurait dire que l'amour et la grandeur de l'homme en général ou de tel homme en particulier sont les "signes" de l'amour dont Dieu nous a aimés dans le Christ, et encore moins l'univers matériel. A partir d'eux, à partir de l'univers, à partir d'événements humains, de "faits de vie" humains (qui ne sont pas explicitement reliés au Christ), jamais je ne pourrai entendre la Parole qui m'annonce l'amour "surnaturel" de Dieu: celle-ci se dit dans le Christ et les chrétiens.[28]

The revelation of God in the history of salvation—OT, Christ, Church—assumes fundamental importance in the theology Colomb proposes. On the basis of his extrinsicist view of revelation, the role of everyday, secular, human experience in catechesis can never constitute a locus of divine revelation; human experience can never provide examples of divine immanence. At best, secular experience provides weak analogies for the contents of doctrine.

Colomb's understanding and use of human experience, however, proves more complex than these comments suggest. On the one hand, he limits experience to an instrumental role in the overall educative

---

[26]. Baum, *Man Becoming*, 3-4. Bracketed material mine.
[27]. Baum, *Man Becoming*, 5.
[28]. Colomb, *Service*, I, 376.

process. On the other hand, his understanding of human experience is shaped by the findings of educational psychology and sociology. As described by psychology, experience is understood as intellectual capacities and social propensities that may be generalized to entire age groups within the human population. Hence, Colomb's comments regarding individualization of instruction[29] must be understood against the backdrop of his treatment of the psycho-social profiles of the catechetical audience, i.e., a single content and method for all children within a given age group. Colomb understands individualization of instruction to consist first and foremost in grouping according to age and offering a curriculum suited to the evolving intellectual capacities of children, and second as a sensitivity to the learning style and the mentality of individual students. He sees the structures and goals of a programme as providing a useful counterweight to the superficial interests a child might exhibit.[30] His treatment of the social and educative role of the *family* remains abstract and no sense of the day-to-day living conditions of children is evident.[31]

It seems clear that the originality of Colomb's approach takes its inspiration largely from advances in the behavioural sciences. Pedagogical influences aside, the role Colomb assigns experience in his methodology appears to be heavily influenced by his understanding of the nature of revelation and its relationship to secular history. For Colomb, the centre of revelation is found in Jesus of Nazareth and without his advent in history humanity would have remained in complete obscurity about the nature and will of God.

In conclusion, we may say that, given the climate of Church life during most of Colomb's academic career, his accomplishments in the field of catechetics remain impressive. The stage he represents in the catechetical renewal proved crucial to the reform of outmoded practices. Other accomplishments and insights would follow, but the most important of these international developments post-dated both Colomb's heyday and the publication of the *Viens vers le Père* series.

---

[29]. Colomb, *Service*, II, 160-166.
[30]. Colomb, *Service*, II, 161.
[31]. See Colomb, *Service*, II, 617-632.

Many of these insights were to come from the historico-prophetic catechesis of Latin America.

Before moving on to a brief discussion of the historico-prophetic emphasis, it seems appropriate to introduce Marcel van Caster, who influenced the catechetical renewal in general, and the *Viens vers le Père* writing team in particular. As it is our contention that one's theology shapes one's interpretation of the Bible and determines many aspect of one's pedagogical method, we will limit our consideration of van Caster to these concepts.

MARCEL VAN CASTER

In the early days of the International Catechetical Centre at Lumen Vitae, the kerygmatic approach was dominant, depending largely on the biblical movement and the Innsbruck Faculty of Theology for its inspiration. An interpretative model known as *Heilsgeschichte* served as the hermeneutical guide for a catechesis based on the Bible. This approach assigned great importance to the use of Scripture, leaving the experience of those to be catechized largely untapped. Marcel van Caster represented a shift in emphasis in Lumen Vitae' kerygmatic approach. He brought reflexion forward by accentuating the role of experience and values in the catechetical paradigm. His reflections, along with the work of Pierre Babin, played a large role in the *catechumenal* or *anthropocentric* phase of catechetical renewal (see Chapter 2).[32] In the context of the International Catechetical Meetings, this emphasis gained wide acceptance at Bangkok (1962) and reached a high point at Katigondo (1964).[33] The theme of *pre-evangelization* expressed a key concern of van Caster and Babin as an anthropocentric adaptation of biblically-informed catechesis got underway.

Van Caster described the task proper to catechesis as the proclamation and interpretation of the Word of God, with faith as the hoped-for outcome of that communication.[34] To achieve its task, Van Caster argued that catechesis should concentrate on three areas: 1) Catechesis should be an instruction regarding the facts and truths of an objective, historical revelation; 2) Catechesis should instil a Christian mentality

---

[32]. Boys, *Biblical Interpretation*, 95.
[33]. Fossion, 198-199.
[34]. Marcel van Caster, *Dieu nous parle: Structures de la catéchèse* (Bruges: Desclée de Brouwer, 1964), 14. Similar statements appear throughout his work.

based on the values found in the Gospel; 3) Catechesis should aim to initiate children into a relationship with Jesus Christ and thus into the mystery of God.[35]

Mary Boys places van Caster's work in the following context:

...van Caster retained the fundamental *Heilsgeschichte* schema, but lead the way in providing a more anthropological appropriation of it. His theory was key in legitimizing stress on the personal, dialogical, relational and present aspects of revelation...[36]

Unlike Colomb, van Caster does not approach the catechetical task from the theory and practice of educational psychology. James Michael Lee, an advocate of a social science approach to religious education, critiques van Caster, identifying him with other prominent proclamation theorists such as Jungmann, Hofinger and Goldbrunner.[37] Lee categorizes van Caster's guiding inspiration: "...proclamation theorists are typically theologians and hence concentrate their attention on theological content rather than on the dynamics of the teaching-learning process."[38] This is certainly the case for Marcel van Caster whose theological anthropology is derived directly from the discipline of theology. Lee concludes that the methodology of the proclamation theorists remained rooted in a cognitive rather than a life-style orientation. Because these Catholic theorists could neither generate nor explain pedagogical practice, they simply carried over the liturgical model of preaching into the classroom setting, confining teacher activity to the deployment of a transmission strategy and the lecture technique.[39] Not only did proclamation theory limit its pedagogy to a highly restrictive concept of the role of the teacher, but it also ignored learner behaviour and environmental variables, thereby seriously im-

---

[35]. Van Caster, *Dieu nous parle*, 14-15.
[36]. Boys, *Biblical Interpretation*, 240.
[37]. James Michael Lee, *The Flow of Religious Instruction* (Dayton: Pflaum, 1973). See the chapter entitled "Theoretical Approaches to the Teaching of Religion," 149-205.
[38]. Lee, 192.
[39]. Lee, 190.

pairing its ability to explain and predict teaching outcomes.[40]

Van Caster developed a theological anthropology which sought to achieve, in its own way, a thorough adaptation of the Word of God to the human subject who hears it. Nevertheless, van Caster's concept of revelation differs little from Colomb's. As with Colomb, the contents of revelation (God's will for the world, God's love for creation etc.) are outside the grasp of humanity until God reveals them in salvation history. It is only through this special history with God—through the stories of Adam, Noah, Abraham, Isaac, Jacob, Moses, the Prophets, David and most fully in and through Jesus of Nazareth—that humanity has come to know God.[41] Despite an elaborate treatment of anthropology in the work of van Caster, the *point d'arrivée* of his method is the historically revealed Word of God, a reality he understands to be extraneous and largely foreign to learner experience. Like other kerygmatic theologians, his understanding of the Word of God accepts the Catholic doctrinal interpretation of the Scriptures and understands the Church as the prime locus for an initiation into the mystery of the divine. Human experience is employed analogically in van Caster, resembling closely the method outlined in the *Viens vers le Père* series above.[42]

Translated into theological terms, the chief goal of this catechesis remains the proclamation of a doctrinal content, although that content appears in a new dynamic format, drawing from "biblical" sources a new vocabulary and inspiration. The teacher holds knowledge which is extraneous to the student; the student remains dependent upon the teacher in a learning process centred on the teacher and the content the teacher supplies. In similar fashion, the catechist as a representative of the Church, holds the truths of revelation which he/she transmits in a catechesis which is necessarily Church-centred. The acquisition of unassailable knowledge is the goal in this model—a goal shared by van Caster and the *Viens vers le Père* series.

An intriguing feature of van Caster's theology lies in the Christology implicit in his treatment of revelation. Van Caster speaks from time to time of a Christology of the Word Incarnate[43] but, to my

---

[40]. Lee, 190.
[41]. Van Caster, *Catéchèse et dialogue*, 50-51.
[42]. For an example of how his method functions see *Catéchèse et dialogue*, 66.
[43]. Van Caster, *Dieu nous parle*, 23.

knowledge, never draws any direct connection between the role of the Logos at creation and the salvific effects of Jesus' advent in history. In other words, he makes no connection between God's transcendence and God's immanence in creation. The closest he comes to drawing a connection between secular human history and salvation history (and therefore to asserting an implicit connection between the role of Christ's mediatorship at creation and his mediatorship in the act of redemption) does not occur in the discussion of protology (i.e., the role of Christ in the creation of the world), but rather in a discussion of eschatology. He cites the work of DuQuoc, which links (but does not identify) human and Christian progress.[44]

Like Colomb, van Caster was not the originator of a new theology or of a new understanding of revelation. Both scholars instead were involved in translating the broad lines of the anthropological shift in intellectual life to the catechetical arena. With respect to pedagogical strategy, the French school clearly surpassed (the early) Lumen Vitae. Theologically, however, no major differences in the notions of revelation and christology are discernible between the French and Belgian schools of thought. As we shall see, historico-prophetic catechesis allowed the life experiences of the catechetical audience to become a source of critique and illumination for the theological tenets proposed. Proponents of historico-prophetic catechesis sought to push anthropological models to their limit.

HISTORICO-PROPHETIC CATECHESIS

The International Catechetical Meetings moved beyond anthropological catechesis and did so by emphasizing the unrealized intent within the anthropological model to take full account of the experience of the person to be catechized.[45] Eurocentrism (Europeanism) was as ubiquitous in the anthropological approach as it had been in the earlier catechetical models of the international study weeks. It was squarely challenged by the leaders at the Manilla and Medellin conferences.

---

[44]. Van Caster, *Dieu nous parle*, 110-111.
[45]. Fossion, 216-228. Fossion understands the historico-prophetic emphasis to be in continuity with its anthropological predecessor.

The assumptions informing eurocentric catechesis clearly conflicted with the social, economic and political realities of the Third World. In Third World settings, avowed and unavowed systems of apartheid give rise to gross social inequalities and leave large portions of the population suffering from malnutrition and starvation, homelessness and joblessness, political oppression and economic colonialism as well as educational deprivation. To take the experience of those to be catechized into full account, given these conditions, requires more than adjusting instruction for psychological development. The challenges third world theology posed to first world theology were far-going and incisive.

Historico-prophetic catechesis was an emphasis inspired by the insights of Liberation Theology. Proponents of this model wanted to do more than transmit doctrine or proclaim a Gospel which talked only of the afterlife. This prophetic model redefined the relationship between Church and world; its programme was supported by socio-political and cultural analyses of concrete historical situations. Historico-prophetic catechesis understands the Gospel to call for a change of heart that would transform relationships between human persons, liberating those in various forms of bondage and leading to justice.

The catechetical movement benefited from insights arrived at beyond its own borders, i.e., in theology, psychology and pedagogy. The renewed interest in experience in Catholic theology, in general, had taken place slowly and with the consistent effort of many now famous theologians and Patristics scholars. The liberalization of theology within the Roman Catholic Church, which began in the 1930s was ratified at Vatican Council II—it involved a profound dialogue with the world. Earlier, the *world* had been understood largely as hostile to the true ends of the Gospel.

The critique of Manilla and Medellin, inscribed within a larger critique "from below," proffered a corrective to the optimism of the liberal theology of Catholic theologians in the industrialized world. *Viens vers le Père* reflects a first world mentality. The liberal theology underlying *Viens vers le Père* shapes its understanding of the relationship between Church and world and thereby the relationship between the biblical message and the socio-political and cultural context in which it finds itself. This series issues from a theological situation in the process of reform. In many ways it reflects the developments ratified at Vatican II, while in a few others it continues older currents.

We turn now to the reform of Catholic theology, perceived chiefly through the contributions of two pre-eminent scholars, Henri de Lubac and Karl Rahner. We will focus on the role which experience plays in renewed Catholic theology, analyzing its effect on the concepts of revelation and christology, moving finally to a discussion of its importance for the interpretation of the Bible. Our goal is to situate the theological options of the series under study in order to trace their influence on the interpretation of Scripture.

"EXPERIENCE" IN RECENT CATHOLIC THEOLOGY

De Lubac's *Surnaturel: études historiques* (1946) was a landmark as far as the rejection of the neo-scholastic, two-tiered vision of the world is concerned. In neo-scholastic theology, the supernatural appears as an add-on or overlay to the natural realm. Karl Rahner later offered what must be the most significant contribution to the modern understanding of how human experience may be read in light of the Christian faith.

DE LUBAC'S *SURNATUREL*

Catholic Tradition maintains that the acts of creation and redemption constitute two distinct divine initiatives. Expressed in terms of the notions of nature and grace, this distinction has been important to Catholic theology as it allows the gratuitous character of the act of redemption to be preserved. Redemption constitutes a second act of mercy on the part of God, distinct from creation, and hypothetically unnecessary. In 1950, the encyclical, *Humani Generis*[46], stated clearly that the gratuitousness proper to the supernatural order cannot be accounted for unless one allows that God could have created thinking beings without gracing them with the vision of God.[47] In other words, God could have created rational beings without communicating that "knowledge" of God which finds its full expression in Jesus of Naz-

---

[46]. Many commentators concluded that the section of *Humani Generis* which upheld the gratuity of the supernatural order was a direct attack on the position of de Lubac. See Gustave Weigel, "Gleanings from the Commentaries on *Humani Generis,*" *Theological Studies* XII (1951): 540.

[47]. Juan Alfaro, "Nature," *Sacramentum Mundi,* 174.

areth. The grace of God has made God known to humankind; *a grace which Catholics understand not exclusively as liberation from sin but principally as communion of life with God through Christ.*[48]

Nature is not a biblical concept; rather, it is a notion which theologians arrived at by abstraction from divinizing grace in human persons. In defending the faith against the contempt for the world found in the Gnosticism of the second and third centuries, the Church affirmed the goodness of creation. In that context, Clement of Alexandria gave the Platonic doctrine of the divinization of human persons a Christian interpretation.[49] Theologians reasoned that, if the human person received grace from God in an act separate from his/her creation by God, there must have been a "moment" when the human person was not yet graced—the state of humanity in this hypothetical moment was understood to be *pure nature*. Augustine already had occasionally used the concept of nature in this strict sense, prescinding from sin and in contrast to 'grace.'[50] As a theological category, pure nature was defined by a kind of extrapolation from the state of grace and as such was not intended to describe an enduring state of humanity in history. Theology has come to refer to this kind of intellectual creation with the term *vestigial concept*.

Some theologians of Post-Tridentine scholasticism missed the distinction between a vestigial concept and a description of a real, historical state of humanity.[51] While most theologians of the period worked with the hypothesis of a *natura pura* (considered necessary to explain the gratuitousness of the elevation of human persons to participation in the divine life) some unwittingly historicized the hypothetical state of pure nature, considering it a real situation of human persons in the world today.[52] Following this mistaken assumption, it was thought that grace first came to persons only through baptism. This position could explain neither the immanent character of grace within the human person nor the internal character of original sin.[53]

The Reformation doctrine of the total depravity of man by sin was

---

[48]. Alfaro, 172.
[49]. Johann Auer, "Grace: Theological," *Sacramentum Mundi*, 2: 412-413.
[50]. Alfaro, 174. De Lubac discusses this notion in a more general way in *Petite Catéchèse sur Nature et Grâce* (Paris: Fayard, 1980), 17.
[51]. Auer, 414; Alfaro, 174.
[52]. Alfaro, 174.
[53]. Alfaro, 174.

reflected in Catholicism in Baianism and Jansenism. Baius (condemned, 1567) ignored the divinizing function of grace and explained its gratuitousness solely with respect to the forgiveness of sin; and Jansen, some decades later, denied the possibility of a pure nature, thereby imperiling the gratuitous character of the act of redemption.[54] The negative attitude towards the world implied in Baianism and Jansenism was condemned by Church authorities.

De Lubac set out to show that the hypothetical state of pure nature was not essential to an explanation of divine grace. In coming to the defense of St. Augustine, de Lubac wanted to dissociate the Bishop of Hippo from the theology of Baius and Jansen by showing that their negation of a certain *pura natura* was not the heart of their error.[55] De Lubac underlined the errors of Baius and Jansen by recovering elements of Augustine's theology. De Lubac demonstrated that creation and redemption were understood in Augustine as two distinct, divine acts, both of which precede human history in the world. For Augustine, grace is thus not understood as a necessary result of the Fall, but is the loving act and will of God who invites human persons into a relationship with God. Humanity is thus created and graced before the Fall. Even though humans are weak after the Fall, they are still accompanied by God's grace. In other words, the Fall does not eradicate or render completely ineffective the indwelling grace of the Creator within the creature.

De Lubac's study argued that the two-tiered concept of nature and supernature is not an appropriate description of the historical state of humanity. From the beginning of human history in the world, God has offered grace to men and women. Hence there never was a period within the history of humanity when the grace of God was not available. The supernatural was not a reality added on from outside, but exists as an indwelling of the Holy Spirit, immanent within the human

---

[54]. Alfaro, 174.

[55]. Henri de Lubac, "Letter to Dennis Joseph Burke." This letter appears in the appendix to Burke's Ph.D. dissertation, *The Prophetic Mission of Henri de Lubac: A study of his theological anthropology and its function in the renewal of theology* (1967). Available on demand from University Microfilms International, Ann Arbor, Mi.

person from the dawn of creation. For de Lubac, the supernatural gift was not simply a sequel to creation. He argued that the necessary and unacceptable by-product of separating nature and the supernatural is a self-contained and self-sufficient humanity.[56] For de Lubac, humanity has always been dependent on God from the moment of its creation. De Lubac presents a view of grace which is historicized; a view wherein all of history is understood as supernatural history.

The idea that the sacraments operate almost mechanically as the nearly exclusive conduits of the grace of God to the world toppled. This vision of the sacraments as windows between the supernatural world and the natural world was not the only casualty of de Lubac's work; a host of other concepts in theology which rested on this dualistic view of reality went by the wayside as well. If the whole of history, despite human sinfulness, stands under the grace of a benevolent God, then the possibility exists that natural experiences can disclose the divine. Pure nature then, never appears except as a "hypothetical moment" of the total event of salvation history; the nature of humanity in history has always been "supernatural" nature.[57] De Lubac was convinced that the Christian tradition did not intend us to see the world as a neutral place, troubled by sin, divorced from God's gracious rescue and left to its own limited and fragmented resources. God's gracious intent to save humanity does not float above history in this view. Divine history subsists within human history. If the vicissitudes of everyday life were understood as something antithetical to or cut off from revelation, then it is obvious that one could never depend on this tainted experience as a source for knowledge of the God whom Jesus reveals.

KARL RAHNER

Faith and Experience

The notion of faith underwent theological development between Vatican Council I and Vatican Council II. Karl Rahner was prominent among those theologians who prepared the work of Vatican II, in

---

[56]. Henri de Lubac, "Le mystère du surnaturel," *Recherches de sciences religieuses* XXXVI (1949): 88.

[57]. Jörg Splett, "Nature: The Philosophical Concept," *Sacramentum Mundi*, 4: 172.

which the Church adopted a wider and richer concept of faith. [58] Even though faith is characterized by a strong intellectual component, a fact which protects the objective character of the contents of revelation, it addresses more than the cognitive capacities of human persons. Whereas Vatican Council I had already included acts of both the will and the intellect in its understanding of faith, Vatican Council II accentuates the dimensions of trust, commitment, obedience and submission, elements which correspond more to our everyday understanding of the term *faith*.[59] While it may be possible to assent to the truth of a statement and not feel affected by it—as in the affirmation of some abstract mathematical principle—faith requires more than mere intellectual assent. It invokes a response to God's revelation from the entire person.

For Karl Rahner, there are two sources of divine revelation: the revelation of God in history, as recorded in the Bible and an immanent revelation of God in the transcendent nature of all human persons. In these two loci, the "fundamental mystery of the triune God is revealed, because what is in question is the communication of God in himself."[60]

Despite the caveats and fears surrounding the theological appeal to personal experiences of the divine in the Catholic tradition, Rahner wanted to find a place for the experiences of people in his theological method. This required a careful approach, since *Pascendi* and *Lamentabili* (encyclicals of 1907) had condemned Modernism for limiting revelation to a personal experience of the divine, thereby minimizing the importance of the cognitive content of revelation as derived from the history of salvation. Then as now, the Church maintains that the interior subjective pole of revelation must be balanced against the historical, objective pole. The Church feared that if Modernist tendencies were pushed to the extreme, historical revelation would dissolve in a

---

[58]. We are particularly indebted in this section to Herbert Vorgrimler's *Understanding Karl Rahner: An Introduction to his Life and Thought*.

[59]. Fiorenza, 105.

[60]. Karl Rahner, "Concept of Tradition," *Revelation and Tradition*, trans. Wm. O'Hara, Quaestiones Disputatae N°.17 (Montreal: Palm Publishers, 1965), 15.

sea of blind religious sentiment, welling up from the depths of the subconscious, guided by the "heart" and the impulse of the will.[61] Karl Rahner's treatment of faith and revelation was in pursuit of the truth dimensions in faith. "Standing on the shoulders" of Heidegger and Thomas Aquinas in that pursuit, Rahner was unlikely to get bogged down in sentiment. His theology was pastorally oriented with a concern to open a path to the truth, to Christ, for all his contemporaries who found it difficult to have faith.[62]

Rahner's idea of faith moved beyond the intellectual assent of Neo-Scholasticism. There were two main reasons for this: 1) He was affected by the biblical renewal and recognized its significance for theology (even though he resisted the *Verkündigungstheologie* of his colleagues at Innsbruck on other grounds). The renewal championed a more biblical notion of faith with an emphasis on trust, hope and surrender; 2) Rahner was also influenced by the philosophical attention given to consciousness, inwardness and decision, which he encountered in his study of phenomenology and existentialism (especially under Heidegger). Both these influences lead Rahner to understand faith as more than intellectual assent to a body of revealed, heavenly truths. For Rahner, faith is an experience open to all human persons. Of course it is a very special experience in that it is the experience of being the recipient of grace.

Rahner was not alone in his pastoral concern to bring experience and faith together. Several other theologians were busy investigating the experience of grace from the late 1930s on.[63] In his formative years as a scholar, Rahner had been influenced by the major work of the Belgian Jesuit, Joseph Maréchal, *Études sur la psychologie des mystiques* (and even credits it with having provided him with his first

---

[61]. René Latourelle, "Révélation," *DTF*, 1162.
[62]. Karl Heinz Neufeld, "Karl Rahner," *DTF*, 1001.
[63]. Of particular note are the works: J. Maréchal, *Etudes sur la psychologie des mystiques* (Bruges: Desclée De Brouwer, 1938); J. Mouroux, *L'expérience chrétienne: introduction à une théologie* (Paris: Aubier, 1952); R. Vancourt, *La phénoménologie de la foi* (Tournai: Desclée, 1953); F. Grégoire, *Questions sur l'expérience religieuse* (Louvain: Public. Universitaire, 1957); Y. Congar, *La foi et la théologie* (Tournai: Desclée, 1962); M. Nédoncelle, *Prière humaine, prière divine* (Paris-Bruges: Desclée de Brouwer, 1962); Karl Rahner, "Über die Erfahrung der Gnade," *Schriften zur Theologie* (Einsiedeln: Benzinger Verlag, [1956] 1967).

philosophical insight).[64] Maréchal had already asserted that a person, through the bestowal of a mystical grace, could be gratified with an intuition of God.[65] But Rahner went beyond the concept of a special bestowal of grace to mystics to hold that all human persons, by their very constitution, had access to such an intuition about God. Like de Lubac, Rahner rejected the two-storied theology of the supernatural. Against this tendency, he affirmed the intertwining of creation and redemption in human history. Human nature exists historically in a drama defined by sin and grace. Rahner's idea that the grace of God is universal in humanity resonates not only with the patristic evidence brought to light by de Lubac and others, but also with the witness of Scripture. Several passages dealing with the preexistence of Christ—1 Cor 10:4, 1 Pet 1:10f., Col 1:15-20, the Prologue of Jn, Heb 1:3—carry a soteriological significance. Colossians 1:15-20, in particular, links Christ's *universal* mediatorship in creation (15-17), to his *universal* mediatorship in salvation (18-20).[66] In this salvific economy, the coming of Jesus in history is the advent of the eternal Logos in time, the unique Logos, the creative principle through which humanity is graced. From the beginning, God's grace has *always already* been present in humanity and God's plan has always been to save all people. This theological position does not deny the effects of the Fall but holds that the grace of God at creation prevented the Fall from leading to the total depravity of humanity. It maintains that the nature of the human person, though damaged by sin, still bears the *imago Dei*, and that primordial prevenient grace was always present as the remedy to human sinfulness. Human persons can choose to resist grace or to surrender their lives to it.

Thus humanity comes into the world created, graced, fallen, but not lost. Secular human history is already supernatural history. The secular, for Rahner, is not as secular as it appears, for looking at it

---

[64]. Karl Rahner, *Karl Rahner im Gespräch*, I, ed. P. Imhof, H. Biallowons (Munich: Kösel, 1982), 32.

[65]. Pierre Ranwez, "Le discernement de l'expérience religieuse chez l'enfant," *Lumen Vitae* 19 (1965): 223.

[66]. Walter Kasper, *Jesus the Christ*, trans. V. Green (New Jersey: Paulist Press, 1977), 185-186.

deeply, enlightened by revelation, we recognize in secular activity the interaction of sin and grace. The theological concepts of universal grace and 'secular history as supernatural history' challenge many traditional ideas about the role of the Church. The Church is no longer the gate keeper of the supernatural order but rather the community where a mystery of universal dimensions is known, proclaimed and celebrated.

In emphasizing new consciousness and a new life orientation as aspects of experience, Rahner did not limit Christian faith merely to sentiment or feeling. Even though faith has a subjective pole, it also includes a cognitive dimension. For Rahner, Christians (in addition to the revelation immanent within the constitution of all persons) receive a message. Unlike others, Christians do learn about the *mirabilia Dei*; they hear the story of salvation.

Rahner's Understanding of Revelation

It was on the strength of his own experience that Rahner became convinced that God has been revealed to every human being and that this form of inner, personal disclosure is the most genuine and original form of revelation. Understanding revelation as the illumination of human life, Rahner rejected every form of *extrinsicism*. Revelation brings to light that which is hidden; it articulates the deep things of human existence and discloses not only the wounds and self-destructive trends in human life, but also reveals God's gracious presence in it.

Rahner opposed a view of grace in which God bestows grace upon the sinner from the outside as something foreign. He thought of grace as the self-communication of God which transforms the inner lives of believers and which brings it about that a person does not sin continually.[67] Grace is immanent in the human person.

In this theological view, human experience is not used as a source of second-rate analogies for understanding a doctrine which is foreign to it. Rather, the movement goes in the opposite direction. Doctrine attains meaning as it is interpreted against the background of life. Thus for example, the paschal mystery, the death and rising of Jesus Christ, assumes new meaning for one whose life has been threatened by death or the "shadows of death" and has been able to emerge to new hopefulness and a new life. Such experiences of disintegration and

---

[67]. Vorgrimler, 119.

reintegration are the *praeambula fidei* which prepare the ground for the Christian to accept, *in faith*, that a definitive reintegration of life can be our ultimate future. In this way, humanity does not explain God, but God explains humanity. Rahner's point of departure for theology lies with the questions stirred up by life itself and then moves towards the Christian message, lifting the subject to a recognition of dogmatic truth.[68] The emergence of the questioning subject and the theological point of departure in human questions represents what has been referred to as the *anthropological shift* in theology.[69] By beginning in human questions, the approach to the Christian Tradition cannot help but be pertinent to the questioner's existence.

For Rahner, revelation as the self communication of God signifies that God "in his own most proper reality makes himself the inner-most constitutive element of man."[70] Rahner's phenomenological approach understands the human person primarily as spirit in the world, in space and time. His understanding of revelation is not limited to a spatio-temporal analysis of the conditions of human existence but leads rather to an extensive reflexion on the meaning of corporeity and our perceptive faculties, which he calls "world," as well as on history as the locus where one may exercise a conditional freedom.[71] It is by turning to the phenomenon, to as many phenomena as possible, that the human person experiences itself as spirit, since the richer and more varied the phenomena, the more there appears in them, the goal of the human spirit, Being itself.[72] Human persons, as spirits, are the fullest manifestation of Being in creation and are, by their very constitution, open to each other as experiences of the transcendent, of the divine. Thus to miss the possibility of experiencing God is to miss the greatness and significance of oneself and to risk not recognizing the true magnitude and significance of one's fellow human beings. Wher-

---

[68]. Vorgrimler, 22.
[69]. Vorgrimler, 22.
[70]. Karl Rahner, *Foundations of Christian faith: An Introduction to the Idea of Christianity*, trans. William V. Dych (New York: Crossroad, [1978] 1992), 117. (Hereafter cited as *Foundations*.)
[71]. Neufeld, 1001.
[72]. Vorgrimler, 63.

ever this ultimate greatness of the individual is not acknowledged, the danger exists that human persons will not be perceived as ends in themselves but merely as a means to some higher good.

At the same time that Rahner defended the doctrine of the universality of divine grace, by affirming the universal character of "original" revelation, he could also say that Scripture contains all that God has revealed for our salvation. He was able to affirm both propositions by making a connection between the generalized, interior revelation in humanity and the particular, historical revelation which culminates in Jesus of Nazareth. It is in this context that Rahner speaks about his now famous idea of *anonymous Christians*. He expresses the connection in this way:

> Since the transcendental self-communication of God as an offer to man's freedom is an existential of every person, and since it is a moment in the self-communication of God to the world which reaches its goal and its climax in Jesus Christ, we can speak of "anonymous Christians." But it still remains true: in the full historical dimension of this single self-communication of God to man in Christ and towards Christ, only someone who explicitly professes in faith and in baptism that Jesus is the Christ is a Christian in the historical and reflexive dimension of God's transcendental self-communication.[73]

What follows from this is that faith, hope and charity are realities offered in the lives of people everywhere, even if they have never heard of Jesus. It should therefore be possible to describe faith, the experience of faith, without necessarily relating it to Jesus. Faith or the rejection of faith exists in the lives of all humans. For secular people faith would mean that they feel that life is a gift to them, that they have a sense of living out of inner resources over which they have no power, that they are humble and do not see themselves as proud authors of their own achievements, that they feel life is "for" and not "against" them (even when they suffer), that they are capable of marvelling at the good things in this world and so forth. These characteristics do not belong to "feeling" but to human consciousness.

Because Rahner believed in the possibility of spiritual transcendence in every human life, he was convinced that truth and morality are to be found outside Christianity, in the other world religions, in the sciences, in various ideologies. One gets a taste of how completely his theology became open to the perception of truth outside the confines of

---

[73]. Rahner, *Foundations*, 176.

the Christian tradition, in the dialogue Rahner carried on with Marxists. Vorgrimler writes:

> In conversation with Marxists Rahner developed his important distinction between absolute future and future in the world. He said that Christianity has no recipes for shaping the future within the world and that it therefore can and must associate itself with any real humanism so that the future within the world may become worthy of humanity. He said that it was the task of Christianity to show humanity as being on the way to an absolute future, to a future which cannot be planned and cannot be made, but comes of itself and consummates all things—humanity, history and the world: the absolute future which is only another name for God. But he learned from the Marxists that there must be a connection between the two futures, without Christianity being a mere consolation with the beyond. Therefore, Rahner emphatically said that a man misses his absolute future—God—if he does not work with all his power for the human realization of the future within the world.[74]

Divine Presence in Day-to-day Life

It is clear that Rahner did not identify the experience of grace exclusively with religious activity such as prayer, cultic acts or the study and contemplation of religious themes. Rahner held that the original, self-communication of God "can be so universal, so unthematic and so 'unreligious' that it takes place, unnamed but really, wherever we are living out our existence."[75]

Rahner wanted to disclose to others the possibilities for experiencing God in the 'everyday', because he thought that anyone who does not recognize the innermost nearness of the incomprehensible mystery (God) or at least have intimations of it, does not know him/herself.[76] To initiate others into faith is to initiate people into this very special experience. Such an initiation requires more than simply transmitting doctrine. It includes uncovering grace at work in human life. Sometimes, in order to uncover this inner revelation in the life of a person

---

[74]. Vorgrimler, 113.
[75]. Rahner, *Foundations*, 132.
[76]. Rahner, *Foundations*, 51-71.

the help of another is required, since not all human beings are in a position to understand and interpret their lives and what happens to them. It is at this point that one may speak of catechesis and religious education.

Rahner's theology understood that it was God's grace, operative within all human persons, that brings about the will, the ability and the performance of all that is good, such that no person ever stands on the merits of their own actions before God. In this way, he could affirm the Reformation principle of *sola gratia*.[77] He continued to understand faith as a gift, a gift which is the work of the Holy Spirit, a spiritual dynamic involving will and intellect and leading to a transformed consciousness.

Rahner looked to human experiences of the spiritual as the locus in which one may discover the gift of faith, to experiences which are more than simply an exhibition of intellectual, cultural and social activity—more than evidence of thinking, studying, deciding, acting, cultivating a social life, living in community and so forth. In all of these experiences, Rahner maintained, "spirit" is (or may be) only that ingredient which serves to make this earthly life more human, more beautiful and in some way meaningful.[78] The transcendence proper to the spirit does not need to be called into play to accomplish those sorts of activities. Rahner looked elsewhere for evidence of the progress of grace in human lives.

Creation itself can be seen as a gift, as a graced reality. More than that, redemption is operative in people as they turn away from pride and selfishness toward humility and love, as they leave a destructive past behind and open themselves to a new future, as they weep with others who suffer and rejoice with others who are glad. Some of the best examples of experiences of spiritual transcendence for Rahner, were to be found in incidents characterized by loving gratuity and disinterestedness on the part of the one who acts. Acts such as making a sacrifice without thanks or recognition, without even an inner feeling of peace; being good to a fellow person without any glimmer of thankfulness or reciprocation, without even the self-gratulatory feelings to which a selfless act might give rise.[79]

For the Christian, this is the life of discipleship, but people who do

---

[77]. Rahner, *Foundations*, 127.
[78]. Rahner, "Über die Erfahrung," 105-106.
[79]. Rahner, "Über die Erfahrung," 106.

not know Jesus may be led by divine grace along the same path. The inclination of "everyman" touched by grace is a self-forgetfulness and the turning to the other in love, where the other is both neighbour and God.

For Rahner, to seek oneself in these life experiences of selfless giving is the path to the transcendent spiritual in humanity. These experiences have little to do with a kind of charismatic revelry wherein the evidence of God's grace becomes confused with personal feelings of religious uplifting. In vivid contrast, they have a great deal to do with the self-emptying of Jesus on the cross. For Rahner, this interior, kenotic movement of the spiritual person is the locus of the eternal, the eternal which emerges within our everyday world, bringing the assurance that the human spirit is more than the rational capacity of a thinking animal.

> Wenn wir solche finden, haben wir die Erfahrung des Geistes gemacht...Die Erfahrung der Ewigkeit, die Erfahrung, dass der Geist mehr ist als ein Stück dieser zeitlichen Welt, die Erfahrung, dass der Sinn des Menschen nicht im Sinn und Glück dieser Welt aufgeht... [80]

Summary:

Karl Rahner's intuition that all humanity stands under God's grace proved crucial in shaping his theological project. His reflexions began with the questions philosophy raised about human existence and moved to a renewed fundamental theology in search of answers. Rahner wished to do away with the distinction between doctrine and life. He wanted to rescue from scholastic theology, in a form recognizable to moderns, those abiding and indispensable elements of the Christian tradition which are food for life.[81] It was this opening to the questions of human existence which inspired his theology of rescue and convinced Rahner that the existing system ought to be turned on its head.

Instead of persons needing to adapt their thinking and experiences to a pre-set pattern of cultural and social religiosity, Rahner put the system at the service of life. Of course this position assumes that there

---

[80]. Rahner, "Über die Erfahrung," 107.
[81]. Vorgrimler, 21.

is a precious core in the Christian tradition which can and should be recovered. He wanted to make theology and doctrine transparent as a response to the existential questions which men and women are wrestling with in the latter part of the 20th century. His theology seeks to offer indications, hints to help the individual find a path to the truth, a truth which already lies unconsciously within.

With this goal in mind, his method begins with the gamut of human experiences, *especially* those limit experiences which lead us to question our existence. The method then moves to Christian revelation as the hermeneutical key to our life. Finally, it returns to the point of departure, to experience, now transformed and understood. The Gospel serves as the interpretative key which permits meaning to emerge from experience, an experience which may have seemed random and incomprehensible to the pre-evangelized person. The meaning which emerges, while surprising and unexpected, does not appear foreign to personal experience; on the contrary, it is the illumination of that experience.

Rahner understood Christology to embrace not only the life, death and resurrection of Jesus, but also the role of the Logos at creation. His is a christology writ large, wherein the salvific effects of the death and resurrection of Jesus are already present as the original will of the Creator. The eternal—that which was from the beginning—becomes known in time. Scripture, theology and doctrine become midwives at the birth of meaning in the lives of believers.

Rahner also attempted to listen to people in order to detect the *de facto* catechism by which they live. He found that these *de facto* catechisms were far from containing everything that is officially presented as the content of faith.[82] In Rahner's attempt to listen to his contemporaries, one hears echoes of Marie Fargues' catechetical project. Fargues sought to listen to her students to discover what it was they really believed. She wished to catechize the *lives* of her children. Marie Fargues wanted to move towards the personal stories of her pupils in order to be able to translate the Gospel message into the vocabulary of their existence.[83]

---

[82]. Rahner, *Foundations*, 450-451. Note the striking similarity between Rahner's conclusion and Louis Racine's understanding of the goal of catechesis (Cf. Chapter 3).

[83]. Throughout Fargues' chronicle of the catechetical movement, she emphasizes the need to consider socio-economic and cultural factors in the devel-

Rahner's theology affected Vatican Council II greatly and his international reputation dates from that time. Although his rise in popularity after the Council was meteoric, prior to Vatican II his work had been known only to professional theologians. His reflexions have managed to be faithful to the best in Catholic Tradition while rehabilitating the role of experience in the life of grace. His work supported the research of many other theologians in virtually every theological field of inquiry.

GABRIEL MORAN

In the area of catechetics, Gabriel Moran dealt with the question of revelation and experience in a still more radical way than did Rahner. In his books *Design for Religion* (1971), *The Present Revelation* (1972) and *Religious Body* (1974), Moran proposed an expanded idea of revelation and re-introduced a concept, consciously or not, which F. Schleiermacher and A. Sabatier had developed in reaction to Kant.[84] Schleiermacher sought to rehabilitate a theological role for religious feelings and experience. For Schleiermacher, revelation blends with personal, immanent, religious experience. What happens in the believer is the personal but imperfect repetition of the awareness of God which Jesus possessed perfectly.[85] For Sabatier, who depends on Schleiermacher, the essence of Christianity is found in a religious experience, in an interior revelation of God which took place for the first time in Jesus of Nazareth but which is repeated, albeit in a less illuminating way, in all his true disciples. Moran, like Sabatier and Schleiermacher before him, identified revelation with interior personal experience. In this view, revelation is an experience which happens between two persons, subject to subject.[86] Moran all but abandons the objective pole of historical revelation in favor of a personal, existential

---

opment of catechesis. Her degree of sensitivity to these questions, while not yet radicalized, surpasses that of her catechetical colleagues at work in those years.

[84]. Latourelle, 1181-1182. We follow Latourelle's analysis of Moran closely.
[85]. Latourelle, 1181.
[86]. Latourelle, 1182.

enlightenment.

The equilibrium Rahner manages to achieve between the objective and subjective poles of revelation is missing in Moran. Rahner's stance permits contemporary theology to continue to dialogue with the ancient Tradition of the Church. Moran's approach has great difficulty in achieving this goal. Moran's position, while producing many useful insights and new perspectives on old problems, suffers from this methodological flaw and will not be pursued further here.

CONNECTIONS TO THE VVLP SERIES

Using the background provided above for contrast and perspective, we will now paint, in broad strokes, a theological portrait of the *Viens vers le Père* series. A few questions will guide our reflexions. First, to what extent may we describe the inspiration of this programme as theological in origin? Second, to what extent do the insights uncovered by the work of scholars such as de Lubac and Rahner influence the theological perspective of the series? Third, how may we describe the role assigned the Scriptures in this series? In other words, how do the theological and pedagogical options of the series shape its understanding of the Scriptures and their overall function in the catechetical process?

PEDAGOGICAL INSPIRATION PREDOMINATES

The *Viens vers le Père* series depends more upon the new pedagogy of the French school of catechetical renewal than on the theology of the proclamation theorists at Lumen Vitae or the new theological outlook of men such as Rahner and de Lubac.

During an interview conducted with Françoise Bérubé, (Sr. Marie de la Visitation of the writing team) the pedagogical origins of the *Viens vers le Père* series became evident. At the same time *Viens vers le Père* was being written, Françoise Bérubé was in contact with colleagues at work in the development of catechetical resources in Europe. Bérubé's European colleagues insisted that, in their view, catechetical themes ought always to begin with a christological reference or emphasis. The Canadian writing team resisted this restriction and preferred to maintain a more dynamic and flexible pedagogy. To allow the starting point for a lesson to be an event from the child's life, a story from Scripture, an ecclesial rite or *any concrete reality* which could open the door to the child's understanding and enable the child to grasp the significance of doctrine, was unquestionably a pedagogical and not a theological decision.[87] The christological emphasis of Bérubé's European colleagues reflected their theological concerns.

The significance of the Canadian team's decision may be clarified with a typical example of their approach to scriptural narratives. Narratives are presented in such a way that the telling of the story itself becomes a concrete experience for the child. Later in the lesson, this story-experience— now part of the child's life and present as a concrete, human event (even if a contrived one)—could be exploited as a source of analogies for the doctrinal content which lay beyond the child's *natural* experience.[88] *Célébrons ses merveilles* (Week Three, Session One) supplies a typical example. Jesus' cure of a man born blind (Jn 9:1-38), is the scriptural passage to be explored. The children, in order to imagine what blindness might be like, are asked to close their eyes as the story unfolds. Later in the narrative, on the teacher's cue, they re-open their eyes, re-enacting the man's recovery of sight. The child's experience with the story and the simulation of blindness leads later in the lesson to a treatment of the theme, *Jesus is the light of the world*, where the physical blindness of the man in the narrative is extended to a spiritual blindness caused by sin.[89]

This notion of concrete learning, of learning that involves doing, is traceable to the methods of the *École active* discussed in Chapters 2 and 3 above and intends clearly to respect the psychological development of children.[90] Discernible here is the influence of the French pio-

---

[87]. Sr. Marie de la Visitation (F. Bérubé) expressed similar views in her published work as well. See: "Le Dieu de Jésus-Christ présenté aux enfants de 6-7 ans," *Communauté chrétienne* 2 (1963): 274-275.

[88]. Here we see the passage from the known to the obscure, the primary goal of the process being the cognitive acquisition of doctrinal content.

[89]. As the articles of the Creed form the main doctrinal backdrop for the series, many weekly themes may be devoted to the same section of the Creed. Thus one finds several weeks devoted to themes dealing with God as Father, God as Son, or God as Spirit. This particular theme relates to creedal statements about Jesus Christ.

[90]. Françoise Bérubé, interview by author, St. Lambert (P.Q.) March, 1991.

neers of the catechetical renewal: Fargues, Derkenne, Lubienska de Lenval, Colomb, Boyer et al. Despite the imaginative techniques of presenting Scripture to young children in this pedagogy, its obvious goal is to tap the experience of the child for analogies suitable for illuminating doctrinal content, a content frequently delivered in the form of biblical "themes." Where no suitable experiences exist, one creates them. This is perhaps the most unambiguous evidence of the fact that experience serves primarily as a means and not as an end in this pedagogical set-up. The handling of scriptural passages was intended to throw light upon the doctrinal content and on the meaning of the scriptural passage. The object of the exercise is not chiefly or even necessarily to illuminate the everyday experiences of the child. The experiences of the child at home, in his/her neighbourhood, in the school yard and so forth may be incorporated into the pedagogical process, but never for their own sake and always with the goal of clarifying another reality.

While the primary goal of the *Viens vers le Père* series is cognitive acquisition, behavioural objectives constitute an important secondary goal. In Chapter 3, we presented Bernard Grom's opinion that the writing team depended heavily for its methodological choices on the thought of Pierre Ranwez. Ranwez, it was argued, investigated the possibility of discerning religious experience in the life of the young child. While Ranwez freely admits that the progress of grace is not empirically verifiable per se, evidence of actions characterized by disinterestedness and self-sacrificing concern for others may be a good indicator of its presence. Relying on the work of Maréchal, Mouroux, Vancourt, Grégoire, Congar, Nédoncelle and Rahner, Ranwez outlines several elements which may be helpful in the discernment of the action of grace in the life of a person:

> a) la nouveauté d'un état spirituel qui apparaît à la fois dépendant de la volonté et "donné," et dont les caractères positifs tranchent d'avec les caractères négatifs de l'état précédent;
>
> b) un attrait vers Dieu se développant dans un contexte de recueillement et d'unification intérieure;
>
> c) parallèlement une propension à se détourner de ce qui est contraire à Dieu (détachement de soi et du monde) avec une disponibilité à l'égard du prochain;

d) un climat de paix et de joie à la fois profond et presque impalpable.[91]

Ranwez' model expresses the progress of grace in the life of a person in terms of differences in behaviour before and after an act of conversion.[92]

Educational achievement is also assessed in terms of measurable change from a previous to a subsequent state. Within educational circles, the concern to plot change arises from the pedagogical requirement for empirical verifiability of educational outcomes. This pedagogical requirement for verifiability is the guiding principle of an article by F. Bérubé, which deals with childhood catechesis, and refers specifically to the *Viens vers le Père* series.[93]

Even though the catechetical approach of *Viens vers le Père* adds *conversion* to its list of goals, it was still able to maintain sound pedagogical principles. The act of conversion was the hoped-for outcome of the pedagogical strategies of the programme. Such concern for empirical verifiability is typical of educators and quite foreign to the concerns of dogmatic theologians.

Anne-Marie Ricard, in a brief article dealing with the origins of this series, isolates five central aims which the programme seeks to achieve.[94] These aims include: the inculcation of fundamental spiritual and religious attitudes; an initiation into a relationship with the Trinity; the transmission of doctrine through activity-based learning; the incorporation of the Scriptures in childhood catechesis; and the memorization of excerpts from Scripture as a kind of 'food for the spiritual journey of life'.

A study of the pedagogical practices employed in the various themes of the *Viens vers le Père* series suggests a methodology which, in effect, subordinates all other stated goals to the goal of doctrinal

---

[91]. Ranwez, "Le discernement," 224.
[92]. Ranwez, "Le discernement," 224.
[93]. Darcy and Beniskos, 257-268. Sr. Marie de la Visitation, "Introduire un enfant dans le mouvement des relations trinitaires," *Lumen Vitae* 21 (1966): 523-532.
[94]. Ricard, 396-397. Ricard draws this information from articles published by members of the writing team in the 1960s.

transmission. In as much as this is true, the programme remains a form of indoctrination, leaving little distance between course content and the "truth" and thereby tending towards an uncritical appropriation of Tradition. This point deserves some attention here.

Writing in 1965, Pierre Babin argued that the catechesis of the day had slipped into indoctrination and was no longer revelatory.[95] To be revelatory, catechesis not only needs to reveal Christ, but also to reveal persons to themselves, in a manner which is both liberating and original.[96] Although Babin wrote largely about adolescent catechesis, his call for a pedagogy of *invention* rather than one of *transmission* applies equally to all education in the faith.

> Il s'agit moins ici d'une orientation strictement catéchétique que d'un point de pédagogie générale. Il faut transmettre aux jeunes l'habitude de créer, et non seulement de répéter des leçons apprises; l'habitude de poser des questions, et non seulement de prendre des notes de cours; l'habitude de trouver des documents, et non seulement d'écouter un professeur; l'habitude de se référer intelligemment à la communauté chrétienne et à l'autorité de l'église, et non seulement de vivre en conformité passive avec cette autorité, attendant d'elle consignes et impulsions. En d'autres termes, donner aux jeunes le goût et l'habitude de s'orienter aux-mêmes (sic), en pleine liberté, dans un incessant approfondissement de la foi et dans des décisions personnelles inédites.[97]

The influence upon Babin of the theological anthropology of Rahner and of the psycho-analytical orientation of Marc Oraison, a priest psychiatrist, becomes evident in his concept of catechesis as self-revelatory liberation. The catechesis proposed by Babin would not eliminate a doctrinal reference but would make the actual experience of those to be catechized the hermeneutical key for the doctrinal corpus. A critical view of experience would be necessary as one tried to determine which elements of the doctrinal corpus might be usefully taken up in any given stage of the catechesis or with any given audience.

By contrast, the subordination of human experience to doctrinal ends obtains throughout the *Viens vers le Père* series. Moreover, the

---

[95]. Pierre Babin, *Options pour une éducation de la foi des jeunes* (Lyon: Éditions du Chalet, 1965), 48.
[96]. Babin, *Options*, 46.
[97]. Babin, *Options*, 72-73.

catechesis of the *Viens vers le Père* series limits its concept of experience principally to psychological realities, leaving the socio-cultural and economic realities of the child largely unexamined. We conclude then, that the field of educational psychology is the primary interpretative context for the methodology of the *Viens vers le Père* series. We turn now to an exploration of its theological options.

A THEOLOGICAL PROFILE OF VVLP

It is our contention that the choice of pedagogical methodology in a catechetical programme indirectly discloses the concept of revelation operative in that programme. This is certainly true of the *Viens vers le Père* series and it is also true of the work of Joseph Colomb and Marcel van Caster. It is probably true of catechetics in general. In this section, we will attempt to throw light upon the relationship between methodological option and concept of revelation. We begin with a general assessment of the theological influences discernible in the series as a whole. In as much as a catechism does not intend to render explicit a theological agenda, it will be all but impossible to make definitive statements about its theological orientations. One may, however, sketch a portrait in broad strokes of the most salient features of the theology underpinning this catechetical series.

Influenced by the biblical movement, the *Viens vers le Père* series carries into the catechetical arena an understanding of the important role the Scriptures play in the life of faith. This series breaks with the monolith of Neo-Thomism in rediscovering the Scriptures as the privileged locus of God's revelation. By the early 1960s the rich concept of the *Word of God*, borrowed from kerygmatic theology, had become a new source of theological inspiration, an inspiration everywhere present in the *Viens vers le Père* series. The neglect of the Bible, so typical of catechisms inspired by Neo-Scholasticism, had been remedied.

Marcel van Caster promoted the idea that God has communicated the contents of revelation in three languages; the language of events in the Bible, the language of symbolic gestures in the liturgy and the sapiential or notional language of doctrine. The *Viens vers le Père* series also structures its catechesis around Scripture, liturgy and doctrine.

As we noted in Chapter Three, wherever possible, *Viens vers le Père* expresses its doctrinal content in language taken from the Bible. The experiences of the child are a source of analogies for understanding both Scripture and doctrine. Occasionally, when biblical stories are used, the narrative itself becomes subordinate to the doctrinal point in question (as we saw was the case with the story of the man born blind in *Célébrons ses merveilles*). At times, the biblical narrative becomes an illustration of the doctrinal point.

In summary, doctrine and Scripture most often function similarly, except in those cases when Scripture is subordinated to doctrine. Typically, Scripture has been subjected to an interpretative process which precedes the child's virginal reception of the biblical content and fashions his/her reception of the text in terms of the doctrinal content at the centre of the lesson. In as much as the child stands within the Christian tradition of reading Scripture, certain doctrinal pre-understandings of the text are a normal part of the reading process; they are elements of the common cultural and spiritual heritage of the society or community in which the act of reading is taking place.

Although some basic doctrinal assumptions may form part of the child's prejudice (in gadamerian terms), the use of doctrine as the key hermeneutical approach to Scripture poses problems. René Marlé calls into question this sort of relationship between dogma and scriptural interpretation. He wonders whether dogma thus used, does not on the one hand, limit our openness to the scriptural Word and on the other, restrict our inquiries into and questioning of Scripture.[98] While dogma and Scripture wish to witness to the same reality, dogma has always necessarily been subordinate to the witness of Scripture. Scripture can provide clarifications for our understanding and formulation of dogma. Given that in the Catholic community, dogma and Scripture are both accepted as sources of revelation, they have complementary roles to play in the process of revelation. Marlé explains:

> Chercher dans le dogme une vérité qui se suffirait à elle-même et qui n'aurait pas à se référer à cette totalité du mystère révélé dans l'Ecriture, ce serait identifier une interprétation de la révélation, si juste et autorisée soit-elle, avec la Parole de Dieu elle-même, ce serait abolir le temps qui nous sépare de la Pa-

---

[98]. Marlé, *Hermémeutique*, 119.

role fondatrice. Mais inversement, vouloir comprendre l'Ecriture indép-endamment de l'horizon défini par le dogme, ce serait...vouloir privilégier notre point de vue individuel, nos horizons limités d'hommes d'une certaine époque, d'une certaine tradition et d'une certaine culture, par rapport à ceux qui nous sont dévoilés par la tradition authentique de l'Eglise, instituée sur cette Parole, et dont les dogmes jalonnent le cheminement dans la foi.[99]

Walter Kasper moves in a similar direction in his discussion of the role which dogma ought to play in exegesis.

Le dogme ne représente pour l'exégète aucun *fixum* devant lequel il n'aurait qu'à s'incliner. L'exégète n'a pas seulement à justifier le dogme après coup, mais à l'interpréter de son propre point de vue. L'exégète doit dire ce que, du point de vue de sa discipline, un dogme peut et ne peut pas vouloir dire. Tout progrès dans la connaissance exégétique est en même temps un progrès dans l'interprétation du dogme. Dans un rapport dynamique du dogme et de l'exégèse se concrétise l'unité, dans la tension, qui existe entre Evangile (au sens transcendant du mot) et dogme.[100]

The role played by pre-understandings in the interpretation of texts will be dealt with in greater detail in the following chapter. For now, we return to our theological profile of this programme.

From Joseph Colomb, the authors borrowed the concept of the *progressive presentation of revelation*, an idea which underpins the entire series. They were careful to introduce this pedagogical strategy in such a way as to avoid the controversy which Colomb himself faced in 1957. In the introductions to Grades Two through Six, rather than speak of progressive revelation, the authors speak of a "sharpening of focus" of the original, complete picture of doctrine, contained *in nuce* in Grade One. This was likely a skilful ruse designed to avoid attacks similar to those visited upon Colomb in 1957. Although Julien Harvey characterized the deferral of various doctrinal themes to subsequent

---

[99]. Marlé, *Herméneutique*, 120.
[100]. Walter Kasper, *Dogme et Evangile* (Tournai-Paris: Casterman, 1967), 120.

years as a linear rather than a concentric process,[101] he admits to finding the basis of a concentric approach elsewhere in the series:

> ...si on étudie avec soin les manuels du 1er cycle de l'Elémentaire, on constate qu'on y présente une synthèse cohérente et déjà complète de la foi. Il y a donc là un point de départ d'une démarche concentrique, et non pas linéaire. On peut cependant se demander si, lors d'une révision, il ne faut pas recommander un rappel périodique de ce noyau initial, en le développant à mesure de l'avance. Le deuxième cycle de l'Elémentaire le fait en général...[102]

Many insights of the theological renewal are recognizable in the theological fabric of this catechism. The authors, in citing the findings of Patristic research, signal a move away from the neo-scholastic model of theology and towards a theology interested in history. We refer particularly to a detailed reference to Vagaggini's research on the Patristic writings which the authors used to explain their presentation of the doctrine of the Trinity.[103]

The interest in the psychological requirements of the audience is evidence of the *turn to the subject* which characterized the anthropological shift in theology. Neo-Thomism had proposed the same formulæ for all people, no matter what their age, culture or historical setting. To realize that different age groups require different forms of catechesis is significant in that it indicates an appreciation of the historical dimensions of the human subject.

The Patristic research of de Lubac and others had ample time to be digested by the European theological community and to influence profoundly the catechetical scene. Already the first years of the *Viens vers le Père* series clearly signal a move away from an a-historical model of theology and towards a view of history as being open to the action of God. In fact it is this level of theological awareness that allows the writing team to make use of experience at all.

Joseph Colomb's concern to balance respect for the Word of God with the needs, requirements and expectations of the child, constitutes further evidence of the collapse of the artificial distinction between *natural* and *supernatural* worlds. This concern marks the *Viens vers le*

---

[101]. Julien Harvey, "Mémoire sur les manuels de catéchèse de l'OCQ: grandes options des manuels," Unpublished paper, 18 pages (October 1973), 10.

[102]. Harvey, "Mémoire," 11.

[103]. OCQ—Équipe, *Viens vers le Père: The New Catechism,* 256.

Père series, although, as with Colomb, the vestiges of this dualism are never fully eradicated.

This catechism sketches a relationship of continuity rather than rupture between the Old and New Testaments. Not only can OT figures such as Moses serve as spiritual models for Christian children, but sacraments can also be depicted as modern day examples of the *mirabilia Dei* in the history of salvation.

> Ces interventions de Dieu ne se limitent toutefois pas au seul peuple hébreu. L'histoire du salut, l'histoire sainte se continue à travers le temps. Aujourd'hui encore, Dieu sauve les hommes et mulitplie ses merveilles à leur endroit. Ces merveilles de Dieu se réalisent de façon privilégiée dans les sacrements.[104]

The concept of revelation implicit in the *Viens vers le Père* series is virtually the same as that found in the work of both Colomb and van Caster. In other words, this series exhibits an extrinsicist understanding of revelation. Prior to the catechetical renewal, this schema was manifest in abstract, notional catechesis. With proclamation theology, the formulation of doctrine has become scriptural, a move which replaced the highly abstract language of Neo-Scholasticism with the more affective expression of the Bible. Doctrine is presented as a-historical truth in this catechesis. The objective pole of revelation swallows up the subjective pole, as *truth* is depicted, not as something one discovers within oneself, but rather as an objectively established cognitive content. Here, revelation is entirely a reality external to the person to be catechized. What one observes in the *Viens vers le Père* series is not a transformation of the concept of how one attains truth, much less a transformation of the understanding of the nature of truth itself, but rather an improvement of the techniques of transmitting truth. Chief among the new techniques of transmission are the *méthodes actives*. Previously, the dry language of notional catechesis predominated. After the renewal, Scripture and the liturgy offered dynamic language, integrated into animated pedagogical techniques which remain essentially unsurpassed to this day.

While experience has a limited role in the catechesis of *Viens vers*

---

[104]. *Célébrons ses merveilles, Guide du Maître*, 7.

le Père, its methodology continues the transmission model of the old catechisms. Pedagogy may have undergone a profound transformation with respect to its techniques of transmission, but the life of the student never becomes the main concern of its catechesis. The result, read with little sympathy, may be characterized as simply a more subtle form of indoctrination. Evaluated more kindly, one might say that the turn to historicity is limited to an appreciation of the psychological evolution of the growing child. The Bible and doctrine have been judged revelatory apart from their reference to the life of the child and apart from their ability to illuminate that life. The locus of revelation is never the life of the child.

The theology of the *Viens vers le Père* series clearly breaks with Neo-Scholasticism and attempts to incorporate many of the insights of the leading theologians at work in the years prior to its publication. Grades One to Four appeared before the work of Vatican Council II had become widely known. In Grades Five and Six, the theological language used clearly indicates a familiarity with the work of the Council. In Grades Five and Six, the themes of freedom and hope play a large role in the discussion of the world and the Christian's place in it. Christian and non-Christian heroes, the Apollo moon shots, ecumenical dialogue, technological and scientific advances such as satellite technology and medical discoveries—all are praised as signs of the love God has for humanity. The sinful face of humanity plays an insignificant role in this whole presentation.

The work of the Council was perhaps too fresh and too far-reaching in its implications to be quickly assimilated and adapted for use in this catechetical programme. The theological content of the Teacher Manuals for Grades Five and Six lacked the integration of the manuals for the first four years, undoubtedly because of the magnitude of the changes that were taking place within the Church at the time of their writing. While liturgical reforms were still in the implementation stage, *Préparer la terre nouvelle* (Gr. 5) had to find ways of presenting their significance to 10-11 year olds and to their teachers. *Selon ta promesse, Fais moi vivre* (Gr. 6) cites Council documents and theologians such as Karl Rahner. Often these references proved problematic for many teachers working in the field.[105]

---

[105]. Even after many years of use and revision, the Grades Five and Six programmes were criticized for using theological language and concepts beyond the grasp of lay teachers. My own experience with the programme dates

This new catechetical series intended to move away from a morose fixation on sin and a religion of rules and to recapture a religion of the "heart" within a religion of the "head." In the text books of the younger grades, words like sin and sacrifice were used sparingly indeed. Julien Harvey evaluates the theological shift with a reference to the work of Rudolph Schnackenburg.[106]

> Cette option fondamentale pour une catéchèse trinitaire dynamique a des conséquences importantes pour la découverte de la vie morale chez l'enfant. Dans les grandes lignes, on pourrait parler d'un passage d'une morale de type paulinien à une morale plus spécifiquement johannique. Dans la 1ère, le péché apparaît comme l'arrière-fond de la situation humaine, si bien que seule une morale "surnaturelle" est possible, le péché étant omniprésent et fatal sauf si on le combat avec la force de Jésus-Christ; dans la 2ième, le péché apparaît plutôt comme un accident, la situation normale chez le croyant étant la grâce et la fidélité qui en découle. Une autre conséquence de l'option fondamentale est l'insistance sur l'expérience spirituelle de l'enfant, sur "la grâce à l'oeuvre dans la question bien posée"...[107]

As the *Viens vers le Père* series was *in embryo* during the period in which Rahner's work became widely known, the general methodology of the programme could not really profit from the insights of this important thinker. Rahner and the Council documents may have been cited in the teacher manuals of Grades Five and Six, but the foundational, methodological options of the series had already been established. The die was cast and it was simply too late for an about-face, assuming the writing team saw a need for one. Human experience continues to be used chiefly as a source of analogies in Grades Five and Six. Only those experiences are selected which serve to elucidate the point of doctrine in question. The methodology is consistent

---

from my days as a Religious Education Consultant, where one of my first duties was to gather teacher reaction to the *Come to the Father* series, which was then in the process of being replaced.

[106]. Rudolph Schnackenburg, *Le message moral du Nouveau Testament* (Paris: Le Puy, 1963). German original: *Die sittliche Botschaft des Neuen Testaments*, 1954.

[107]. Harvey, "Mémoire," 3-4.

throughout and despite some ambiguous statements of intent to the contrary, the notion that revelation is meant to serve as the interpretative key of history and of the life of the individual is never embraced.

The theological method suggested by Rahner's transcendental Thomism clearly is not in view in the *Viens vers le Père* series. Rahner sought to listen to the questions which the modern age was stirring in the lives of people in search of meaning. Having listened, he pored over the Christian Tradition (Bible, doctrine, Church history) in search of wisdom and insight useful in the clarification of the present situation. The role of doctrine for Rahner was to throw light upon the experiences of men, women and children today. Anything in the Bible or in Tradition, whatever its objective (ontological) worth, was of no practical value if it could not accomplish this task. The goal was not to adduce the whole of the contents of the Tradition, but rather to evangelize the life of the person who was on a quest for meaning. Doctrine is clearly not the epistemological object of Rahner's theological method. Life is.

INTERPRETING SCRIPTURE IN VVLP: PRELIMINARY CONCLUSIONS

The production of a set of age-appropriate catechetical resources, covering a wide range of doctrinal and spiritual themes, requires competence in several disciplines. The skill and scholarship of the writers of the *Viens vers le Père* series was impressive and perhaps unequalled in North America. Each of the authors had completed a licentiate degree in either theology, philosophy or catechetics; several held doctorates in theology. In addition, the team was fortunate to have among them Françoise Bérubé (Sr. Marie de la Visitation), a person skilled in both the theory and praxis of the new pedagogy. Any expertise that the team lacked was enlisted from various academics and professionals. In the decades previous, catechetics had not been considered an area of great interest or import in theological or ecclesiastical circles in North America. In the school curriculum, it occupied an intellectual space, akin though superior to the requirement for mastery of the multiplication tables.

At its height, the catechetical renewal did much to advance the popular renewal of the Church. The movements behind the catechetical renewal (the Biblical and Liturgical Movements and Catholic Action) were the very movements which had inspired the

Verkündigungstheologie at Innsbruck and which affected theological renewal at large. As catechetical renewal took hold, the biblical and liturgical emphases informing it insinuated themselves into theological faculties steeped in Thomism or Neo-Scholasticism. The kerygmatic theology associated with the catechetical renewal had a short life in faculties of theology, as it was soon replaced with a plurality of theological models which tried to make room for modern experience.

The emphasis on educational psychology which guided the renewal of the Canadian Catechism, reflected the new interest in the human subject within catechetics. An accommodation to the psychological possibilities of the audience is a first important step in a wider shift to an existential methodology, a methodology still largely underrepresented in catechetical circles today. The old emphases of a rule-ridden, ritualistic religion have made way for a new and invigorating notion of faith grounded in the Scriptures.

The *Viens vers le Père* series with its emphasis on educational psychology offered a corrective to American catechisms published in the late 1950s and early 1960s which incorporated a *Heilsgeschichte* theology without a renewed pedagogy. This series understood the need to adapt its content to the learning requirements and styles of children.

When suspicion of human experience and suspicion of the world at large were beginning to fade in theological circles, the problem of how to establish the correct relationship between the content of revelation and the existential reality of the inquirer came into focus. Scripture was but one element in a trilogy of languages of revelation for the *Viens vers le Père* series. The languages of the liturgy and of doctrine were the other expressions of revelation.

It is our contention that the approach to dogma (or doctrine) in the *Viens vers le Père* series has the effect of limiting the witness of Scripture in a way similar to that suggested by René Marlé and Walter Kasper above. This series tends to limit its approach to Scripture to those themes which more or less relate to the central elements of the Church's doctrinal heritage. In this series, the meaning of Scripture is not so much something one discovers as it is something one recovers from the doctrinal heritage of the Church. While this is one of the goals of catechesis, students should be encouraged to explore Scripture as more than a repository of doctrine. In the same manner in which culturally and historically-bound human experience was sacrificed to the ultimate goal of the elucidation of doctrine, so too the content of Scripture became hemmed in by a doctrinal framework and goal.

Viens vers le Père adopts an extrinsicist concept of revelation which, in its methodology, translates into an emphasis on doctrinal transmission, realized in and through activity-based learning. The goal of the catechesis derived from these concepts consists in finding ways of accommodating and relating human experience to fixed understandings of the content of revelation.

Karl Rahner's theological method and his concept of revelation suggest a critique of this methodology. Rahner recommends the opposite movement to that suggested by extrinsicism. For Rahner, what Jesus reveals through his life, death and resurrection is the truth about all human life. The Christ event has the power to throw light on every aspect of human life, uncovering the hidden reality of grace found there. Human life and human being are intimately related to the contents of revelation. This implies more than an adaptation of a message to the *psychological* requirements of the person to be catechized and it implies more than using human experience only as a source of analogies to explain the divine. It implies that the profound significance of the Word of God may only be discovered in the context of life and as such its meaning could never have the appearance of a reality whose origins are extrinsic to the world of our experiences. A catechism structured on Rahner's understanding of revelation would seek less to proclaim and explain the Gospel, than to find the Gospel hidden within the particular culture, history and religious traditions within which the Church seeks to make the Word known. In contrast to Rahner's views, the ruling concept of the *Viens vers le Père* series does not see catechesis as a convergence of the subjective and objective poles of revelation in an act of insight and spiritual enlightenment. This series seeks rather to transmit the objective contents of revelation by passing from the known (the experiences of the child) to that which is unknown (the contents of revelation). In contrast to Rahner's view, this idea of revelation maintains that if it were not for the divine revelation in Jesus Christ, humanity would have no knowledge of God's will for us.

As in the catechetics of Colomb, the genius of the *Viens vers le Père* series is found in its adaptation of the findings of educational psychology to the catechetical process. The series also rescues catechesis from the periphery, re-placing it within the pastoral mission of the Church at large. Buoyed by an optimistic, liberal theology, this catechism accepts an optimistic view of human history,[108] which seems strangely at odds with large portions of the scriptural witness. The influence of liberal theology on the interpretation of Scripture is considerable. The de-emphasis of the reality of sin in the work of liberal theologians leads to a reading of the Bible which became preoccupied with passages dealing with grace, leaving the biblical treatment of sin largely untouched.

One effect of the choice to de-emphasize sin in this catechesis is the exclusion of doctrinal themes dealing with the broken and fragmented character of human life. Once these "negative" themes are removed, one is left with what might be described as an optimistic view of the Christian religion (e.g., God is love, God makes me live) in which the struggles of the Christian life have all but evaporated. These themes were selected ostensibly for their appropriateness for young children. Two assumptions seem to underlie this selection criterion. First, as we have maintained throughout, the programme assumes that the contents of revelation are not available in secular human experience—they convey a special kind of knowledge available to humanity only since the advent of Christ in history. By designing a programme, which by all appearances seems to wish to address middle class urban children, the second assumption seems to be, that children in this country have little or no first hand experiences of evil, that they "normally" live in cheery, well-balanced and secure home environments.

Unfortunately, Canada was no more utopian in those years than it is today. Health and Welfare Canada (1997) reports that one in six Canadian children lives below the threshold of poverty. Without embarking on a barrage of statistics, the rates of child abuse—sexual, physical and psychological—of unemployment and family break-up, of malnutrition and of dropping out of school, continue to be alarmingly high. Despite the best intentions of the writing team to leave the diffi-

---

[108]. The optimism regarding the modern world is especially evident in the Grades Five and Six programmes.

cult questions of evil and sin until later in the catechetical process, it seems as though Canadian children were not and are not isolated from the reality of evil and sin in our world. Liberal theology, of the variety informing the *Viens vers le Père* series ignores many of the messy realities of social evil, compartmentalizing them into a theme or two entitled "evil in the world." The methodology buttressed by these theological assumptions cannot adjust for the real-life situations of individuals. This methodology assumes an average child (from the point of view of psychological development and social status), a single profile for an entire country which is characterized by regional economic disparities and differences in culture. A methodology which seeks to elucidate experience would make no such assumption and would, within the bounds of the possible, individualize catechesis. At the very least, such an experience-centred model would attend to the cultural, social and economic conditions prevalent in the region where catechesis is to be given.

Historico-prophetic catechesis critiques liberal theology as inadequate, calling for a recovery of the notion of sinfulness in the theological paradigm. This prophetic catechesis does not want to see a return to moral scrupulousness or a rule-book concept of (personal) sin. Radical theologians, especially those of the Third World, set about uncovering the systemic, social sinfulness in the fabric of collective human relationships. Their socio-political critique challenged the work of theologians from wealthy countries. While catechisms for young children could not hope to deal directly with such issues, their design can be such that room is made for these concerns.

While Karl Rahner did not escape the critique levelled against liberal theology,[109] he did acknowledge the importance of the questions raised by political theology. This critique notwithstanding, Rahner's "historical," theological method remains a thoroughgoing critique of every form of extrinsicism and as such provides us with a source of critique for the *Viens vers le Père* series.

With Rahner we agree that the Church can initiate people into an experience of faith. Children can be made aware of the experience of grace as a reality which is already hidden in their daily lives. If a person can become aware of the reality of grace at work in his/her life,

---

[109]. J.B. Metz, a political theologian and a friend of Rahner until his death, levelled a biting critique at Rahner's work. See Metz' *Pour une théologie du monde*, trans. Hervé Savon (Paris: Editions du Cerf, 1971).

then forging links to the corpus of doctrine and to the biblical witness will carry a significance and a pertinence it would otherwise lack. Faith, if it comes, will be a response to that reality identified for the listener.

To paraphrase Dilthey, texts are to be understood as 'expressions of life fixed in writing.' If the texts of the Christian Tradition are understood in this way, the gap separating revelation and life may be bridged. The preoccupation with doctrinal transmission, prevalent in *Viens vers le Père*, not only exploits the experiences of its learners in the attainment of a higher goal, but limits the students approach to the texts of the Bible. Catechesis must find a way to bring together the experiences communicated in the texts of the Christian Tradition and the life experiences of its listeners. This brings us to the threshold of the general hermeneutical questions raised by *Viens vers le Père*'s methodology and thus to our next chapter.

CHAPTER 5

HERMENEUTICAL OPTIONS IN *VIENS VERS LE PERE*

The difficulties related to the critical reconstruction of the hermeneutical options discernible in the *Viens vers le Père* series are not minor. Consider these points. The programme had not one but ten authors. These authors were divided into two teams which worked consecutively on the project. The corpus, distributed over six separate grade levels, consists of some 3167 pages of text. Each grade level subdivides into texts intended variously for teachers, students and parents—and although Scripture plays an important role in the programme's design, the series nowhere makes pretence of introducing a *new* biblical hermeneutic into the catechetical arena. Pedagogical concerns predominate. Since *Viens vers le Père* exhibits no overt interest in hermeneutical theory, its method of interpreting the Bible must be reconstructed from its use of biblical excerpts which figure prominently in each of the programme's weekly themes.

Despite these obstacles, several factors augur well for our proposed metacritique. Biblical excerpts and often whole narrative passages occupy a central role in each theme of the series. The deployment of these passages leaves behind clues of the redactors' interpretation and allows a reconstruction of key hermeneutical presuppositions, even if these presuppositions were never articulated by the catechism's authors. An examination of the redactional process itself helps reduce the complexity of the task, as one finds there evidence of both cohesiveness and unity. First, strong leadership within each of the teams offered a focus of unity and clear methodological reference points. Second, a consistent, pedagogical approach and a single concept of revelation informs the entire project. Third, the elementary writing team expressly intended its efforts to be a continuation of the methodology and inspiration begun in the first three years, i.e., *Initiation chrétienne.*[1]

At this point, a summary of those observations offered earlier regarding the programme's approach to Scripture may prove helpful. Typically, the biblical witness is harmonized with Catholic doctrine, especially the Creeds. In many instances, no clear line of demarcation separating doctrine and Scripture is discernible. For Grades One, Two and Three of the series, biblical excerpts are kept brief, as passages were selected for their appeal to the senses and for their ability to foster the nascent spirituality of its young learners. The use of biblical narratives, restrained for pedagogical reasons in the primary years, becomes more frequent throughout the elementary grades. When they are employed, narratives (in the same way as shorter biblical excerpts) aim at the elucidation of a point of doctrine, usually an important tenet of Christian faith. The approach to doctrine itself is also intended to nuture the spirituality of the child. Because *Nous avons vu le Seigneur* (*We Have seen the Lord*, Grade 4) introduces children to the New Testament as the primordial expression of the Word of God, and because it renders explicit key understandings of the nature, formation and transmission of the New Testament, it will hold particular interest for the question of biblical interpretation in this series.

Following the theological insights garnered in Chapter 4, it is our contention that certain key theological pre-understandings condition biblical interpretation in important ways. Christology—in particular the interplay of protology, eschatology and Christ-in-history—plays a specific, crucial role in shaping one's concept of revelation and thereby one's notion of biblical interpretation. The idea that human beings, because they live within traditions of interpretation which have shaped their personalities and intellects, never approach texts without some pre-understandings, came to prominence in the phenomenology of Martin Heidegger and was more fully developed in the work of H.G.

---

[1]. A consensus emerged around these points in the interviews I conducted with members of the writing teams. With respect to the title, the first three years of the programme were identified collectively as *Initiation chrétienne*, until the project gained national scope and changed its name to *Catéchisme canadien.*

Gadamer.[2] As the question of the effect of theological prejudices on biblical interpretation fits the category of "reading in a tradition," we will begin with a few words about the quest for an *objective* interpretation of texts in the field of biblical criticism. In the wake of this discussion, we will attempt to situate the hermeneutical options of the *Viens vers le Père* series in the context of biblical hermeneutics today. The goal of this chapter will be to adumbrate the principal features of the hermeneutical strategy of the *Viens vers le Père* series by comparing and contrasting it to three basic approaches to the interpretation of the Bible today. In presenting these three approaches, we have chosen one or two scholars whose work is representative of each emphasis. Our goal is to provide a backdrop for a description of the hermeneutical approach of this series.

THE IDEA OF REVELATION IN VVLP

The interest of the present study lies in the reception of the Bible and biblical scholarship in a popular, ecclesial setting which, unlike academia, has no interest in concealing its theological assumptions and purpose. Quite to the contrary, the raison d'être of catechesis is the dissemination of an *interested* interpretation of the Bible and Tradition. Within this context, as in the context of Systematic Theology, a Christian interpretation of the Bible hinges on one's understanding of the relationship of Christ to history. Most christologies imply theological anthropologies, and one's anthropology conditions one's view of the relatedness of sacred literature to secular experience.

The methodology of the *Viens vers le Père* series, which may be described theologically or pedagogically, demonstrates a sophisticated understanding of the psychological development of the child. While it was not the sole intent of its authors, the "system" implied by this catechism has as its chief end, the clarification of the Church's doctrinal heritage. The elucidation of the lives of the children taught remains, at best, secondary. With respect to the existential or "anthropological" orientation of this programme, the experience of the child is not plumbed for its own sake, but always with the intention of finding analogies capable of illuminating the doctrinal object in view.

---

[2]. Hans Georg Gadamer, from *Truth and Method*: "The Elevation of the Historicality of Understanding to the Status of Hermeneutical Principle," *CTSN*, 842.

In contrast to this method, the rescuing theology of Karl Rahner sought precisely to recover from Tradition those elements capable of imbuing the lives of his contemporaries with meaning.[3] This represents a reversal of earlier theological approaches in that it shifts the focus of interest away from philosophical and theological clarifications of dogma, and towards an existentialist-theological clarification of experience.

The extrinsicist notion of revelation in Joseph Colomb—a view shared by the great majority of Catholic theologians prior to de Lubac and Rahner—is reflected in this programme's understanding of the relationship of human experience and divine message. The synthesis in Rahner of the protological, eschatological and historical roles of the Christ, leads to the view that all of human history has always been under the offer of grace. In the anthropology which results, grace is understood to accompany fallen humanity on its journey through history in an *immanent* way. The divine message, far from being extrinsic to the human situation it addresses, emerges as the expression of an implicit reality, a reality perhaps unconscious or only vaguely fathomed by the person prior to coming to faith, but nevertheless already present. The presence of grace remains ambiguous in humanity, as men and women waver in their fallen state, between co-operation and resistance with the work of the divine within them.

This understanding of Christology, with the theological anthropology it implies, opens a wide path for an approach to the interpretation

---

[3]. The correlation method of Paul Tillich, similar to the transcendental anthropology of Rahner, seeks to analyze and understand the human situation, for its own sake. Tillich's goal was to use the analysis of the situation offered by the various scientific and humanistic disciplines to fashion a specific response from the Gospel to that particular alienation which is the angst of 20th century humanity. Like Rahner, he wished to reformulate the Christian message in order to allow people of today to come to an understanding of it in the context of their own lives. For a comparison of the methods of Tillich and Rahner see Gilles Langevin, "Méthode de corrélation et anthropologie transcendentale—Paul Tillich et Karl Rahner," *Religion et Culture*, ed. M. Despland, J.C. Petit & J. Richard (Québec: Les Presses de l'Université Laval, 1987), 605-616.

of the NT which does not exclude the concrete, historical circumstances of the reader as a constitutive element in the hermeneutic process. If one accepts a link between the creative and salvific roles of Christ, then the immanent witness of God in the consciousness of all human persons may be affirmed.[4] In Rahner's system, the relationship of the life of the secular person *before* confessing faith, to the life of the believer *after* that confession, has the possibility of being one of continuity. In other words, the unevangelized person who implicitly guides his/her life by Gospel values (for example: selflessness in service to others, readiness to forgive, love of fellow person, trust in an Absolute Good etc.,) already implicitly possesses that primordial interior revelation of God of which Rahner spoke. What has become known in time, through the life, death and resurrection of Jesus Christ was the will of the Father "in the beginning" and at every point in history. Christians, those privileged to hear and respond to the Gospel, arrive at a conscious appreciation of the offer of salvation which God makes to every person—regardless of their historical circumstances. In this view, the light of revelation subsists not only in the consciousness and interior life of individuals, but also manifests itself in other religious systems which seek to bring the divine to expression; albeit, from the Christian point of view, an imperfect expression. Rahner provides the ground for a sincere respect for the plurality represented in the great religions of the world as well as for the plurality of the gamut of humanizing choices exercized by individuals in all contexts.

Theologically-interested approaches to biblical interpretation offer indicators as to whether the notions of revelation which underpin them may be understood as "extrinsic" or "immanent" in character.[5] If secular human experience is fundamentally dissimilar to the message which the Bible brings in Jesus Christ, if grace is an entirely new reality, extrinsic to the sinner's experience, then one will not find in ex-

---

[4]. In the view of Rahner and other Catholic theologians, the consequences of the Fall do not imply that grace was rendered of no effect. Supported by the biblical witness for a natural theology (esp. Romans 1 and 2), these theologians hold that grace and sin coexist within human persons.

[5]. One may also use the choice of pedagogical options in catechesis as another indicator of the underlying concept of revelation.

perience, symbols of the Gospel's content. By symbol[6], I wish to refer to more than simply the value of a sign, wherein one reality points to another. Symbol has also the quality of participating in the reality it signifies, of making it present, of being imbued with its power. For Rahner, secular human experience is pregnant with the possibilities of symbolizing the divine, of being an implicit communication of the divine. For the extrinsicist position, secular human reality may at best be a sign of the divine, a source of analogies for the divine, but may never symbolize that sublime reality, which completely eclipses and surpasses the fallen human state.

In brief, the *Viens vers le Père* series adopts an extrinsicist view of revelation which leads it to limit the role of human experience in its pedagogical, theological and hermeneutic methods. Human experience can do no more than provide a source of analogies for the clarification of its doctrinal goals. This instrumental use of human experience sets this programme apart from thoroughly anthropological or existentialist theological paradigms. It remains to be seen, where in the range of available hermeneutical options of the Bible, one may locate the hermeneutical options of this catechetical series. It is to this task that we now turn our attention.

THREE HERMENEUTICAL APPROACHES

Three centres of interest have frequently attracted the attention of scholars who reflect on the problem of interpretation. These hermeneutical *axes* constitute three loci of meaning, all of which elude attempts to neatly define them. No credible theory of interpretation may completely disregard any one of the three. In broad terms, we may speak of meaning as determined principally either in (1) the context in which the text was produced, (2) the context in which the text is interpreted or (3) the context of the text *in ipso*, bereft of its historical moorings.

The degree of complexity involved with all three options is not

---

[6]. The term *symbol* is used in this context as an heuristic device and the qualifications offered here do not represent our position in the context of current hermeneutical debates.

immediately evident. It seems as though one need only propose and defend the author or reader or text as the *primary* home of meaning. But which author, which reader and which text, since the notion of what constitutes each is determined within a given model of interpretation? For instance, is the critic referring to the Implied Reader, the Informed Reader, the Narratee, the Model Reader, the Reader-in-the-text, the Flesh-and-blood Reader, the Competent Reader, the Literent, the Encoded or Inscribed Reader, the Subjective Reader, the Newreaders, or the wilful Misreader?[7] The *author function* of a text generates complexity comparable to that of the reader function, with scholarly reflection on the subject stretching at least from St. Jerome's *De Viris Illustribus* to Michel Foucault's *What is an Author?*[8] As for the text *in ipso*, does one refer to the deep structures and architecture of the writing (Greimas), to the possible world conjured in front of the text (Ricoeur), to the rhetorical direction of the reading process which the text effects (Fowler), to the stylistics and structures at the "surface" of the text (Fokkelman, Ska), to the text in the context of the canon (Childs), or to the text as an example of a genre, and so forth.

H.G. Gadamer adds further involution to the subject, insisting that readers belong to communities of interpretation which shape their reading. Many interpreters proceed with their task, unaware of the way in which their hermeneutic strategies are inscribed in a tradition of interpretation much larger than their own thought. Because the assumptions within which they work prove so all-enveloping, these assumptions often remain subliminal. Today, the challenge of philosophical hermeneutics to the regional hermeneutics of the Bible has awakened a new consciousness of the role of the subjective in the process of interpretation. This new consciousness remains, however, far from ubiquitous.

Many exegetes continue to work within what Gadamer has called the Enlightenment's *prejudice against prejudice*, subscribing uncritically to the notion that interpretations should be as completely objective as human capacities allow. Hayden White has observed that it is most difficult to be at once both "practitioner" and "critic" of a disci-

---

[7]. Stephen D. Moore, "Stories of Reading: Doing Gospel Criticism As/With a 'Reader'," *SBL 1988 Seminar Papers*, ed. Kent Harold Richards (Atlanta: Scholars Press, 1988), 141. Moore provides this list drawn from an extensive bibliography on reader-oriented criticism.

[8]. Michel Foucault, "What is an author?" *CTSN*, 143.

pline in which one is engaged.[9] Exegetes are not alone in this—historians and academics of all stripes encounter the same difficulty. In other words, most scientists and historians are far too engaged in the application of received research methods—methods whose validity and reliability were established prior to their entry into the field—to be able to critically analyze those methods.

Similar discussions take place in NT studies which involve the author-function of texts. Were the evangelists no more than compilers of traditional material over which they had little control—a position recently defended by George Johnston[10]—or, were they deliberate authors who very carefully shaped a theological view of Jesus, giving it their personal stamp[11]? Or, is a middle position possible, wherein the evangelist (Mark) shapes our experience of the traditional material by carefully controlling the conditions under which we receive it, as Robert Fowler contends?[12] The question of the degree to which NT writers were affected by tradition remains one of considerable interest.

Having scratched the surface of one area of discussion in NT hermeneutics, we move now to a description of the three major hermeneutical options, attempting to evaluate the *Viens vers le Père* series in the light of each. Our strategy here consists in introducing one or two proponents of each basic orientation, providing a specific example of the approach at work. In this way we hope to avoid vague generalities.

VVLP AND "MEANING BEHIND THE TEXT"

Few are the exegetes who dismiss the contribution which histori-

---

[9]. Hayden White, "The Historical Text as Literary Artifact," *CTSN*, 395. One sees a similar dilemma explored in the work of Thomas Kuhn. See Kuhn's "Objectivity, Value Judgment, and Theory Choice," *CTSN*, 381-393.

[10]. George Johnston, "Should the synoptic evangelists be considered as theologians?" *Studies in Religion/Sciences Religieuses* 21 (1992): 181.

[11]. See Johnston, 184, (note 12) for a bibliography of authors dealing with Mark as theologian. The list includes works by E. Best, R. Pesch, M.D. Hooker and J. Schreiber.

[12]. The middle ground which Fowler marks off in his book, *Loaves and Fishes*, provides a compelling argument in this regard.

cal-critical research has made to NT interpretation.[13] Historical critics, still in the majority, understand the constraining meaning of the text as closely bound up with the author's original intent and with the original situation. Scholars of this school practice a recognitive hermeneutics. In recognitive hermeneutics, the reader attempts to sympathetically reconstruct in him/herself, the thoughts of the author. The reader imaginatively reproduces the probable mental processes which led to the production of the text. The first task of the exegete is to imaginatively reproduce the author's mental processes, his attitudes and cultural givens, in short, his world.[14] Biblical exegetes are not alone in their defence of this position. E.D. Hirsch has ably defended this direction in interpretation theory for the past quarter century. For Hirsch, "interpretation is the construction of *another's* meaning...It is natural to speak not of what a text says, but of what an author means, and this more natural locution is the more accurate one."[15] Gone is the sense that one's interpretation may be verified, in a manner analogous to the natural sciences. Hirsch proffers this nuanced position:

> Of course, the reader must realize verbal meaning by his own subjective acts (no one can do that for him), but if he remembers that his job is to construe the author's meaning, he will attempt to exclude his own predispositions and to impose those of the author. However, no one can establish another's meaning with certainty. The interpreter's goal is simply this—to show that a given reading is more probable than others. In hermeneutics, verification is a process of establishing relative possibilities.[16]

But how does one go about reconstructing an author's intention (i.e., the intentions of a *probable* author) in such a way as to explain all the linguistic elements of the text, in a manner appropriate for the genre in question, within an interpretation that is coherent? Hirsch explains that the criterion of coherence can only be evoked with refer-

---

[13]. See, however, Gerhard Maier, *The End of the Historical-Critical Method* (St. Louis: Concordia, 1977) and W. Wink, *The Bible in Human Transformation* (Philadelphia: Fortress, 1977). For a more balanced critique see P. Stuhlmacher, *Historical Criticism and Theological Interpretation of Scripture* (London: SPCK, 1979).

[14]. E.D. Hirsch, *Validity In Interpretation* (New Haven: Yale University Press, 1967), 242.

[15]. Hirsch, 244.

[16]. Hirsch, 236.

ence to a particular context. But no context can be inferred without positing a probable horizon for the author, one which is likely to explain his disposition to a particular type of meaning.

> When the interpreter posits the author's stance he sympathetically reenacts the author's intentional acts, but although this imaginative act is necessary for realizing meaning, it must be distinguished from meaning as such. In no sense does the text represent the author's subjective stance: the interpreter simply adopts a stance in order to make sense of the text, and if he is self-critical, he tries to verify his interpretation by showing his adopted stance to be, in all probability, the author's.[17]

Hirsch shows no interest in assigning a truth of correspondence to the historical critic's reconstruction, i.e., he is not concerned to establish the postulates of a critical reconstruction as facts. A text, once it has been produced, possesses a meaning not strictly limited to the author's intent. Textual meaning is constrained, in the first instance, by the general rules of the linguistic system in which it is elaborated and, more specifically, by the norms established for the particular class of utterances (genre) to which it belongs.[18] In some cases the author may have missed his mark and expressed his ideas poorly; the written text remains the final arbiter of meaning, regardless of the original, irretrievable intent of the author. Ultimately, the reference of the text cannot be to the meaning of the flesh-and-blood author who is inaccessible to the reader but must content itself with the sense of the text as construed from its historical, social, literary and linguistic contexts. But for any reconstruction to be possible, the interpreter must imaginatively recreate a plausible author and his/her horizon:

> Even with anonymous texts it is crucial to posit not simply some author or other, but a particular subjective stance in reference to which the construed context is rendered probable. That is why it is important to date anonymous texts. The interpreter needs all the clues he can muster with regard not only to the text's *langue* and genre, but also to

---

[17]. Hirsch, 237.
[18]. Hirsch relies on Saussure's distinction between *langue* and *parole*, which relate as *possible* and *actual* uses of language. He refers also to the work of Wittgenstein. See Hirsch 68-71.

the cultural and personal attitudes the author might be expected to bring to bear in specifying his verbal meanings. In this sense, all texts, including anonymous ones, are "attributed."[19]

Hirsch posits a possible, or to be more precise, a probable author as a key heuristic strategy. On Hirsch's view, without an historical context for that probable author, meaning cannot be plausibly reconstructed.

Hirsch's position, developed in the realm of secular literature, sidesteps a major concern of many biblical exegetes. For most historical critics of the Bible, it has not been enough to demonstrate that the Bible makes sense, i.e., that the narrative world it creates is plausible. They are also interested to establish its truth with reference to extra-textual, historical reality. An analogy inspired by Gottlob Frege's distinction between meaning as sense (*Sinn*) and meaning as reference (*Bedeutung*), may help clarify this distinction.[20]

Within the canon of Western literature and consequently within occidental culture at large, the unicorn may be an entirely plausible entity, i.e., a fabulous, horse-like animal with a single horn—reputed to possess magical and medicinal properties—in the middle of its forehead. Intratextually, the unicorn makes sense and has a meaning, but one should not too quickly mount an expedition to find its fossil. The unicorn, it is generally admitted, is a creature which has no reference of the four-legged, flesh-and-blood variety in historical, extra-textual, extra-linguistic reality. Texts therefore, may produce coherent meanings and yet not be true.[21] Historical critics of the Bible are wont to insist on the truth value of texts. They understand these texts as referring to an extra-linguistic world, the world "behind the text."

Among the practitioners of biblical criticism, eloquent defenders of historical research methods are not lacking. James Barr in an essay

---

[19]. Hirsch, 240.

[20]. See Gottlob Frege, *The Philosophical Writings of Gottlob Frege*, trans. Max Black, Peter Geach (Oxford; Oxford University Press, 1952), 56-78.

[21]. We might offer Rudolph Bultmann's position as an example of an author who adopts a two-fold attitude to the literature of the NT. On the one hand, Bultmann considered the Synoptics to possess a significant, historical reference while on the other, treated the Johannine and Pauline corpuses apart from this concern. Bultmann seeks the sense of these latter, without pressing the question of historical reference.

entitled "The Spiritual and Intellectual Basis of Modern Biblical Research" peppers opponents of this approach with a barrage of lucid arguments in its defence, while demonstrating great openness to other research models.[22] Barr begins his reflexions with the observation that the historical nature of biblical research is tied up with the nature of Christianity, which is to "an unusual degree a historical religion."[23] He situates the rise of biblical criticism, historical and otherwise, within that struggle for intellectual and spiritual freedom which was at the core of the Enlightenment and the Reformation.[24] The values of these movements, maintains Barr, reached a high point in the American Revolution and in particular in the Declaration of Independence.[25]

> In sectarian Christianity there was a quite exclusive emphasis on the Bible: confessions, creeds, ministries, Church authorities and the like were regarded as largely or purely human quantities, while the Bible came from God. In such groups the struggle for political freedom was also a struggle for freedom to interpret the Bible in ways that differed from those authorized by the prevailing establishment. The question of religious tolerance on the social level corresponded with the question of exegetical freedom in the understanding of the Bible.[26]

The objectivity which biblical studies seeks has been defined not in relation to the natural sciences, but in relation to state and ecclesial authority. On Barr's view, "Critical biblical scholarship *is* objective in the sense that its results are not predetermined by a given authoritative ideology."[27]

Like Hirsch, Barr understands the reconstructive work of the exegete as existing in the realm of the *probable* and not that of the *certain*.[28] He further stipulates:

---

[22]. James Barr, *Holy Scripture: Canon, Authority, Criticism* (Philadelphia: Westminster, 1983), 105-126.
[23]. James Barr, 106.
[24]. James Barr, 34.
[25]. James Barr, 33, 124-125.
[26]. James Barr, 33.
[27]. James Barr, 114.
[28]. James Barr, 107.

...biblical criticism never belonged other than to the humanities in its methods and inspiration. Only late in the development of biblical criticism, and probably only in the United States with its high evaluation of scientific objectivity, was the model of the sciences much used as the image of biblical scholarship. The motivation behind biblical scholarship derived overwhelmingly from theology and from the conviction of the authority of scripture.[29]

Barr even allows for the concept of a 'creative prejudice' (of the theological variety) in the realm of biblical criticism.[30] Despite his insistence on the need for freedom as foundational in biblical research, he remarks that "biblical criticism and traditional doctrine have succeeded in living remarkably well together," and that research need not necessarily be critical in order to be productive of valuable insights.[31] In the end, the exigencies of research, and not those of Church doctrine, remain the yardstick against which the results of biblical criticism are to be measured.

Firmly ensconced in the tradition of F.C. Bauer, Wm. Wrede et al., Barr rejects canonical criticism as an unnecessary restriction on the scope of research. He also argues that sectarian concerns of another sort may have led to biblical criticism's sore neglect of the *Nachgeschichte* and *Wirkungsgeschichte* of the biblical texts.[32]

In summary, the research model of historical criticism which Barr offers, intends to provide the scholar with freedom by creating a critical distance between the exegete's object of study and doctrinal pre-interpretations of Scripture. The best way to achieve this distance is to understand the text in its original setting, a setting free of contemporary prejudices. His theory, however, engages no polemic with doctrinal concerns. Having read Barr, one is left with the impression that he perceives the fruits of free research as one of the few sources of constructive critique of doctrine in contemporary Church settings.[33] He argues throughout that the variety of approaches are complementary in the attainment of a critical appreciation of the text.

Obviously, much more could be said of the historical-critical ap-

---

[29]. James Barr, 112.
[30]. James Barr, 113.
[31]. James Barr, 108.
[32]. James Barr, 114-115.
[33]. On this point, Barr's position resembles that of Walter Kasper as set out in Chapter 4 above.

proach today. We have tried to sketch some key understandings through the work of two of its noted theorists. The question must now be put: To what extent may the hermeneutical approach of the *Viens vers le Père* series be understood to be inspired by the historical-critical method? On the basis of our observations in Chapter 3, we may conclude that the writers of this catechetical series were generally aware of the scope and value of the findings of historical-critical research. The reader will remember that the entirety of the programme was submitted to a scholar in order to insure that its proposals in no way contradicted the surer findings of historical work. The reader will also remember that the creedal structure of the primary years gave way to a more christocentric catechesis in Grades 4, 5 and 6. In particular, Grade 4 concentrates on the historical manifestation of Jesus in Palestine. As one might imagine, the theme of Grade 4 lends itself particularly well to an incorporation of the conclusions and speculations of historical-critical research. It is equally clear that no other grade level of the programme concerns itself *directly* with the data provided by this critical approach. Elsewhere in the series, one might say that the positive results of historical research provided the series with its hermeneutical point of departure, but did not form the basis of its hermeneutical strategy.

The first two weeks of *Nous avons vu le Seigneur* sets the broad goal of leading the children through a process similar, in significant ways, to the one which (many believe) produced the Gospels. The aim was that students should understand that the Good News, which the Church hands on today, began in the preaching of the apostles (oral tradition) and was only subsequently fixed in written form (the 4 gospel narratives).[34] To achieve this end, activity-based learning strategies were designed to reveal the importance which *point of view* can make to a story-teller's reconstruction of an event. The Gospels are presented as the narration of historical events, interpreted from different points of view. The question of whether or not the evangelists were

---

[34]. Collaboration: OCQ—NORE, *Nous avons vu le Seigneur, Guide du maître*, 46.

eye-witnesses to the events is never raised. De facto, students begin to appreciate that different points of view may result in contrasting accounts of the same person or event.

Throughout Grade 4, one finds a constant reference to historical details from first-century Palestine: the topography and climactic conditions; the spiritual atmosphere of Jewery under Roman oppression; the distinction among different sects of Jews; details about typical daily life with illustrations of the style of dress and so forth. The colour photographs, which dot the student text, are exclusively drawn from modern day Israel and show the traditional sites associated with Jesus' life, death and burial, as well as scenes of the typical daily life and dress of its Semitic inhabitants.

At times, historical information does serve to clarify the meaning of individual texts in Grade 4. We find an example of this in Theme 3 which deals with Matthew 9:9-14 (the call of Matthew, the tax collector, and the Pharisees' criticism of Jesus who ate with sinners). The teacher explains the position of the Pharisees to the children:

> What were the Pharisees' hearts like? Their hearts seemed closed. The Pharisees were Jews who formed a group apart. They had a great desire to be perfect, and they wanted to practice the law of God exactly. They said many prayers, gave alms to the poor and often fasted. Because they were so faithful, they were inclined to despise those who were not like themselves.[35]

We submit that the reasons for the inclusion of historical detail in *Nous avons vu le Seigneur* (which is the only grade to include any significant amount of historical detail about the Scriptures) are two-fold. The first and most important reason is to be found at the religious level; Grade 4 wants to create a sense of contemporaneity with Jesus (in the manner of Kierkegaard) in order to provoke an "encounter" with the Lord. This is in keeping with the series' ultimate goal of establishing a relationship with the Trinity. On the pedagogical level, the satisfaction of the 9-10 year old's fascination with concrete facts and gestures also favours the inclusion of historical detail. Insights derived from the historical background of the NT are few in number, while the spiritual import garnered from scriptural messages stands central.

Of course, it may not be reasonable to think that a catechetical pro-

---

[35]. *We Have Seen the Lord, Teacher's Manual*, 131.

gramme could adapt its pedagogy closely to the requirements of the historical-critical method. The latter suspends the very belief the former wishes to promote. If Barr's contention that the élan of the historical-critical spirit may be traced to the *enlightened* desire for freedom and critical distance from doctrinally-interested readings is correct, no catechesis could operate if such premises were foundational to its method.

A further difficulty in the use of a strategy of interpretation such as this lies in the degree of intellectual sophistication it assumes of its neophytes. The ability to deal credibly with historical criticism's suppositions far outstrips the intellectual capacities of young children and in most cases even that of adolescents. While the products of historical criticism may reasonably be incorporated into a religious education programme, it is difficult to see how the method itself might be adapted for such use.

Our observations of the use of the Bible in *Viens vers le Père* lead us to conclude that this series understands the meaning of the scriptural passages it cites to be perspicuous. The passages selected by the authors of the series have a clear and unequivocal meaning from which doctrine may be formulated. In as much as the authors of this programme seem to hold that the texts of the NT ordinarily have one meaning, which is clear, they accept one of the most basic tenets of historical criticism as it has been practised by generations of scholars.

It seems reasonable then, to describe the relationship of the hermeneutical strategy of the *Viens vers le Père* series to the historical-critical approach as ambivalent. This catechism respects the findings of historical criticism but rarely makes reference to them in the clarification of a text. While the series' use of the Bible does betray methodological traits one normally associates with the work of historical critics, it clearly does not bracket the question of faith in its biblical interpretation (as does historical criticism). We submit that, on balance, the incorporation of historical detail in this series has more to do with spiritual aims and youthful curiosity (i.e., with pedagogical exigencies) than with its hermeneutical strategy.

VVLP AND MEANING "IN FRONT OF THE TEXT"

The "turn towards the subject," that sea change in Western intellectual life, brought with it challenges to the hermeneutics of recovery. Prominent among the dissenters to recognitive hermeneutics were Freud, Marx, Nietzsche and Feuerbach, the masters of what Paul Ricoeur has dubbed the *school of suspicion*. Each of these authors, in his own way, has been carried by the concern to unmask, demystify and reduce illusions in the process of interpretation and for this reason we may refer to their strategy as a hermeneutics of reduction.[36] The school of suspicion exposed and challenged implicit, ideological assumptions underpinning the hermeneutics of recovery.

One of the first casualties of this offensive was the notion that the human subject forms a coherent, unified and stable whole. This assumption has been applied to the personalities of both author and reader. Texts, as extensions of the stable human consciousness of their authors, are perceived as repositories of stable meanings inscribed in language. The task of readers, interpreters and exegetes is to *de-scribe* a meaning originally *in-scribed* in the text by the author. The process of deriving meaning is understood as one of *extraction* and the observer must remain vigilant to exclude any subjective influences which might obscure the object in view.

David Tracy discusses the assumptions Westerners have about the notion of the *self* and offers an example of how these assumptions affect textual interpretation.

> ...every Westerner is initially startled when attempting to interpret the seeming dissolution of the self in classic Buddhist texts. The belief in individuality among Westerners is not limited to substance notions of the self. Even radical critiques of the notion of the 'self as substance' in the West live by means of the history of the effects of Jewish and Christian senses of the responsible self in the presence of the radically monotheistic God; the Greek and Roman senses of the ethical, political, the contemplative and active self; and all the other reformulations of the importance of a self from Burckhardt's Renaissance individual through Kierkegaard's or Nietzsche's radical individual to modern suspicions of traditional understandings of the self-as-individual. The history of the effects of the Jewish, Greek, Roman, Medieval, Renaissance, Reformation, and modern senses of the reality and importance of a 'self' mean that some such effect is likely to be present in the

---

[36]. René Marlé, *Herméneutique*, 77.

preunderstanding of any Western thinker....When attempting to interpret a classic Buddhist text, therefore, we are startled not only by the questions and responses of the meaning of self in these texts. We are startled as well into a recognition of how deeply any language, any tradition, and, therefore, any preunderstanding is affected by this Western insistence on the importance of the individual self.[37]

The challenge which recent hermeneutical theory mounts against the notion of a stable, coherent consciousness (and therefore against stable meanings deposited in texts) finds its origins in a variety of disciplines, all of which have come to conceive the human condition as fragmented.

Jacques Derrida's famous essay, *Différance*, mounts a challenge to western metaphysics as it critiques philosophy's method for deriving meaning. Derrida holds that, by ignoring or flattening the divisiveness, gaps and inconsistencies in language, interpreters have constructed the illusion of an authorial consciousness that is coherent and unified.[38] Working within the field of linguistic philosophy and responding to the work of structuralists, this deconstructionist takes inspiration from Freud's reflections on the unconscious in order to dispute some of the fundamental assumptions which have informed hermeneutical practice. If, before *Différance* one's image of consciousness resembled a coherent and vital body, after Derrida's play on language has worked its effect, that body has slipped into unconsciousness and lies riddled with enigmatic holes.

Michel Foucault in an essay entitled, *What is an author?*, also challenges the notion that one can refer to a flesh-and-blood figure as the ultimate reference for textual meaning. Foucault maintains that once a text has been written, it stands alienated from its author and as such, the latter's intentions can be of no importance for textual interpretation.[39] He notes that in the act of writing, the writing subject endlessly disappears. The text annihilates its author; and this obliteration is voluntary on the author's part.[40] In suggesting a connection

---

[37]. Tracy (Grant), *A Short History of the Interpretation of the Bible*, 157.
[38]. Jacques Derrida, "Différance," *CTSN*, 120-136.
[39]. Foucault, 139.
[40]. Foucault, 139-140.

between writing and death, Foucault characterizes the goal of all writing as an attempt at objectification of its contents. In writing one wishes to remove the subjective element of one's thoughts and offer them for contemplation and acceptance by others. Once the text has been written, the author is free to move on to new ideas and produce new texts, some of which may even repudiate earlier work. For this reason, Foucault chooses to speak about the "author function" of a text rather than about the author as such.[41] Defined by the textual evidence, a single figure in history, subject to intellectual growth and conversion to new ways of thinking, may give rise to a series of "different" authors. This allows one to speak, for example, of the *Sturm und Drang* Goethe, the romantic Goethe and the neo-classical Goethe. Similarly, one speaks of the early and later Heidegger. For Foucault, the historical personality behind such writings—subject to change and evolution in thought—can no longer supply the illusion of coherence and unity among the variety of disparate literary monuments which bear his/her name. The evidence of the self-divisiveness in authorial function demonstrates the dynamic historicality of the human subject. Many philosophers contend that what Foucault asserts of the authorial function of texts, holds for the discussion of all human subjects. As we shall see, the idea that the human subject comes into being and develops in language, occupies an important space in recent discussions in the philosophy of hermeneutics.

One might fruitfully pursue either Derrida or Foucault in search of a critique of *ontos*, as post-Enlightenment metaphysics has described it. Both stand in that line of trumpeters whose blasts have, in the view of many, already brought the walls of objectivist ontology tumbling down. Rather than launch his attack from the parapets of Derrida's linguistic philosophy or Foucault's panopticon, another critic adopts a strategy of subversion from within the field of metaphysics itself. Paul Ricoeur also draws inspiration from Freud, also insists on the importance of the alienation of the text from its author for hermeneutical practice and also understands the subject as coming to existence in language.[42] René Marlé qualifies Ricoeur's method as a dialectic be-

---

[41]. Foucault, 141-144.
[42]. Other than Ricoeur, we could have introduced the work of Edgar V. McKnight, another eminent scholar in the field of biblical hermeneutics who reflects on meaning "in front of the text." As this would have likely been excessive in this context, we limit our discussion to Ricoeur. McKnight has

tween faith and suspicion.[43] Ricoeur began his career following the recognitive path, but under the influence of the idea that consciousness is radically false and misleading, shifted to a hermeneutics of suspicion. His hermeneutics of suspicion was not intended to destroy faith, but rather to become its dialectical partner. It is in this dialectic of faith and suspicion that Ricoeur sees the emergence of the art of interpretation. His reduction of illusions gives way to the re-establishment, of a new reign of meaning and a new post-critical faith. Ricoeur summarizes the connections in this way:

> Le contraire du soupçon..., c'est la foi...Non plus sans doute la foi première du charbonnier, mais la foi seconde de l'hermeneute, la foi qui a traversé la critique, la foi post-critique...C'est une foi raisonnable puisqu'elle interprète, mais c'est une foi parce qu'elle cherche, par l'interpretation une seconde naïveté...Croire pour comprendre, comprendre pour croire, telle est sa maxime; et sa maxime, c'est le "cercle herméneutique" lui-même du croire et du comprendre...Le souci de l'objet, ce fut pour nous la docilité au mouvement du sens qui, partant de la signification littérale...pointe vers la saisie de quelquechose dans la région du sacré.[44]

One of the key consequences of Ricoeur's turn to the hermeneutics of suspicion has been his critique of ontology. We turn now to that critique.

The Idea of the Subject in Ricoeur

In his essay, "On Interpretation," Ricoeur critiques the phenomenology of Husserl, tracing the roots of Husserl's notion of *Being* to Descartes and Kant.[45] Building on Descartes' *dubito ergo sum*, Husserl judged that the consciousness the self has of itself stands su-

---

authored books dealing with literary criticism, focusing especially on reader-oriented and narrative criticism. Three of his key works appear in the bibliography at the end of this work.

[43]. Marlé, *Herméneutique*, 79-80.

[44]. Paul Ricoeur, *De l'interprétation* (Paris: Editions du Seuil, 1965), 36-37.

[45]. Paul Ricoeur, *From Text to Action*, trans. K. Blamey and J.B. Thompson (Evanston, Illinois: Northwestern University Press, 1991), 1-23.

perior to all forms of positive knowledge.[46] Nothing could be known about the material world outside human consciousness with the same certainty with which Being knows itself to exist. In other words, self-consciousness, self-immanence provides the only example of indubitable knowledge. All other reality becomes reduced to phenomena present to human consciousness. The world outside the mind ceases to have importance, and meaning is established, not with reference to that outside world, but rather within the web of relationships established among the phenomena present to the conscious subject.[47] Questions concerning things-in-themselves are excluded and the concept of establishing statements as facts, that is, as having a truth of correspondence to the material world outside consciousness, is abandoned. Husserl's system might be described as intending meaning but not truth. In this philosophical system, the human subject, removed from the vagaries of history, is the solid foundation upon which all meaning is built.

Ricoeur's hermeneutical theory opens up a dialogue with two partners: the linguistic sciences and the hermeneutic tradition of Schleiermacher, Dilthey, Heidegger and Gadamer.[48] Insisting that one of the primary characteristics of human being is that it is being-in-the-world, Heidegger rejected Husserl's bracketing of the world.[49] Husserl's separation of the human subject from the background of human existence in which natural consciousness is originally immersed, had an epistemological end in view, contended Heidegger. This bracketing is intended to create a critical distance between the human subject and the world in which it is immersed, so that the subject becomes capable of setting up objects in opposition to itself in order to judge them and to submit them to human intellectual and technical mastery.[50] Ricoeur reminds us that this setting up of the world as an

---

[46]. Ricoeur, *From Text to Action*, 13.

[47]. Frege's contrast of *Sinn* and *Bedeutung*, i.e., the distinction between truth and meaning, is already implicit in Husserl's phenomenological reduction of sense to the self-contained world of the self-conscious. Meaning, for Husserl, does not refer to the world, but to syntheses effected in the mind.

[48]. Lynn M. Poland, *Literary Criticism and Biblical Hermeneutics: A Critique of Formalist Approaches* (Chico: Scholar's Press, 1985), 163.

[49]. Ricoeur, *From Text to Action*, 14.

[50]. Ricoeur, *From Text to Action*, 15. Ricoeur uses the term *distanciation* to refer to this separation.

object to be studied is a characteristic of both common and scientific knowledge.[51]

It is this complete objectification of the material world, this separation of the human subject from it, in a way that allows the subject to evaluate and manipulate the world *from outside*, which Heidegger rejects. The understanding a human subject has of the world cannot be from outside the world, since the subject has no means of escaping the world in which it finds itself—short of death. For Heidegger, all human understanding contributes to self-understanding and comes about only in history. The *hubris* of the Enlightenment was to suppose a kind of self-possession of the human subject, without reference to history. The claim was that the self was founded on itself.[52] With Heidegger, Ricoeur rejects this possibility. Human Being finds itself immersed in the world from which it cannot consciously extract itself. Ricoeur summarizes Heidegger's position in this way:

> *Verstehen* for Heidegger has an ontological signification. It is the response of a being thrown into the world who finds his way about in it by projecting onto it his ownmost possibilities. Interpretation, in the technical sense of the interpretation of texts, is but the development, the making explicit of this ontological understanding, an understanding always separable from a being that has initially been thrown into the world. The subject-object relation—on which Husserl continues to depend—is thus subordinated to the testimony of an ontological link more basic than any relation of knowledge.[53]

Ricoeur, like Heidegger, understands language to be a projection of human possibilities onto the world. Because we are in the world, we have *the world* to speak about, and Ricoeur insists (contra Derrida) that language is fundamentally referential; it intends to say something about the world.[54] Ricoeur's insistence on the ontological foundation of language, not only undercuts the position of the deconstructionists,

---

[51]. Ricoeur, *From Text to Action*, 15.
[52]. Ricoeur, *From Text to Action*, 15.
[53]. Ricoeur, *From Text to Action*, 14.
[54]. Poland, 169. Derrida, by contrast, understands language to refer to nothing but itself. All meaning is reduced to *sense*, and language does not refer to extra-textual reality.

but also challenges the presuppositions of structuralism. Meaning does not reside exclusively in the text, nor in the world of the reader. Methods which concentrate exclusively on either the subjective or objective poles of interpretation never establish the dialectic between explanation and understanding which Ricoeur views as essential to interpretation.

Ricoeur recognizes that it is the organizing principles of language which allow us to order our ideas of the world. Our knowledge of the world comes into being in and through the rules governing grammar and genre. Language does not discover a pre-existent order in the world but creates order by a conscious human act of projection onto the world. As Northrop Frye explains, even syntax in a sentence is the projection of a fiction onto reality; a projection which does not inhere in the reality observed but one that is imposed by the observer. Frye explains:

> In truth of correspondence a verbal structure is aligned with the phenomena it describes, but every verbal structure contains mythical and fictional features simply because it is a verbal structure. Even the subject-predicate-object relationship is a verbal fiction, and arises from the conditions of grammar, not from those of the subject being studied.[55]

On Ricoeur's view, the ontological status of the human subject, its being-in-the-world, conditions its every act of knowing. With Heidegger, Ricoeur agrees that understanding is hermeneutical; it comes about through interpretation. Human subjects are finite, historical and limited to the world into which they have been thrown. Gadamer's observation—history does not belong to us, but we belong to it—echoes Heidegger's view.[56] How then is it possible for the subject to form any objective idea of itself or the world, if it is tied to the world in this way? In Heidegger's system, an *absolutely* objective idea of either *self* or *world* is ruled out. Ricoeur endorses this view. We may form ideas of *self* or *world*, but these will be from within a consciousness immersed in the world. Any ideas we may have of the self or the world come into existence only in language. Before its expression in language, no thought exists.

Self-understanding, like all understanding, is not a given, but a

---

[55]. Northrop Frye, "from *The Critical Path,*" *CTSN*, 258.
[56]. H.G. Gadamer, from *Truth and Method*, 846.

task to be achieved by way of interpretation of our experiences *in the world.*[57] But in order to reflect on our experiences in the world, one must find some way of delineating (of bracketing) them, so as to be able to consider them. Heidegger does not disagree with Husserl that some distance needs to be created between subject and object, if any knowledge is to emerge. Rather, his disagreement with Husserl turns on the historical nature of the human subject in general and of its consciousness in particular. This discovery radically tempers claims for objectivity in epistemology. Some degree of objectivity needs to be sought. It is the objectivizing of our experiences in language, that allows us to reflect on them and opens up the possibility of understanding—understanding of both self and the world. Without language, what happens to us in the world is inaccessible to analysis.

Ricoeur rejects the notion of an intuitive self-knowledge (i.e., one that is innate in the human subject before its interaction with the world) and holds that no shortcut to self-understanding is possible:

> It is the task of hermeneutics to show that existence arrives at expression, at meaning and at reflection only through the continual exegesis of all the significations that come to light in the world of culture. Existence becomes a self—human and adult—only by appropriating this meaning, which first resides 'outside' in works, institutions, and cultural monuments in which the life of the spirit is objectified.[58]

The human subject comes at the same time into both consciousness and speech.[59] This coming-to-consciousness in language, shifts the project of self-understanding (and of all understanding) from the field of phenomenology to that of hermeneutics.

The Consequences of the New Ontology for Hermeneutics

Language allows the human subject to assume a critical distance from itself. But the human subject must learn language before it can

---

[57]. Kevin J. Vanhoozer, *Biblical Narrative in the Philosophy of Paul Ricoeur* (Cambridge: Cambridge University Press, 1990), 29.

[58]. Paul Ricoeur, *The Philosophy of Paul Ricoeur*, ed. Charles E. Reagan and David Stewart (Boston: Beacon Press, 1978), 106.

[59]. Ricoeur, *From Text to Action*, 17.

use it and so the very means by which the subject comes to consciousness has its source outside the self. The circular nature of understanding appears once it has been realized that language not only allows the human subject to externalize and objectify its experience, but the very language by means of which the subject accomplishes this act, is itself the condition of possibility of experience. In other words, language is the primary condition of all human experience (of all knowledge and thought) and language is heard before it is uttered.[60] Consciousness, the gift of self, comes from beyond the self. The coming-to-consciousness of the subject occurs in dialectical relationships with others, established in language.

For Ricoeur, the home of meaning is not consciousness, but something other than consciousness.[61] In order for understanding to take place, a de-centring of the subject must occur. Understanding is the process by which the human subject is lead outside itself in order to gain an idea of itself and the world. Ricoeur states it this way: "...there is no self-understanding that is not *mediated* by signs, symbols, and texts; in the last resort understanding coincides with the interpretation given to these mediating terms."[62]

Recognitive hermeneutics assumes a stable, coherent self, underpinning acts of knowing. The notion of self implicit in this hermeneutic programme is one which pre-exists language and history, one which stands sovereign before the world, capable of judging it. Ricoeur's hermeneutical theory, by contrast, conceives of a self in the process of becoming, through acts of interpretation and reflection; a self tied to a world from which it can manage only a limited autonomy. "To understand oneself is to understand oneself as one confronts the text and to receive from it the conditions for a self other than that which first undertakes the reading."[63] Ricoeur's idea of the self is not one constantly threatened by annihilation by the subconscious (Derrida), nor an immutable self which floats above the vicissitudes of history (Husserl). Ricoeur's self is rather a dynamic reality, which during its life-in-the-world never arrives at being (understood as stasis), but remains constantly in a process of becoming, always contingent on history. The self emerges through the process of interpretation

---

[60]. Ricoeur, *From Text to Action*, 16.
[61]. Ricoeur, *De l'interprétation*, 62.
[62]. Ricoeur, *From Text to Action*, 15.
[63]. Ricoeur, *From Text to Action*, 17.

and interaction with others through language. One of the most fruitful forms of that interaction occurs when individuals confront the valued literature of their culture, and of the world in general. Literature, reflected upon, has a transformative power in that it can challenge, complicate and extend our visions of the world and our perceptions of what it means to be human.[64] The Bible has challenged generation upon generation of readers in this way—for occidental readers, the test of time has demonstrated that it does so in a way that no other text has or is likely to do.

In light of this new ontology, what regard does Ricoeur have for objectivist, exegetical practices? In other words, what does he make of historical criticism and semiotics? Convinced of the gains for interpretation realized by a hermeneutics of suspicion, Ricoeur resists the derridean temptation to toll the death knell on objectivist models. He situates his hermeneutics of reduction in a productive dialectic with the hermeneutics of recovery. For Ricoeur, this dialectic opens up a new field in hermeneutics.[65]

Because he understands texts to be alienated from their authors, Ricoeur rejects a connection between the meaning of a text and the intentions of the composing author. He draws a sharp distinction between textual interpretation and face-to-face conversation. In face-to-face conversation, the dialoguing partners share a situation, a common ground uniting both and providing a context of interpretation replete with clues to meaning. When the speaker-hearer relationship is replaced by that of writer-reader, the meaning fixed in a text no longer enjoys, that "direct link of congeniality between the two subjectivities" characteristic of a face-to-face conversation—this link is forever lost to the author and reader of a text.[66] When the spatial and temporal distance between writer and reader replaces the shared situation of the speaker and hearer, the text may refer to something other than the world "behind the text" which gave rise to the text. Despite a distanciation from his/her work, the author does not disappear, but leaves a

---

[64]. Poland, 179.
[65]. Marlé, *Herméneutique*, 78.
[66]. Ricoeur, *From Text to Action*, 18.

trace in the structures of the text. Instead of speaking of the flesh-and-blood author, one now more properly refers to the *implied author*.

The very fact that a text is cast in a *genre* insures that its work (what it says) does not perish with the loss of its original situation; its generic qualities preserve it from distortion and make it available to be understood in new situations.[67] This appears especially true in the case of the Bible. Relying on Gerhard von Rad's understanding of the relation between the form of discourse and theological content, Ricoeur explains how biblical narratives possess a double reference. Biblical narrative possesses at once a historical *and* a kerygmatic dimension; it manifests an unshakeable solidarity between the profession of faith and the narrative.[68] A work's form and content are thus inextricably linked.[69] It is for this reason that interpreters ought to pay attention first to literary forms when reading. Only after the genre has been determined, should one move on to the question of content.

Ricoeur's programme reacts to a modern tendency to limit discussions of truth to a consideration of the claims of individual propositions.[70] Generally, a proposition's claim to truth depends on whether it corresponds to external reality or not. Before Ricoeur, discussions of the truth rarely considered literary units longer than a sentence. Textual forms such as narratives, never got considered.[71] On this view, a story cannot be evaluated as true or false, only individual statements within the story can be assigned that status. Ricoeur challenges this position, insisting that stories *do make* assertions about the world. Unlike purists in the field—who contend that the meaning of narrative does not refer beyond the narrative's textual borders—Ricoeur is a narrativist who believes that biblical narrative wishes to say something that is true about the world. Beyond philological and grammatical work, beyond the analysis of the word and the sentence, Ricoeur

---

[67]. Poland, 173.
[68]. Ricoeur, *From Text to Action*, 91.
[69]. Poland, 179.
[70]. The argument presented here follows Gary Comstock's article, "Truth or Meaning: Ricoeur versus Frei on Biblical Narrative," *The Journal of Religion* 2 (1986): 117-141. Comstock's analysis corresponds very well to Ricoeur's own account of his intellectual path in *From Text to Action*, Chapter 1.
[71]. Comstock, 123.

pushes for an analysis of the *textual level* of discourse. Ricoeur wants to examine the context in which we read words and sentences—he is especially interested in the textual form of the story or narrative. Comstock summarizes:

> Ricoeur finds it necessary to describe a level of discourse that has been ignored by modern philosophy and linguistics. This is the level of the *text*, and Ricoeur insists that we grant it a place alongside the more familiar units of *word* and *sentence* (or name and propostion)...Each new level of discourse adds a new order of reference to the previous level. A name can denominate, but it takes a sentence both to denominate and predicate. In the same way, it takes a text to denominate, predicate, and create a possible world.[72]

For Ricoeur, the text, as a formal generic structure, achieves an autonomy with respect to its author and original situation and projects potential horizons of meaning which may be actualized or constructed in different ways.[73] Meaning, as *sense*, can be established within the narrative world projected by the text. For Ricoeur, therefore, narrative does not refer to the world behind the text but to a "possible world" in front of the text. He understands the biblical story to be a story *for someone*, and in the case of the Gospels that someone is a reader. Therefore, one should not say that the referent of the story is confined to the text itself.[74]

As is now evident, the distance separating a text from its author and original situation forms an integral element in understanding for Ricoeur.[75] Texts do not therefore have a truth of correspondence with the original world which gave rise to their production. Ricoeur specifies:

> Thanks to writing, discourse acquires a threefold semantic autonomy: in relation to the speaker's intention, to its reception by its original audience, and to the economic, social, and cultural circumstances of

---

[72]. Comstock, 134.
[73]. Poland, 175-176.
[74]. Comstock, 132.
[75]. *Vanhoozer, 36, note 42.*

its production.[76]

Ricoeur rejects the significance for interpretation of the links between the text and the circumstances of its production when these links are understood to constrain the meaning of the text or to exclude other possible meanings.[77] Since language is a projection on to the world of the human subject's ownmost possibilities, since it is not simply, the description or recovery of a meaning already inhering in the world, biblical narrative (like all narrative accounts) is largely linguistic fiction. It does not (and could not) have a truth of correspondence with the world that produced it. The truth of the biblical narrative is related rather to the possible world to which it gives rise. In biblical terminology the possible world of the Bible's narrative may be understood as the "kingdom of God," a concept which makes demands on readers and challenges their view of reality. Biblical narratives recreate—in language—*a* view of the world, which arose in a given historical context, but which through the process of writing, has been cut free of its historical moorings. The world of the text has an autonomy and it has power.

If the alienated text does not refer backwards to the context of its production, if its reference is rather to a possible world which the reader construes in front of the text, then the task of interpretation is double. In a first movement, interpretation must discover the alterity of the text and in a second, it must seek its possible meaning for the reader. In uncovering a *possible world* that may be revelatory to the reader, Ricoeur's theory shifts the interpreter's gaze from the conditions of the text's production to the conditions of the text's reception. He understands the historical, economic, cultural and social conditions of the reader to be critical in the reading process. If the text is to be revelatory, it will be so in the context in which it is received. Ricoeur criticized Bultmann for neglecting this aspect of interpretation and attributes the oversight to Bultmann's insensitivity to the later Heidegger's treatment of language. Bultmann, in Ricoeur's opinion, limited faith too much to its personalist dimensions and neglected the more general factors affecting the reception of texts—socio-economic and

---

[76]. Ricoeur, *From Text to Action*, 17.
[77]. Ricoeur, *From Text to Action*, 18.

cultural factors, for example.[78]

Ricoeur understands the biblical narrative as bearing down on the world of the reader. The text is not a flight away from the reader's world into a heavenly and ultimate world. The narrative challenges readers to act, to transform their own world in the image of that possible world projected by the narrative. It challenges the person to work to bring about the kingdom of God. Biblical narrative does not allow for a passive attitude before the world, but calls the reader to do something about what they have discovered to be actually the case.

Ricoeur defines interpretation as the dialectic of explanation and understanding at the level of the "sense" immanent in the text, where *explanation* refers to the ability to reconstruct the internal dynamic of the text (the objective pole), and *understanding* refers to a second-order operation, which consists in restoring to the work its ability to project itself, in the representation of a world that the reader could inhabit (the subjective pole).[79] In the end, Ricoeur rejects any interpretative practice which excludes *understanding* and thereby excludes the relevance of the text to the world of the reader. Here, meaning is always "contextualized meaning" and never an essential truth, uniform for all ages and changeless. Meaning does not inhere in the biblical text or in any text, (although structures do inhere in the text which allow the sense of the text to be construed). The biblical text has the capacity of producing another world for the reader, a *text-world* that surpasses mere structures. Ricoeur, like Gadamer, understands interpretation, to lead to the fusion of horizons; the horizon of the possible world to which the text gives rise and the horizon of the reader's world. The text achieves its meaning within the context of the reader's situation.

Just as Ricoeur rejects the author-text link as the key to interpretation, he likewise rejects structural analysis which "gives rise to the positivist illusion of a textual objectivity closed in upon itself and

---

[78]. Gilles Raymond, "L'autorité de la foi sur les normes de l'éducation de la foi," *Enseigner la foi ou former les croyants?* (Montreal: Fides, 1988), 47.

[79]. Ricoeur, *From Text to Action*, 19 and more completely in the section entitled "What is a text?"

wholly independent of the subjectivity of both author and reader."[80] Despite the caveats he offers regarding structuralism, Ricoeur's programme insists on the objective dimension of literary meaning; a point which distinguishes it from all critical orientations which define meaning wholly in terms of the reader's consciousness or response.[81] He supplants this *either/or* dichotomy presented on the one hand, by historical criticism and structuralism and on the other hand, by reader-response criticism and deconstruction, by a *both/and* dialectic of explanation and understanding. Ricoeur rules out methods of interpretation which contend that the home of meaning may be discovered exclusively either in the objectified text or in the consciousness of the reading subject.

In the pre-critical exegesis of the Middle Ages, it was common for a text to be given several levels of meaning in addition to the *sensus litteralis*.[82] With the rise of critical methods, other levels of interpretation were discredited as eisegetical and unreliable. Ricoeur's theory, far from wishing to obliterate the gains that other forms of criticism have brought to an understanding of the text, intends to provide a critical foundation for additional meanings for the text. Thus, unlike medieval efforts, his project is post-critical and not fideistic. Ricoeur wants to restore to the Bible a revelatory power which surpasses our critical capacities:

> If the Bible can be said to be revealed, this is to be said of the "thing" (the possible world) it says, of the new being it unfolds. I would then venture to say that the Bible is revealed to the extent that the new being that is in question is itself *revealing* with respect to the world, to all of reality, including my existence and my history. In other words, revelation, if the expression is to have a meaning, is a feature of the

---

[80]. Ricoeur, *From Text to Action*, 18.

[81]. Poland, 170. Poland's position, while appropriate as a critique of certain forms of reader-response criticism does not take into account the nuanced approach of Stanley Fish. Fish rightly claims that the responses of the reader are not as variable as is often assumed and that they allow for a certain objectivity to be attained. He also establishes a connection between the reading and writing processes. See Stanley Fish, *Is There a Text in This Class? The Authority of Interpretive Communities* (Cambridge, Mass.: Harvard University Press, 1980)

[82]. Grant and Tracy, 83-91, esp. 85.

HERMENEUTICAL OPTIONS 231

biblical *world*. (i.e., the possible world, in front of the text.)[83]

Ricoeur's idea of revelation maintains both an objective and a subjective pole. *Revelation* emerges through a dialectic between text and reader, in the fusion of horizons of the biblical world and the world of the reader. The reader begins to see the possibilities within the world he/she inhabits by comparing it to the possible world of the text, to what we have referred to as the kingdom of God.

Ricoeur's idea of revelation resembles Karl Rahner's idea of revelation in at least two ways. Not only did Rahner make every effort to emphasize the two-fold nature of revelation, its objective and subjective poles, he also laid the groundwork for a universalist idea of how human persons interact with God. Significantly, Gary Comstock asks whether or not Ricoeur's impure narrativism might not be the most recent attempt to turn Christianity into a universalist religion of being and language.[84] Comstock further contends that for Ricoeur, the Bible which contains the possible world offered by Jesus, the Parable of God, possesses the highest capacity to challenge and shape the reader.[85]

Ricoeur uncovers a link between the Bible's capacity to interpret the world for its readers and the historical appearance of Christianity itself. Just as the Bible helps men and women today to interpret the world and the traditions into which they are born, other avenues of interpretation were available at the dawn of Christian existence. In his

---

[83]. Ricoeur, *From Text to Action*, 96. Bracketed material mine.

[84]. Comstock offers a lucid explanation of some distinctive features in Ricoeur's method. "On Ricoeur's view, the claims of artistic and religious discourse challenge the presuppositions of ordinary discourse. Truth claims of ordinary discourse are based on two assumptions: that truth is objective and can be measured by the criterion of empirical falsification, and that truth appears to an autonomous thinking subject, a consciousness completely in control of itself. Ricoeur says that religious truth (revelation) "violates" these two assumptions. Truth, according to religious texts, is not transparent (it cannot be assessed simply by using methods of adequation or falsification). Nor, according to the biblical stories, are human beings sovereign, self-possessed individuals who can objectively survey such claims. See Comstock 135, note 33.

[85]. Comstock, 137.

Preface to Bultmann, Ricoeur contends that the origins of Christianity present a hermeneutical problem. It is the problem of the relationship between the two Testaments. Ricoeur develops this idea:

> Originally, there were not, properly speaking, two Testaments, two Scriptures; there was one Scripture and one event. And it is this event that makes the entire Jewish economy appear ancient, like an old letter. But there is a hermeneutic problem because this novelty is not purely and simply substituted for the ancient letter; rather it remains ambiguously related to it. The novelty abolishes the Scripture and fulfils it. It changes its letter into Spirit like water into wine. Hence the Christian fact is itself, understood by effecting a *mutation of meaning* inside the ancient Scripture. The first Christian hermeneutics is this mutation itself.[86]

Elsewhere, Ricoeur adds that the newness of the Christ event became expressed in the available and written signs: Jesus had interpreted the Torah; Paul interpreted Christ in terms of the prophets and the old covenant; the christological titles of the Gospels reinterpret OT and Hellenistic figures; finally the NT itself became a text to be interpreted.[87]

Instead of understanding literature as an "endless labyrinth" which refers to nothing but itself (Derrida), Ricoeur understands narratives to produce a world of meaning capable of changing the life of the reader. Ricoeur rejects the insistence within pure narrativism on the self-referentiality of narrative (Hans Frei). Ricoeur wishes to foster the emergence of critical reading. He would probably agree with Northrop Frye who wrote: "...it is clearly one of the unavoidable responsibilities of educated people to show by example that beliefs may be held and examined at the same time."[88] Ricoeur believes that Gadamer has so stressed the condition of "belonging-to" a tradition for understanding, that a critique of that tradition is no longer possible.[89] Within a dialectical notion of interpretation, Ricoeur opens up the possibility of believing, while continuing to question. It creates the possibility of a

---

[86]. Paul Ricoeur, "Preface to Bultmann," *The Conflict of Interpretations: Essays in Hermeneutics*, ed. Don Ihde (Evanston: Northwestern University Press, 1974), 382.

[87]. Paul Ricoeur, "Philosophical Hermeneutics and Theological Hermeneutics," *Studies in Religion: Sciences Religieuses* 5 (1975): 19-20.

[88]. Frye, 254.

[89]. Vanhoozer, 36, note 42.

critique of tradition. As Frye's statement suggests, critical thinking ought to be the goal of all education.

Can it be said that the *Viens vers le Père* series educates in this sense? Does it begin the process of forming critical thinkers? Does it offer the students any interpretative distance? In other words, does it show signs of a hermeneutic which places the locus of meaning "in front of the text," de-centring the subject in a search for meaning?

If the *Viens vers le Père* series reflects Ricoeur's method, one should be able to identify in its approach, the two-fold task of interpretation, i.e., explanation and understanding.

On the one hand, the adaptation of Lubienska de Lenval's approach to biblical narrative demonstrated considerable ingenuity in helping the children come to an appreciation of the text's own structures. Encouraged to reconstruct imaginatively in themselves a narrative world, children transported themselves to the streets of first century Palestine, to encounter Jesus with the main players of the synoptic dramas. Historical detail helped children re-invent the text's world as a world different from their own; it helped them to discover the alterity of the text. All this is accomplished with considerable care, as we noted in our treatment of *Nous avons vu le Seigneur*. This method, allied with other strategies, it appears, went far in the direction of helping children *explain* the biblical texts selected for study.

On the other hand, once the children have inhabited the text-world, the pedagogical method arrogates to itself the task of *understanding* the text's meaning. This approach does not help the children discover the pertinence of the text to their own situation. Instead, it defines the meaning of the text outside the context of the lives of the children. And *what the text means*, seems invariably to be some point of doctrine or other. The text's ability to project a world, which makes meaningful claims on the world(s) into which the text is being received, is never realized. The communication of the meaning held within the structures of the text, to the situation in which the text is received, gets short-circuited. The text's ability to project its meaning to a possible world in front of the text is suppressed. Instead of transposing the text's significance from the text-world to the world of the child, the text's significance is transferred to an earlier and, more or less, "definitive" reception of the text within the tradition. The biblical text is shown to refer not to life, but to another text, i.e., the doctrinal tradition of the Church.

While the child may indeed stand within a tradition, that tradition cannot supply a personal understanding of Scripture. The catechist may tell the children in a later movement, how others have read this or that text, in an effort to encourage further reflection on the text, but this is another matter entirely from providing an explanation of the text using doctrinal statements which are distant from the child's life. At best, Tradition becomes another text to be interpreted. If the child is to come to an understanding that is personal, to a faith that is personal, doctrine (dogma) cannot be used as the pre-determined outcome of biblical interpretation. Doctrine, as text, becomes the object of another hermeneutical process of explanation and understanding, i.e., if doctrine is to become in its turn *revealing*. A main feature of Ricoeur's method of interpretation—the recognition of the social, cultural, economic and general historical conditions obtaining at the moment of the text's reception—remains neglected in the *Viens vers le Père* series.

The theologically extrinsicist notion of revelation which shapes the pedagogy of this programme, has far reaching repercussions. From every angle—theologically, pedagogically and hermeneutically—the elucidation of the life of the child takes a back seat to the presentation of doctrine. Gilles Raymond, in a comment aimed at the catechetical series which replaced the *Viens vers le Père* series in Quebec, enunciates a critique which in some ways seems applicable to its predecessor:[90]

> La réforme actuelle des programmes de catéchèse, loin de faire progresser la fidelité à l'activité du sujet croyant dans son acte d'interprétation, a plutôt remis en valeur une catéchèse d'assimilation dogmatique mieux structurée au niveau de la démarche éducative par des objectifs cognitifs et affectifs.[91]

---

[90]. Of course one should not lose sight of the fact that the *Viens vers le Père* series was a ground-breaking catechesis in that it brought catechetical thinking in Canada in line with the psycho-pedagogical revolution in 20th century educational theory. Its reactionary successors can make no such claim to breaking new ground.

[91]. Raymond, 48.

The *Viens vers le Père* series does not create for children any critical distance from the text it studies. This approach does not foster the child's capacity to understand or to disagree with the programmatic presentation of meaning.

A quick example may help explain the difficulty. In Lesson 5 of Grade I, the doctrine to be learned is that "God is a Father who loves us," God is the Father of Jesus, and thanks to Jesus, He is our Father too. The illustration shows a boy and his father embracing. The teacher manual makes allowance for the fact that not every child will have a father and that some children will not have a healthy relationship with the father they have. Caveats are provided, which draw the teacher's attention to these *unusual* cases. For the child who has an absent or unfit father, for the child whose father is preoccupied by unemployment or poverty, one might say that there is a dissonance between the child's world and the catechism's understanding of Scripture (expressed as doctrine). The young child, to a greater degree than adults, is tied to his/her situation, unable to take a critical distance from it. This inability to assume a critical distance from his/her situation coincides with a less developed capacity to articulate on the part of the child, when compared with adults.[92] The programme, instead of paying attention to the conditions under which the text is being received, instead of paying attention to the social/familial situation—so critical to the development of the child—provides suggestions for working around the problem. It is at this very stage, that the programme ought to alert the catechist's attention to the types of difficulties in the lives of average (and not so average) children in society.

It is a fact worth noting, for instance, that in Quebec, the provincial government maintains that one in 10 children is born into circumstances of abject poverty. In 1992, in a city as large as Montreal, school board officials discovered that 28% of all children in the primary-elementary grades came to school in the morning without having eaten. While a catechist in a classroom and a religious education programme can do little, if anything, to remedy such wide-ranging social

---

[92]. This point is worth noting, given Ricoeur's thesis about the coming-to-being of the subject in language.

problems, catechesis must do everything it can to eradicate the impression that God (the object of catechetical discourse) remains indifferent to the plight of those in need. A Christian catechetical programme should make it clear that Jesus is God's message to the world and that his priority is the establishment of the kingdom of God. The images of that kingdom are of sharing and abundance. Unjust social structures are not part of the kingdom, if one is to believe Scripture. Catechetical programmes which skirt the question leave the lingering doubt that the existing world order is inevitable and even willed by God. God appears to be silent on these issues and this impression is reinforced whenever Chrisitan Churches employ theological, hermeneutical and pedagogical methods which lack a social dimension. Does the Gospel, proclaimed in the context of a Christian school, have anything to say about such situations? If the text will be revealing, it must be revealing to those children, in the world into which they have been thrown. And today in Canada and of course more pitifully elsewhere in the world, the world into which children have been thrown is less and less hospitable towards the poorest new-comers.

Ricoeur's theory does not want to work around problems, it wants readers to be suspicious of texts, challenging them with their own pre-understandings. In the case of children, the pre-understandings are meagre, but every child has at least his/her own experiences. Those who design catechetical programmes may choose to orientate the educative process towards or away from the elucidation of that experience. They may choose to co-opt the great monuments of wisdom and knowledge preserved in our cultural heritage (chief among which is the Bible) towards the self-understanding of the child, or they may choose to make this legacy an end in itself, an end to which children have no choice but to adapt themselves. Reading ought to challenge the child's understandings but paradoxically, it must also give the child faith in his/her own understandings. Text world and reader world must both be open to mutual elucidation and those who promote the Bible ought to have faith in its ability to conquer suspicious readings. While children may need considerable help to achieve these ends, it seems that the critical path may begin at least as soon as schooling does.

VVLP AND MEANING "IN THE TEXT"

The choice to dissociate interpretation from historical, social, political and existentialist concerns (as in the case of structuralism and semiotics) proves seductive in its appeal. Severing a text from the circumstances of its production and reception, dealing with the text 'and nothing but the text,' rids the task of interpretation of a great deal of complexity. The roots of non-historical, critical research on the Bible may be traced to the rediscovery of ancient texts as literature during the Renaissance.[93] In dealing with the classics of antiquity, scholars began to discern generic structures and clues upon which to found an interpretation. Eventually this emphasis became firmly ensconced in the sphere of biblical studies, where today it exercises broad appeal in the guild of professional critics. Several branches of critical research limit their concerns to meaning as defined by the text *in ipso*. Genre criticism, semiotics, structural analysis, narrative criticism and certain approaches to canon criticism all share a number of assumptions. The methodological postulates uniting scholars who choose this hermeneutical path may be clearly seen when they are contrasted with those informing the historical-critical method.

Historical criticism pores over biblical texts, lifting out the disharmony found there, e.g., Source Criticism in the Pentateuch. The lapses in logic and continuity, the contradictions, repetitions and other irregularities of the text, tip the critic off to the possibility that such texts represent the compilation of different sources. The simple observation of textual difficulties, over time, gave rise to a complex network of critical methods. Text Criticism, Form Criticism, Redaction Criticism, Source Criticism—these are among the branches of diachronic study which investigate the genesis, growth and history of the biblical text. The question of the authorship of books got buried beneath a labyrinth of compilers, redactors and sources in oral tradition. Walter Vogels neatly summarizes the task of deriving meaning, in the face of this complexity.

> In some ways the exegete using the diachronic framework of the historical-critical method works as an archaeologist reaching back into the oral tradition and carefully sifting through the various redactions the text has undergone throughout its history in an effort to unlock its real meaning. In his opinion the text belongs to the writer who has

---

[93]. James Barr, 105.

determined once and for all what the text means. This explains the difficulty the reader feels in understanding the text, especially if he is very distant from the writer.[94]

Synchronic approaches to the text, assume the text to be alienated from its author and show no interest in the various stages of the text's history.[95] Interest has shifted from *original text* to *present text*, and depending upon which method one refers to, it is of little import whether the text under study is in Hebrew, Greek, English or any other language.[96] The text itself becomes the locus of meaning. Its grammar, its generic features, its surface and deep structures form a kind of self-contained world of *sense*, which need not refer to anything beyond its borders in order to be understood. Once the text has been distanced from its historical roots, the single meaning intended by the author has been abandoned in favor of a possible plurality of meanings, arising from the plurality of methods applied to the text.[97]

We limit our goal here to an introduction to one representative of the synchronic approach to the text. The author we choose makes a claim for the *sensus litteralis* as *the* meaning of the text. The pure narrativism of Hans W. Frei (1922-1988) makes no appeal to the history behind the text, or to the flesh and blood author in his attempts to interpret the biblical text. Similarly, he sees the historical circumstances of the reader as unimportant to the reading act. Frei is an example of a scholar who understands the meaning of the text to be determined only by the written word. Many of the hermeneutical strategies and guiding theological ideas of the biblical interpretation of *Viens vers le Père* resemble those of Frei and for this and other reasons, he appears to be an ideal candidate for examination in the context of the present

---

[94]. Walter Vogels, *Reading and Preaching the Bible* (Wilmington, Delaware: Michael Glazier, 1986), 27.

[95]. For an explanation of this notion, see the section of this Chapter dealing with meaning "in front of the text."

[96]. Nothrop Frye, the noted literary critic, worked with an English translation of the text without apologies.

[97]. Vogels, 33. In as much as their findings may corroborate one another, several of these methods may prove more complementary than competitive in their claims.

work.[98]

First of all, Frei's method rests upon an extrinsicist view of revelation. We contend that the *Viens vers le Père* series also adopts an extrinsicist view. *Second*, Frei understands the NT as best interpreted within the community for which it serves as Scripture. This also proves to be an implicit assumption of this catechetical series. *Third*, Frei's interpretative method casts biblical interpretation as a trinitarian and christocentric enterprise. Once again, the theological orientation of the catechesis under study here, resembles Frei's option. *Fourth*, since Frei has contrasted his hermeneutical project to the work of Paul Ricoeur, we may gain a new perspective on Frei's work by comparing and contrasting its striking similarities and differences with the account given of Ricoeur above.[99]

Gary Comstock has already given a competent account of several basic similarities and differences in the written work of Frei and Ricoeur. From his article, a list of points which the two narratologists hold in common may be gleaned. Frei and Ricoeur agree that:

1. narrative is not only indispensable to understanding God's work in history, but the NT narrative of Jesus is essential for Christian practice and faith. Hence, the meanings of the scriptural narratives are tied to their Christian audience;

2. the meaning of realistic narrative is to be discovered in, not outside, the story's own depiction of agents and circumstances. Narratives produce a world of sense;

3. hermeneutic theories that convert the text into an abstract philosophical system, an ideal typological structure or simply the occasion for existential decision are to be rejected;

---

[98]. We might just as easily have used the work of George Lindbeck for this analysis. Lindbeck's options closely resemble those of Frei, a fact in some measure attributable to their common roots in the theology of Karl Barth.

[99]. See particularly Hans W. Frei, "The 'Literal Reading' of Biblical Narrative in the Christian Tradition: Does It Stretch or Will It Break?," *The Bible and the Narrative Tradition*, ed. Frank McConnell (New York: Oxford University Press, 1986), 36-77. (Hereafter cited as: "Literal Reading.")

4. narratology should not become an essay in apologetics;

5. the Christian story is true, (however, only Ricoeur thinks it important to try to spell out what this claim might mean);

6. realistic narratives do not refer ostensively to real objects, agents or events behind the text.[100]

For all these similarities, the two scholars disagree in still more basic ways. Rather than view Frei through the optic of Ricoeur's work, let us turn now to our author, letting his own work speak for itself.

We have it on Frei's own words, that the three cardinal influences on his thought were Erich Auerbach, Karl Barth and Gilbert Ryle.[101] From Ryle's book, *The Concept of Mind*, the idea of intentional personal action became "demystified" for Frei. In praising Ryle's refusal to divide intelligent activity into mental and external aspects, Frei makes a thinly veiled attack on the position of Ricoeur and other phenomenologists.[102] As will soon become evident, Frei's difficulties with Ricoeur and others to whom he refers as philosophers of "Existence" or "Being," has as much to do with the universalist claims of their systems, as it does with any practical consequences for interpretation.

Auerbach and Barth have exercised a more thoroughgoing influence on Frei's thinking. To understand Auerbach's contribution, one needs to look at Frei's treatment of the development of the literal sense in the Christian practice of interpretation in the West.[103] Frei explains the genesis of the primacy of the literal sense in early NT interpretation. Its dominance was linked to the function which the sacred story—the life, death and resurrection of Jesus—exercised within the life of the early Church. "This narrative...has a unifying and a prescriptive character in both the NT and the Christian community that, despite the importance of the Exodus accounts, neither narrative generally nor any specific narrative has in Jewish Scripture and the Jewish

---

[100]. Comstock, 117, 118, 121. An account of the differences which Comstock suggests separate Frei and Ricoeur will be better dealt with after our treatment of Frei.

[101]. Hans W. Frei, *The Eclipse of Biblical Narrative: A Study in Eighteenth and Nineteeth Century Hermeneutics* (New Haven: Yale University Press, 1974), vii.

[102]. Frei, *Eclipse*, viii.

[103]. Frei develops this argument in *Eclipse*, 30ff.

community."[104] Since Christians understand the rule of faith to be based on NT narrative, one has to be able to determine clearly what it means.

From earliest times, and still for the Reformers, *literal* and *historical* readings of biblical narratives were in effect the same thing.[105] A biblical narrative, judged not to be metaphorical or allegorical, was read as an historical text. In the 18th century a major shift occurred. Historiograhpy, in weighing its evidence, came to place the highest value on empirical verifiability. In the wake of this development, the interpretation of biblical narratives became dissociated from their historical factuality. In Frege's terms, the meaning of NT narrative as literal sense had become isolated from the extra-textual, historical reference of the NT narrative. As the distinction between these two concepts came clearly into view, the truth claims of the Bible (*qua* historical document) appeared to many, to be in jeopardy. This uncoupling of the *sensus litteralis* from the historical sense had, Frei makes clear, crucial consequences for the principles of interpretation.

Prior to the empirical shift in historiography which gained prominence in the 18th century, the literal sense (or sometimes the figurative) gave the sense of a narrative passage. The historical factuality may have been assumed, but played no major role in determining what the passage was about. As the concepts of *story* and *history* became clearly separated and were applied to biblical interpretation, the sense

---

[104]. Frei, "Literal Reading," 39.

[105]. Drawing his argument from James Preus' book on Christian interpretation of the OT, *From Shadow to Promise*, Frei reconstructs the early Christian notion of the literal sense of the NT. Early Christianity intended to read the Scriptures spiritually. As those directly privy to the truth, Christians saw the heavenly, spiritual and religious, rather than the earthly, empirical, or political significance of the Scriptures. The OT was understood as carnal, the NT as spiritual; the OT was cast as the "letter" and the NT as the "spirit." In order to retain the OT, it had to be interpreted spiritually as referring to Christ. The literal sense of the OT required interpretation if it was to be properly understood. The NT, by contrast, referred to the Christ. It was already a spiritual book and so its literal sense was already a spiritual sense. But the NT was not about earthly things. See Frei, "Literal Reading," 40-41.

of a passage "came to depend on the estimate of its historical claims, character and nature."[106] With the rise of historicism, proponents of the primacy of historical data for determining meaning parted company with proponents of the primacy of literal criteria for determining meaning. On the question as to whether the OT could be referring to events reported in the NT, the two camps split. On the one hand, historical interpretation suggested that OT texts could not be referring to events that had not even taken place when they were written. On the other hand, an overarching figural interpretation of the Bible as a single literary unit suggested they could.[107]

In the end, Frei understood the consistently historical approach to be fundamentally wrongheaded and misleading with respect to the significance of the NT. He rejected historical criticism's claim that the real meaning of the text lies outside the text, i.e., with the intentions of the original author. Frei contended that historical criticism, by insisting that meaning lay with the intentions of the author, had alienated the biblical narrative from the community for which it functions as Scripture. It was the dissociation of sense and reference in biblical interpretation which allowed this to occur. Once sense had become severed from reference, the biblical narrative could be read either *symbolically* for a moral lesson or religious truth, or *historically*, as a document relevant only to its original audience. Frei's method wished to overcome this chasm, opened up in the 17th century and still gaping today. In order to bridge the gap, he needed to find some means to reunite sense and reference. Erich Auerbach provided just such a means.

Auerbach's *Mimesis: The Representation of Reality in Western Literature* offers a new view of the relationship between the biblical text and the world outside. In Auerbach's opinion, the Bible is not satisfied with claiming that it offers an historically true vision of reality, but "insists that it is the only real world" and as such is "destined for autocracy."[108] The Bible, for Auerbach, wishes to reduce or assimilate the world outside the text to the narrative world of the text. Before the decline of Christendom, most of Western civilization found little

---

[106]. Frei, *Eclipse*, 41.
[107]. Erich Auerbach, *Mimesis: The Representation of Reality in Western Literature*, trans. Willard R. Trask (Princeton: Princeton University Press, 1968), 73, 555. (Hereafter cited as *Mimesis*)
[108]. Auerbach, *Mimesis*, 14-15.

difficulty with accepting the biblical world as the only real world. In that earlier context, the whole process of biblical interpretation consisted in ranging "extra-biblical thought, experience and reality into the one real world detailed and made accessible by the biblical story—not the reverse."[109] Frei cites a revealing passage from Auerbach which illustrates the claim biblical narrative makes on its reader:

> Far from seeking, like Homer, merely to make us forget our own reality for a few hours, it seeks to overcome our reality; we are to fit our own life into its world, feel ourselves to be elements in its structure of universal history...Everything else that happens in the world can only be conceived as an element in this sequence; into it everything that is known about the world...must be fitted as an ingredient of the divine plan.[110]

For Auerbach, and for Frei, the biblical story does not seek to infiltrate the world, but rather to absorb it.

Like other text-oriented approaches, Frei understands the circumstances of the production of the text to be extraneous to the process of interpretation. Frei does not understand meaning to be tied to the beliefs, intentions and practices of either author or reader.[111] Frei argues that the truly distinctive trait of biblical narrative does not lie in its extra-textual, historical reference, but in its quality of being *realistic*. One of the key characteristics of realistic narrative is that its events unfold in a history-like, chronological sequence. Frei fleshes out this skeletal description:

> Realistic narrative is that kind in which subject and social setting belong together, and character and external circumstances fitly render each other... Believable individuals and their credible destinies are rendered in ordinary language and through concatenations of ordinary events which cumulatively constitute the serious, sublime, and even tragic impact of powerful historical forces. These forces in turn allow the ordinary, "random," lifelike individual persons, who become their bearers in the crucial intersection of character and particular event-laden circumstance, to become recognizable "types," without

---

[109]. Frei, *Eclipse*, 3.
[110]. Auerbach, *Mimesis*, 15 as quoted in Frei, *Eclipse*, 3.
[111]. Comstock, 123.

thereby inducing a loss of their distinctively contingent or random individuality.[112]

The biblical narrative provides the master-story into which all other stories fit. Rather than stylized heroes, realistic narrative is of the sort that allows the reader to identify the *types* of individuals cast in the story from their own world. The story is not thereby reduced to the reader's world, but invites the reader to see their world in the characters and events, realistically portrayed in the story. Even miracle stories may conform to the notion of realistic narrative. Frei cites the work of Henry James, wherein the latter understands narrative events and character to be mutually interdependent.[113] Each defines the other. Events are the means of illustrating a character and character the means of defining events. If the action depicted in miracle accounts seems indispensable to the portrayal of a particular character, divine or human, then the miraculous accounts may be deemed history-like and realistic.

The novels of Charles Dickens offer a marvellous example of realistic narrative at work in literature. Despite the exaggerated instances of Victorian serendipity in a novel like *Great Expectations*, the many characters it creates have become a part of the intellectual furniture of literate people everywhere in the English-speaking world. They have become so, in as much as they offer typical characters and social types, readily identifiable even to today's readers, despite their chronological distance from those readers. Miss Havisham, the jilted spinster; Pip, the hopeful foundling; Joe Gargery, the simple but faithful smith—all resemble types which occur and recur in the most varied of social contexts. The events of the narrative create the characters and the characters determine the events; the two cohere.

Since Frei understands biblical narrative to be self-referential, i.e., referring only to itself and to nothing else, what the text is about is identical to its verbal meaning.[114] Frei contends that the subject matter of biblical narrative is the identity of Jesus Christ.[115] At the heart of Christianity, he sees "a unique affirmation about Jesus Christ, viz., not only that he is the presence of God but also that knowing his identity is

---

[112]. Frei, *Eclipse*, 13, 15.
[113]. Frei, *Eclipse*, 14.
[114]. Comstock, 120.
[115]. This is the point of his book of the same name.

identical with having him present or being in his presence."[116] Frei insists that the identity of Jesus in the text coincides with the experience of the Risen Christ by the reader.[117] Gary Comstock points out a *non sequitur* in Frei's position. First, Frei holds that the subject matter of biblical narrative is the identity of Jesus Christ. Second, he contends that biblical narrative fits the category of realistic narrative which has a meaning that is obvious, transparent and open to every reader, "no matter how he disposes himself toward the story on a personal level."[118] If biblical narrative is realistic narrative with a publicly accessible meaning and if the subject matter of the biblical narrative is the identity of Jesus, then any reader ought to be able to gain access to the identity of Jesus through the narrative. But this is not so, Frei implies. For Frei, the identity of Jesus as subject matter is *one of a kind* and not comparable to any other example in literature.[119] The identity and presence of Jesus are linked in a unique way, such that "...it is not the power of our thinking that makes him (Jesus) present; it is he who presents himself to us."[120] In other words, interpretation cannot lead us to Jesus. Comstock rightly levels a charge of fideism against Frei—in order to understand the Gospel one must first believe in Christ.[121] Moreover, Comstock reveals Frei's departure from the theory of realistic narrative upon which Frei's own hermeneutical theory rests. He describes Frei's conundrum with some levity: "The logic of his view entails that he get tremendous theological mileage out of a literary vehicle he does not really own."[122]

It is not surprising that Frei shies away from a general hermeneutic theory. In his definition of hermeneutics, Frei is very careful to avoid any universalizing tendency:

---

[116]. Hans W. Frei, *The Identity of Jesus Christ: The Hermeneutical Basis of Dogmatic Theology* (Philadelphia: Fortress Press, 1975), vii.
[117]. Frei, *Identity*, 156.
[118]. Frei, *Identity*, xvi.
[119]. Frei, *Identity*, 15.
[120]. Frei, *Identity*, 14.
[121]. Comstock, 126.
[122]. Comstock, 126.

Hermeneutics I define in the old-fashioned, rather narrow, and low-keyed manner as the rules and principles for determining the sense of written texts, or the rules and principles governing exegesis. This is in contrast to the more recent, ambitious, indeed all-encompassing view of hermeneutics as inquiry into the process that goes into all understanding or interpreting linguistic phenomena. In the latter instance, hermeneutics becomes practically equivalent to general philosophical inquiry; and the language-to-be-interpreted becomes shorthand for a whole philosophical or theological anthropology, a view of man as language-bearer.[123]

Frei's interest in Auerbach and his reticence to become involved in universalizing philosophical inquiry may be traced, we contend, to his grounding in the theology of Karl Barth. Auerbach judges the intent of the biblical narrative to be the absorption of all reality into its narrative world.[124] Barth's theology, as we will see, offers a similar judgment of the intent of biblical revelation. Like Barth, Frei rejects every form of natural theology, denouncing theological systems which try to find symbolic connections between biblical revelation and general human experience. The very possibility of treating biblical narrative in this fashion may be traced, claims Frei, to the dissociation of sense and reference in the rise of critical research. Once the sense of the Bible was dissociated from its reference, its message could be interpreted as referring to "Everyman," But the heart of the Bible (for Barth and Frei) is not the story of "Everyman"—it is the story of Jesus, the story to which all human experience must be assimilated, if it is to be truly understood. In this view, the Word of God judges the world and not the reverse. The relation between the Word of God and the Bible, however, is unclear. For Frei, the *sensus litteralis* of the biblical narrative appears to be the Word of God (but perhaps only for a special class of believing readers).

The number who have fallen into the theological trap of dissociating sense and reference in narrative, in Frei's opinion, are legion. Among the prominent theologians of the 20th century who have strayed down this perilous path, Frei lists Bultmann, Rahner, Ebeling,

---

[123]. Frei, *Identity*, xvi.

[124]. Absorption is a term taken not from Auerbach but from George Lindbeck, *The Nature of Doctrine: Religion and Theology in a Post-Liberal Age* (Philadelphia: Westminster Press, 1984). It seems apt to describe the action intended.

Pannenberg and Moltmann. Frei rightly contends that these, and a great many other theologians, agree(d) that in one way or another religious *meaningfulness* must "be perspicuous through its relation to other accounts of general human experience."[125] James Barr levels a biting critique at scholars who yearn for pre-critical simplicity in biblical interpretation. Frei's position, with its emphasis on an overarching figural interpretation, fits loosely into canon criticism, the target of Barr's attack.

> ...the movement of canonical criticism, as we have seen it in recent times, can be understood as very much an attempt to dispose of the Enlightenment, to destroy its values and drive out its way of dealing with biblical materials. According to this view, the Reformation was a good time, and pre-critical exegesis in general has great values to offer, but the Enlightenment introduced a damaging and distorting set of questions. One could not say that this, if meaningful at all, was because it introduced the idea of history...but rather it made more familiar the idea of religion, as distinct from theology, and with it the notion of pluralism in religion. There was only one God, but there were different human ideas of God, different religions.[126]

Extrapolating from Barr's critique, one may see a possible connection between Frei's rejection of the historical reference of biblical narrative and his wish to side-step the question of religious pluralism. Gary Comstock suggests that Frei's commitment to the self-referentiality of biblical narrative allows him to excuse himself from those arguments that try to compare the beliefs and practices of Christians and non-Christians.[127] Frei's bracketing of the question of religious pluralism, coincides with a notion of Christology which limits its explanatory strategies to material found within the NT. To delve further into this foundational theological presupposition of Frei's hermeneutic, we turn now to a brief summary of the theology of Karl Barth.[128]

---

[125]. Frei, *Eclipse*, 128.
[126]. James Barr, 122-123.
[127]. Comstock, 129.
[128]. As we make no claim to being a Barth scholar, we rely for the following account on summaries of Barth's theology provided by Ronald F. Thie-

Barth's theology of revelation represents a clear example of extrinsicism. For Barth, revelation denotes the content of our knowledge about God and is nothing other than the 'being of God in verbal form.'[129] Again, revelation brings a knowledge of God from beyond history and it introduces into word and history what Barth has called the "reiterated being" of God, i.e., God's inner, trinitarian being.[130] Following Barth's example, Frei clearly understands the identity of God and of Jesus Christ to be at the heart of revelation. Understood in this way, it is reasonable to posit with Barth and Frei, that no amount of human speculation could arrive at the content of revelation. Revelation comes as a surprise to humanity, which could not have fathomed the mercy, generosity and goodness of God.

Barth's trinitarian theology focuses on the inner-life of God. It is his understanding of that inner life, which allows him to reject every form of natural theology. Ronald Thiemann explains Barth's position in this way:

> The possibility for knowledge of God, Barth argues, is grounded not on any human capacity or capability but within God's own trinitarian being. The possibility for relation to and knowledge of God is primarily and properly God's own possibility...The triune God lives in self-differentiated relation. The differentiated "persons" of the triune reality are unified precisely as they participate in one another. And that participation establishes a relation of mutual love and self-knowledge within God's being *ad intra*. Thus God is knowable *in se*, that is, in God's own inner being. So, also, God is in loving relation *in se*, independent of any relation to reality external to God. God's knowability is not established in relation to human beings. But in the act of sheer grace, God's knowability is shared with us.[131]

The sublime origins of divine revelation have occasioned considerable trepidation among those whose duty it is to speak about it. From the beginning of his career as a theologian and pastor, Barth had encountered the dilemma of preaching: How could a human mouth pre-

---

mann, "Response to George Lindbeck" in *Theology Today* 43 (1986): 377-382, and R. Marlé, *Hermémeutique*. Lindbeck, like Frei, shows great affinity to the work of Barth. Thiemann offers a summary of Barth's theology while responding to an essay by Lindbeck appearing in the same issue.

[129]. Thiemann, 378.
[130]. Thiemann, 378.
[131]. Thiemann, 379.

tend to truly hold forth the Word of God? In the preface to the second edition of his great commentary on the Epistle to the Romans (1922), Barth refers to the angst pastors experienced as they assumed their duty to preach. Like himself, many clergymen had only been initiated into a respect for scientific objectivity (history), but were unprepared to preach; they enter the pulpit in fear and trembling.[132] His extrinsicist view of revelation offers a solution to the problem of proper speech about God. Since God is identified solely through revelation, theology ought to begin its task by reflecting exclusively upon God's identity as communicated in the Bible. "Barth argues that God's revelation provides the only possible basis for proper speech about God. Because God is available to us in the one Word, Jesus Christ, we are now able to undertake an interpretation of that revelation."[133] Here one gets a glimpse of Frei's reason for insisting that the identity of Jesus Christ as the subject of a narrative is a unique instance. Jesus does not reveal an identity which is typical; there are no corresponding *types* in our experience of humanity which we may read into the biblical narrative about Jesus, since Jesus is the revelation of a heavenly truth, an other-worldly truth.

Given that the only proper speech about God is God's own Word about God, a special concept of biblical interpretation comes into view. One of the foundations of this hermeneutical concept lies in the relation of the interpreter to the contents of revelation. Thiemann expresses Barth's view:

> Barth, sometimes spoke of revelation as "God's self-interpretation," almost as if to suggest that our interpretative faculties play no role in understanding that revelation... .Theology is for Barth a hermeneutical activity in which the theologian in the context of the Christian community seeks to give, in Hans Frei's helpful phrase, a faithful *redescription* of the biblical narrative... .Christian theology must always have that dual emphasis on God's guiding grace and free human inquiry, but if priority is to be given (as Barth believes it must) to God's free grace, then the two elements can never be systematically correlated... .Revelation is thus both God's self-interpretation and our in-

---

[132]. As recounted in Marlé, *Herméneutique*, 22.
[133]. Thiemann, 379.

terpretation of God. But our interpretation of revelation can be true only as it seeks to conform itself to the pattern and structure of God's being as shown in revelation. Theology is the search to discern the being of God in the words of the biblical text.[134]

Placed in the context of Barth's theology, Frei's hermeneutical programme becomes transparent. It is obvious that nothing in human history *behind* or *in front of* the text could contribute to explaining the divine subject matter of the text. Thiemann explains this point in Barth: "Jesus Christ as God incarnate is God's sacramental presence among humankind, but even that sacramental presence cannot be known directly, for God is known in Jesus Christ only through the witness of the biblical narrative."[135] For Barth and Frei, the world is not a sacramental reality. Secular human history, then as now, contains no trace of the underlying reality to which the biblical text witnesses. The literal sense of the text, cut off from history, contains the real subject of revelation, Jesus Christ in verbal form. It is, however, only by a free act of the grace of God, that any reader comes to see the identity of Jesus Christ which is *the* meaning of Scripture. By a free act of grace, Jesus makes himself present to the reader who is then able to identify him in the reading of the text. Frei's theological world, like Barth's, centres on the Bible and on the advent of Christ in history to the exclusion of all natural knowledge of God.

It is significant that Ricoeur, in contrast to Frei, does not understand the identity of Jesus Christ to be the centre of Christian revelation. Ricoeur chooses to describe the core of the Christian message in terms not of who Jesus was, but like Bultmann, in terms of what Jesus wanted, viz., the kingdom of God.[136] As Comstock contends, the choice of the *kingdom of God* as the central theme of the Gospel gives Ricoeur's interpretation a more universalistic and pragmatic emphasis than Frei's.

If Frei understands the stories as passion narratives with long introductions, Ricoeur understands them as extended parables about the kingdom. For Ricoeur, the texts are the end result of a process in which the oral kerygma was transferred to written form. In them, he sees Jesus the teller of parables becoming Jesus the parable.[137]

---

[134]. Thiemann, 379-381.
[135]. Thiemann, 381.
[136]. For Bultmann's intentions see Marlé, *Herméneutique*, 24.
[137]. Comstock, 136.

Ricoeur has a universalist understanding of the possibility of revelation. The imagery of the kingdom of God, Ricoeur has written, is dominated from above by apocalyptic imagery that, through forms difficult to number, turns on *reconciliation in a unity*—the unity of a one yet triune God, the unity of humanity, the unity of the animal world in terms of the symbol of the lamb, of the vegetable world in terms of the symbol of the tree of life, and of the mineral world in terms of the heavenly city.[138]

Whereas for Ricoeur, the disclosure which happens in the narratives about Jesus—the *reconciliation in a unity*—can also take place in the creative discourse of any culture,[139] Frei understands revelation to be contained specifically and exclusively in the Bible.[140] While Ricoeur understands the possible world projected by the NT (the kingdom) to be publicly intelligible,[141] Frei sees the identity of Jesus emerging only by the bestowal of grace on the reader. Frei's reader gains access to faith and the presence of Jesus at the same time. For Ricoeur, the significance of the biblical narrative as *kingdom of God* continues to be defined, continues to emerge in the present. Frei, on the other hand, operates under the assumption that the identity of Jesus Christ has been captured definitively, for all time, in the biblical narrative.

Our overview of Hans Frei's hermeneutical programme has been concerned to discover his underlying concept of revelation in order to help us understand his hermeneutic. Several of Frei's key concepts—that biblical narrative is perspicuous, that the Bible interprets itself (both through typological interpretation and determination of the literal sense) and that Scripture preaches Christ—harken back to the pre-critical tenets of the Reformation. Frei's idea seems to be that any truth worth knowing is to be found exclusively in the revelation which God has communicated in the Bible. The Bible communicates knowl-

---

[138]. Paul Ricoeur, "'Anatomy of Criticism' or the Order of Paradigms," *Centre and Labyrinth: Essays in Honour of Northrop Frye*, ed. E. Cooke (Toronto: Toronto University Press, 1983), 10.
[139]. Comstock, 137.
[140]. Comstock, 137.
[141]. Comstock, 138.

edge of the divine, a heavenly truth made known to humanity exclusively in the Bible and unavailable in "natural" human experience. Frei's hermeneutic is thus built on an extrinsicist notion of revelation. For Frei, the Bible does not move towards the world, the world must come to it.

While great strides have been made in ecumenical dialogue since Vatican Council II, it goes without saying that a Catholic catechetical team writing in the 1960s did not depend on Hans Frei and Karl Barth for direct inspiration. Other forces, which also espoused an extrinsicist notion of revelation, were at work in Catholic circles. The reader will remember from our discussion of de Lubac's *Surnaturel*, that proponents of Neo-Scholasticism defended a separation between nature and grace. In pre-Vatican II Catholicism, this separation of nature and grace carried over into the separation of Church and state. In a two-storied view of reality, the Church rightfully occupied itself with matters spiritual and supernatural, leaving the affairs of the world strictly to political powers. The notion that the contents of revelation have a divine origin and an other-worldly import permitted a separation between spiritual and political life. The Church was, from the beginning, the custodian and interpreter of the contents of the deposit of revelation. This concept is remarkably similar to Frei's, except for the fact that in Frei's account, the faculty of interpretation is not given to the Church as a whole but to individual believers. In both cases, the Bible's message is not about life in this world, but about the relation of God to the world.

In considering the role of tradition in the interpretation of the Bible, one may clearly see the abiding difference between Frei's Reformation principles and the Catholic presuppositions informing the *Viens vers le Père* series. For Catholics, the concept of Tradition (as distinct from traditions) reflects the Church's evolving appreciation of the significance of revelation, under the guidance of the Spirit. Tradition means much more than the results of the first few important councils which dealt primarily with christological heresies. It represents the story of how God's people have responded to the divine initiative throughout the centuries since the "death of the last apostle." The reading of Scripture in Catholic tradition is understood as enriched by the way in which those who have gone before us in the faith, have read and lived the Gospel. The fruits of any hermeneutical programme would eventually have to be brought into dialogue with that *normative* Tradition. For this Catholic catechetical series, the relation between biblical interpretation and doctrine is evident, given that one of the characteristics of Catholic biblical interpretation is that it is read within Tradition. On Gadamer's view, all readings of all texts take place within traditions, consciously or unconsciously. In this sense, while Frei and Catholic practice both understand the Bible to be properly interpreted in and for the Christian community, in each case what is understood by this terminology proves to be quite different. Frei understands the Spirit's bestowal of grace in terms of the individual. Catholic theologians understand God's grace as being bestowed on the community as a whole.

CONCLUSIONS:

Our goal in this chapter was to compare and contrast the hermeneutical strategies of the *Viens vers le Père* series to three distinct approaches in biblical interpretation today. In reviewing these pedagogical instruments in this way, we kept their pastoral orientation before us as we attempted to adumbrate a portrait of their method of interpretation. Since these catechetical resources issue from the Catholic Tradition, we highlighted the particular understanding Catholics have of the complementary character of the corpus of Christian doctrine and the biblical witness.

We found that the question of objective and subjective poles within the idea of revelation finds an echo in the question of objective and subjective poles in textual interpretation. At opposite ends of the spectrum lie scholars who approach the question from an either/or perspective. One approach, which includes many historical critics, structuralists and pure narrativists, insists that meaning is located outside the reading subject and is determined either by the reconstructed (flesh-and-blood) author (Barr, Hirsch) or by the *implicit author*, defined in and by the text (Frei). A second approach, the deconstructionist, understands reading as a subjective process where the reading subject construes his/her own unique text using the written words as points of departure for the construction of meaning. In this view, meaning remains radically personalized, an individual affair. The middle ground, which rejects this *either/or* scenario in favour of a *both/and* option, has been staked out by Paul Ricoeur.

In as much as *Viens vers le Père* embodies an extrinsicist view of revelation, it favours what we have referred to as the "objective pole" within the idea of revelation. With generations of historical critics, the authors of this programme seem to hold that texts of the NT ordinarily have one, clear meaning. Another assumption underlying their methodology seems to be that nearly all the vital elements of the NT have been translated into the Creeds and the doctrinal Tradition of the Church. This has lead the authors of this series to cast doctrine in the role of *hermeneutical key to Scripture*. At every level, doctrine stands at the centre of this series' catechetical method. We recall Marlé's caveat regarding this understanding of the interaction of doctrine (dogma) and biblical interpretation (See Chapter 4).

We noted that since historical methods of exegesis bracket questions of faith and questions regarding the truth value of biblical texts, they are unsuitable as the basis for a catechetical programme. Thus, the relationship of the *Viens vers le Père* series to the historical-critical method proves ambivalent. On the one hand, we know that the completed texts of the series were submitted to an exegete in order to ensure that the programme contents did not contradict reliable historical findings. We remarked that only the Grade 4 programme, *Nous avons vu le Seigneur*, included significant historical detail. But even in Grade 4, this series rarely (if ever) looked to the history behind the text *to provide the basis for interpretation*. We conclude that the predominant motivation for the inclusion of historical data in Grade 4 was pedagogical and pastoral rather than hermeneutical in nature. It helped encourage a spiritual encounter between the children and the Risen Jesus, at the same time that it responded to a growing interest on the part of 9-10 year olds in factual detail. The results of historical-criticism provide a starting point for this catechism's programme of interpretation; historical criticism is not, however, its hermeneutical instrument of choice.

Our discussion of meaning "in front of" the text, focused on the work of Paul Ricoeur. Ricoeur maintains a balance between the subjective and objective elements which make up the reading process; he refers to a two-tiered process of explanation and understanding. On the one hand, he understands the architecture of texts (genre) to be an important determinant of meaning; the structures of a text are an objective control on the reading process. On the other hand, he insists on the personal nature of reading and moves to the circumstances of reception as the key to understanding. In this view, interpretation includes a moment of explanation of the text, which relies on textual structures for clues and then moves to a personal moment of understanding, which calls into play the imagination and feelings of the reader as well as his/her cognitive abilities.

Moving beyond the level of word and sentence as the principle units of biblical interpretation, Ricoeur uncovers the *narrative* as a literary unit which conveys a unique level of meaning. While a word can name an object and a sentence can predicate something of that object, only a story can create a possible world. Applied to the interpretation of the Bible, the possible world of the *kingdom of God* confronts the actual world of the reader in a way that challenges the reader to re-evaluate his/her own world. Only in the context of the reader's world can the text of the Bible or any text prove revelatory. Meaning for Ricoeur, while shaped by the text, is always *meaning for someone* and hence does not reside exclusively in the text nor exclusively with the reader. Meaning is an event which takes place when the horizon of the text's world fuses with the horizon of the reader's world. Unlike Frei, Ricoeur contends that narratives refer beyond their own borders to an extra-textual world, a possible world projected in front of the text. When the horizon of the world projected by the biblical text fuses with the horizon of the reader's world, the former bears down upon the latter and claims truth for the vision it projects.

While one may suppose that there is nothing in Ricoeur's method which rules out the possibility that the architecture of texts may correspond to the normative readings of the Bible which form the Church's doctrinal heritage, the use of doctrine as hermeneutical key in *Viens vers le Père* would not constitute a complete notion of interpretation in Ricoeur's terms. Doctrine, which makes normative claims regarding the explanation of a text, cannot be imposed as a substitute for the reader's personal understanding and appropriation of the text in terms which arise from the reader's experiences. In Gadamerian terms, by not allowing children to bring the full gamut of their "cultural" prejudices to the text, by limiting the scope of their prejudice to the Church's doctrinal heritage, *Viens vers le Père* truncates the reading process. This series favours the objective elements in the reading process as it favoured the objective elements in the idea of revelation. This has the effect of limiting the questions which students can put to the text from their own lives and also of eliminating any critique of the biblical text which might arise from their culture. *Viens vers le Père* short-circuits the process of interpretation by not allowing the students to move beyond the stage of explaining the text. It favours a hermeneutics of recovery over a hermeneutics of suspicion.

For several reasons, we conclude that the hermeneutical profile of the *Viens vers le Père* series has most in common with the work of Hans Frei, with the view that meaning is located "in the text." Similar to Frei's work, this catechetical series is underpinned by an extrinsicist view of revelation. The extrinsicist concept of revelation fits very well with Frei's claim that the world created within the borders of the biblical text intends to absorb the reader's world and eventually to supplant it.

Because proponents of the extrinsicist view of revelation understand the content of the Bible to be centred exclusively on things divine—on the secret, inner life of the Trinity as revealed to us in the record of the life, death and resurrection of Jesus Christ—it does not look for the meaning of the Bible in the lives of its readers. It has enlisted the experiences of the children, not in order to elucidate them, but as a means to illuminate the divine contents of revelation. The use of contemporary human experience, especially the experiences of children, was a means to a pedagogical end; it provided a source of analogies for explaining doctrine. In this view, revelation is understood more or less exclusively as a description of the divine, having little to say about the human situation outside the history of salvation. Like Hans Frei, the *Viens vers le Père* series does not understand the Bible to be the story of "Everyman," but rather the story of *the* divine man, Jesus Christ.

Since the contents of revelation are understood largely as defined prior to interpretation (requiring at best a re-description) the goal of preaching and teaching have a doctrinal end in view. Doctrine, as understood in this model, is a description of God which does not address the historically changing human situation. It follows from this view that religious education consists in an assimilation of the contents of revelation. The contents are understood as sublime, and apart from re-description, as immutable. The *Viens vers le Père* series has effectively re-described the contents of Scripture in terms of the doctrine of the Church.

Falling in line with a position championed by Frei, *Viens vers le Père* understands the message of Scripture to be perspicuous. The distance and strangeness of the biblical text have evaporated as its message is handed on to eager neophytes. Hermeneutics may be essentially understood in this programme as a re-description of God as God has been revealed in Tradition, through Scripture and doctrine. It is in order to re-describe the contents of Scripture that *Viens vers le Père* has enlisted the experiences of its audience.

From the first year of the series, the goal of the programme is to dispose the children to be ready to enter into a relation with the Trinity. In Frei's terms, one could perhaps speak of preparing the children to accept the offer to enter into the presence of Christ. The programme explicitly recognizes that only God can grant faith and that ultimately, no catechesis may work without divine participation. As the programme is largely structured around the use of Scripture, the same can be said for its understanding of biblical interpretation. Only divine participation (or in Frei's terms, only being in the presence of Jesus already) will allow the reader to understand the message of revelation. Only in a relationship with the Trinity, through Christ, will students grasp the true significance of Tradition (doctrine and Bible).[142] Like Frei, *Viens vers le Père* seems to favour a fideistic concept of biblical interpretation.

One's concept of revelation conditions greatly one's practice of biblical interpretation and influences teaching and preaching. We conclude that revelation occurs in a *conversation* between, on the one hand, a sinful yet graced human situation and, on the other hand, the biblical-traditional witness. This concept implies a de-centring of the biblical message. The message of the Bible (and of Tradition) finds its real sense not intra-textually, but in its ability to address the world beyond its borders in such a way as to bring about the transformation of that world, spiritually, socially, politically, intellectually. Revelation intends the transformation of the world into the Kingdom of God. While sparks of this concept dapple the fringes of the *Viens vers le*

---

[142]. See *Viens vers le Père, Guide du Maître*, 5 and frequently throughout the programme thereafter.

Père series, its inspiration remains undeniably an extrinsicist concept of revelation. As such it corresponds generally to the hermeneutical programme of Hans Frei.

CONCLUSIONS

The publication of the *Viens vers le Père* catechetical series was a remarkable event. As a result of this single enterprise, catechesis in Quebec and in Canada was catapulted into a new age. Its influence flowed beyond our own borders, as it was translated to several other languages and transposed to other national settings. One of its major achievements is its re-definition of the catechetical task. Intuiting that the social position of the Church vis-à-vis society at large was changing, *Viens vers le Père* supplanted the model of catechesis as *Instruction* by the pastoral model of catechesis as *Initiation*. The old catechisms effectively defined the goal of catechesis as "cognitive acquisition" and worked with pedagogical instruments ill-adapted for use with children. In vivid contrast, *Viens vers le Père* developed a catechesis intended to address the whole person, i.e., intellectually, emotionally and spiritually. Its ultimate goal, the conversion of those it addressed, falls beyond the measurable effects of any educative programme, and in this, it reflects a change in direction for religious education.

Since no chronicle of the catechism's origins existed, we attempted to reconstruct the events which set the stage for the production of the *Viens vers le Père* series (even though the chief interest of our study is not historical). In the first Chapters of this book, we saw how this series revived a number of ideas and practices not seen in catechesis since the days of the early Church, i.e., the time when last the Church found herself at the margins of society.

This series took very little for granted about the pre-understandings it attributed to its young audience. Taking its inspiration from theological thought that had formed in the atmosphere of a largely dechristianized France, *Viens vers le Père* worked on the assumption that the Tridentine-style catechisms were no longer effective. As a remedy to these shortcomings this series set out to co-ordinate the efforts of home, school and parish. It intended to address both children and parents to ensure that the catechesis would be integrated into the daily lives of the children. The *Viens vers le Père* series demonstrates a keen awareness of the importance of parental influences on the religious habits and beliefs of their offspring. It also aimed at the integration of the catechism into the life of the parish by emphasizing the liturgy and sacramental initiation. It would appear that the interpretation of Scripture has been inspired to some extent by the history of salvation recounted in the Eucharistic Prayers of the liturgy.

We noted how this series reflected ecclesial and secular movements that flowered in the middle of the 20th century. Advances in educational psychology and a better appreciation of the educational significance of a child's milieu prepared the way for its publication. In Church circles, the synergism of the biblical movement, the liturgical movement and Catholic Action began to direct the attention of theology towards the laity and to "action in the world." The catechetical renewal was closely intertwined with these movements and served as a vehicle for the popularization of their ideas.

It is clear that the *Viens vers le Père* series was defined by the same movements that culminated in the ecclesial renewal of the Catholic Church at Vatican Council II. Catholic theology was renewed by a process of *'ressourcement'*—a return to biblical and patristic sources. With the cautious acceptance of critical biblical methods by Pius XII, Catholic theologians began to see the Bible from a new perspective, one that challenged many of the notions of Neo-Scholasticism. Some time earlier, the rediscovery of a rich Patristic heritage had begun to exercise a similar critical function with respect to the assumptions of neo-scholastic theology. Among the emphases emerging in the first half of the 20th century, Proclamation Theology gave new life to the role of the Scriptures in Catholic life.

This new, more age-appropriate and more culturally sensitive catechism was intended to be a student-centred curriculum. A change in pedagogical methods was an essential first step in the move to student-centred catechesis. *Viens vers le Père* clearly represents such a renewal in pedagogical methods. It combined the enthusiasm of Proclamation Theology with new developments in educational psychology.

At least three disciplines—theology, pedagogy and hermeneutics—have exerted an influence first, on the way in which this series goes about its catechetical task and therefore, also on the way it reads the Bible. To bring the relevant choices into relief, we presented the principal features of the pedagogical method and content of this programme as well as its theological underpinnings (see Chapters Three and Four respectively). This was followed by an examination of the key hermeneutical assumptions which *Viens vers le Père* borrows from the fields of biblical criticism and theology (see Chapter Five).

An examination of the pedagogy of *Viens vers le Père* shows the unmistakable influence of the French school of catechetical renewal. Borrowing an image from Bernard of Chartres, we might say that the catechetical reformers in France were themselves standing upon the shoulders of their famous colleagues, including such bright lights as Montessori, Binet, Claparède, Decroly, Dewey, and Piaget. The work of Colomb, Fargues, Lubienska de Lenval, Derkenne, Ranwez and van Caster left its mark on their students and admirers who were responsible for the *Viens vers le Père* series in Quebec.

The *méthodes actives* employed in this series represented a great stride forward for educational practice. Children were introduced to textbooks with attractive illustrations and an appropriate amount of written information. They began learning through doing—through physical movement, drawing, singing, exercising their imagination, story-telling, meditation, prayer and celebration. This catechesis for young children addressed the developing child whose early intellectual formation necessarily involves physical activities. The groundbreaking pedagogical techniques pioneered in North American catechesis by *Viens vers le Père* remain largely unsurpassed even today. Indeed, one of the enduring legacies of this series is the variety of pedagogical techniques it introduces.

We examined the fundamental goals of the series in the light of curriculum theory and the philosophy of education. Our goal was to understand how educational options influenced its interpretation of Scripture. Our exploration led us to consider two basic options—the heritage-centred and experience-centred models of learning. On the one hand, we suggest that much of the content of the educational process arises from our intellectual and cultural heritage. On the other hand, in order for education to contribute to personal development and the achievement of one's potential, it must find ways to approach our intellectual heritage in ways that demonstrate its continuing relevance. The central question of the role of critical thinking in the process of education entered our discussion at this juncture.

We found that this catechism adopts a curriculum orientation centred on content—the content being a doctrinal corpus. From a pedagogical point of view, *Viens vers le Père* paid close attention to the psychological requirements of the student and in so doing greatly improved upon earlier methods of communicating doctrine. As we tried to demonstrate, the ultimate object of this method is the transmission of the doctrinal heritage of the Church, and not the elucidation of the lives of children. The experiences of children were examined for analogies which could help explain the doctrinal points under study. The emphasis on psychological development proved to be a sophisticated tool in the service of the assimilation of doctrinal content. Thus, the method of *Viens vers le Père* represents only a more subtle form of indoctrination than that evidenced in its neo-scholastic predecessors.

The intertwining of doctrine and Scripture in this series reflects their complementary character in Catholic thought. Our analysis demonstrates that the interpretation of Scripture is not the central concern of the authors of this series, even though scriptural excerpts appear in virtually every lesson. Since the Church's doctrinal heritage holds centre stage, Scripture was cast in an ancillary role. Generally, the doctrinal content was expressed in biblical paraphrase or in direct biblical excerpts. The use of the Bible does more, however, than provide a more affectively appealing reformulation of doctrinal content. This series typically deals with a single point of doctrine over several class periods and with reference to multiple biblical excerpts. This allows time for the student to gradually assimilate the content of the catechesis.

Even though children were encouraged to commit brief excerpts of the Bible to memory, they were not encouraged to take up the Bible on their own. Passages which Protestant Christians have traditionally read for comfort in times of distress or temptation, or hortatory passages encouraging good conduct, honesty and the like, play almost no role.

The *Viens vers le Père* series presses Scripture into the service of explaining doctrine, even though this reverses the historical relationship between the two. In the past doctrine has often functioned as an explanation or clarification of Scripture, in the same way in which this series used the life experiences of children as a means to higher, doctrinal ends. The series also tends to constrain the witness of Scripture, allowing it to respond only to questions of doctrine. Doctrine exercises a hegemony over human experiences, be they the experiences of the men and women of the Bible or the experiences of its audience.

To the extent which the concept of revelation informing the *Viens vers le Père* series is extrinsicist in nature, one can say that its pedagogical, hermeneutic and theological methods cohere. The question as to whether the students' lives constitute a *means* or an *end* in the educative process has a parallel in the theological method underpinning the series. We asked, on the one hand, whether the contents of revelation correspond to a reality already implicit in human life, or if they communicate a secret, divine knowledge that would otherwise be inaccessible to human persons. In other words, we asked whether revelation is extrinsic or intrinsic to human experience? This discussion reached a high point in our consideration of the theological concepts of nature and grace, and of Christology. Dependent upon one's view of revelation, upon one's notions of nature and grace and upon one's Christology, catechesis may appear either as a process of cognitive transmission or as a process of intellectual midwifery.

When catechesis is perceived as cognitive transmission, the student is regarded as an empty vessel, waiting to be filled with the teacher's knowledge. When it is seen as a maieutic process—as a process of intellectual midwifery—the student is understood already to be in possession of all that is necessary for his/her education. In the latter model, the teacher is seen primarily as a facilitator who helps students discover their own lives as the locus of insight and leads them to autonomous and critical intellectual activity.

If one's claim about revelation is that it speaks about divine realities to which human persons otherwise would not have access, then catechesis (and evangelization) must be understood as a process of transmission. Our conclusion about the *Viens vers le Père* series is that it has an extrinsicist view of revelation and that its catechesis consists therefore, in an assimilation of the contents of Tradition (in a form appropriate to today's people). For the *Viens vers le Père* series, catechesis consists in a recovery of a meaning and a content defined in the Bible and doctrine. Situations drawn from secular human experience are not meant to provide examples of grace already at work, or already present in the world. In the extrinsicist view, the human situation can, at best, provide only analogies for that reality to which humanity gains access through divine revelation. In this view, secular history is not understood as open to supernatural grace.

The task of catechesis is to connect the Christian tradition to life. It must find a way to combine the objective aspects of revelation, Scripture and doctrine, with the life experiences of its audience. Joseph Colomb, despite his intentions to balance the two poles, favoured the objective elements by opting for an extrinsicist view of revelation. Gabriel Moran, on the other hand, insists that revelation is a subjective reality tied to the believer's present. It would appear that the theological method of Karl Rahner offers a balanced approach to the problem of bringing the Christian fact into contact with contemporary experience. Rahner's method is a key source in our critique of the theological method underpinning *Viens vers le Père*.

For Rahner, the whole of human history stands under the aegis of God's grace, such that no history is truly secular, and signs of the grace of God may be found even in the direst periods of human history. In Rahner's view, the revelation of God in salvation history corresponds to a primordial inner revelation which is part of the constitution of every human consciousness. Thus in preaching and catechesis, one need not plumb human experiences for analogies capable of explaining the divine content of revelation. Rather, one plumbs human experience to discover the revelation immanent in it, and to uncover human experience as the locus of God's gracious action. That would mean that catechesis ought not to start with doctrine and then move towards life; it should start with life and put doctrine at the service of elucidating that life as God's gracious gift. It is our conclusion that the *Viens vers le Père* series puts the life experiences of the children at the service of elucidating doctrine, when it might have moved in the opposite direction.

In the final Chapter of our work, we moved from theological questions to a consideration of specifically hermeneutical issues. The practice of biblical interpretation among Christian scholars is affected by certain theological pre-understandings, not the least of which is the idea of revelation underpinning their work. With this in mind we began to situate the *Viens vers le Père* series in the context of contemporary hermeneutics, exploring three options pursued by scholars today. As we saw, recent interpreters locate meaning primarily in one of three loci: "behind the text," "in front of the text" or "in the text itself."

The overview of current hermeneutical trends indicated the complexity of the reading process. Contemporary scholarship has demonstrated the difficulty in determining what is meant by the concepts of "author," "reader" and "reading." This challenges the philosophical positions central to the historical-critical approach, i.e., the idea of a

CONCLUSIONS 265

stable and coherent human subject and the ability of language to convey the "truth." As a consequence, the hermeneutical debate has moved from mere strategies of translation of a stable content and toward hermeneutics as the production of meaning. One may speak of a shift of interest from the circumstances of the production of texts, to the circumstances of the reception of texts.

Just as our discussion of the theological aspects of the *Viens vers le Père* series uncovered objective and subjective elements within the idea of revelation, our discussion of hermeneutics uncovered subjective and objective elements in the reading process. We discovered that this series relates to the historical critical method in several ways. The series appears to function with many of the basic assumptions which govern historical criticism, but does not (and likely could not) employ its strategies actively in the catechetical process. It appears to use historical criticism's findings as the point of departure for its reading of Scripture. With historical criticism, the *Viens vers le Père* series assumes that Scripture normally has one clear meaning. We noted that challenges to historical criticism argue for a multiplicity of possible meanings in textual interpretation.

The method of interpretation in *Viens vers le Père* seems closest to that of Hans Frei. Frei's fideistic approach is also clearly based on an extrinsicist notion of revelation. Both Frei and the authors of this series understand the function of biblical hermeneutics to be that of redescription, since the Christian Tradition delivers a message which is inaccessible outside that Tradition, a message which comes from beyond our world. Neither Frei, nor this series looks to secular experiences (of children) in the world as the locus of revelation.

Frei's extrinsicist notions are incompatible with Paul Ricoeur's universalizing notions of the process of revelation. For Ricoeur, meaning is always *meaning for someone*, and the great literature of any culture has the ability to be revelatory for its people; i.e., all great literature has a religious capacity. This universalizing principle in Ricoeur's theory of reading bears a resemblance to Rahner's notion of a primordial and universal revelation in human persons.

The extrinsicist position of Frei and the universalizing position of Ricoeur translate into hermeneutical positions on textual reference. A universalizing concept of revelation leads to an understanding of the biblical narrative as a text which refers beyond its own borders—a text which challenges our ideas about the world in which we find ourselves. Revelation, in this view, is not limited to a presentation of secrets about God's relationship to humanity but seeks to unlock the hidden possibility of the world to become the kingdom of God. If, as extrinsicists maintain, revelation consists in an uncovering of the divine secrets, unattainable in our common human experiences of the world, then the real goal of preaching and teaching in the faith is to bring the audience away from their familiar world to inhabit the world created in the biblical text.

In general, we may describe the *Viens vers le Père* series as guided by the interpretative methods of biblical criticism while seeking the spiritual significance of the Bible for its young audience. Its view of revelation makes it apt to want to bring the children into the world of Tradition and to have that world become their own. While this is a laudable goal, the relationship between life and Tradition seems too one-sided. Because this programme is a systematic presentation of doctrine which largely ignores questions arising from the lives of its audience, it does not allow room for the questioning of its contents; it has no room for critique. Does one simply ignore a girl's question as to why she may not become a priest in the Roman Catholic Church, or a boy's question as to why his father has no job? While doctrine may not hold answers to such questions, the method of catechesis should not give the impression that God is indifferent to these concerns. The series does not encourage teachers to re-organize the contents of the programme around the children's questions, which emerge in the discussion of the Christian Tradition and life. The child-centred curriculum should be designed in such a way as to listen to the questions of the students, and then to use these questions as the basis for curriculum organization.

As Louis Racine suggests, the goal of catechesis and evangelization ought not to be to preach the Bible, but rather to preach as the Bible preaches. Scripture must be existentially pertinent. It is not enough to use experience in the service of a greater goal. For religious education there is no greater goal than making sense of the student's life. Catechesis and Christian interpretation of the Bible ought to illuminate that experience as the locus of divine revelation. If Scripture is to become revelatory, it must do more than provide a source of doctrinal language. The experiences of the men and women captured in the text must be allowed to be projected to a possible world in front of the text so that we may measure our own world against it and, if necessary, act to change it.

Religious education, like all education, should do more than indoctrinate children. When the social context supporting the indoctrinated view crumbles, as has happened with religious doctrine in secularized societies, little of the value contained in the heritage perdures. If the value of the Christian heritage is to be passed on, the catechetical curriculum must be grounded in the experiences of those it addresses and it must facilitate its audience's encounter with Scripture and Tradition, allowing these to speak to a new situation. Absorption into a world defined by the Bible or the Church is simply no longer an option for the vast majority of Quebecois and Canadians today. Despite a rapid move to secularization, the search for ultimate meaning, for a *religio*, shows no signs of dissipation, and the Bible stands as ready as ever to uncover the possibilities of our world. Catechesis should help the young identify those aspects of social and political life which are examples of the grace of God already at work in the secular and invite them to join in the building of the kingdom of God.

The task of catechesis is therefore to bring together life-in-the-present and Tradition, in a way that illuminates both. Not only must the experience of the child become central in determining one's approach to doctrine, it must also be understood as the locus of revelation, as Ricoeur suggests. While the *Viens vers le Père* series may not go far enough in this direction, those who continue to work in this field are fortunate to be standing on the shoulders of its authors. Their work elevates us to the ongoing task of catechesis, lifting us to where we can "see for ourselves" through the eyes of this landmark catechetical series, which has advanced the cause of catechesis in so many ways.

WORKS CITED

Alfaro, Juan. "Nature: The Theological Concept." In *Sacramentum Mundi: An Encyclopedia of Theology*, edited by Karl Rahner et al., vol. 4, 172-75. New York: Herder and Herder, 1968-.

Audinet, Jacques. "A Tradition for the Future? Social and Spiritual Dimensions of Catechesis." *Living Light* 21, no. 4 (1985):295-304.

Auer, Johann. "Grace: Theological." In *Sacramentum Mundi: An Encyclopedia of Theology*, edited by Karl Rahner et al., vol. 2, 412-15. New York: Herder and Herder, 1968-.

Auerbach, Erich. *Mimesis: The Representation of Reality in Western Literature*. Translated by Willard R. Trask. Princeton: Princeton University Press, 1968.

Ayel, Vincent. "Pedagogical Training for Future Catechists." In *Readings in European Catechetics*, 109-18. Brussels: Lumen Vitae Press, 1962.

Babin, Pierre. *Options pour une éducation de la foi des jeunes*. Lyon: Éditions Du Chalet, 1965.

Bal, Mieke. *Lethal Love*. Bloomington: Indiana University Press, 1985.

Bareille, G. "Catéchèse." In *Dictionnaire de théologie catholique*, vol. 2, cols. 1877-95. Paris: Librairie Letouzey et Ané, 1932.

Barr, David L., and Nicholas Piediscalzi, eds. *The Bible in American Education*. The Bible in American Culture. Philadelphia: Fortress Press, 1982.

Barr, James. *Holy Scripture: Canon, Authority, Criticism*. Philadelphia: Westminster, 1983.

Bauer, Walter, William Arndt, and F. Wilbur Gingrich. *A Greek-English Lexicon of the New Testament and Other Early Christian Literature*. Chicago: University of Chicago Press, 1979.

Baum, Gregory. *The Church In Quebec*. Ottawa: Novalis, 1991.

—. *Man Becoming*. New York: Seabury, 1970.

Bellinger, Gerhard J. "Katechismus II: römisch-katholische Kirche." edited by Gerhard Müller. In *Theologische Realenzyklopädie*, vol. XVII, 729-35. Berlin: Walter de Gruyter, 1988.

Berger, Peter, and Thomas Luckmann. *The Social Construction of Reality*. New York: Anchor Books, 1967.

Bérubé, Françoise. Interview. St. Lambert (P.Q.): 7 March 1991.

WORKS CITED

Bérubé, Jean-Paul, M. Caron, R. Marsolais, F. Darcy, M. Jefferey, A. Julien, R. Legentil, S. Lévesque, R. Marsolais, M. Ordway, A. Turmel, and B. Vezeau. *Viens vers le Père: Initiation chrétienne des enfants de 7-8 ans.* Montreal: Pedagogia, 1970.

Blais, Léo. "Notre catéchèse: de la première à la sixième année inclusivement." Unpublished Paper. Montreal, 1972.

Blondel, Maurice. *Exigences philosophiques du christianisme.* Paris: Presses universitaires de France, 1950.

Bossard, J. H. S. *The Sociology of Child Development.* 2d ed. New York: Harper, 1954.

Bouillard, H. "Le concept de Révélation de Vatican I à Vatican II." In *Révélation de Dieu et langage des hommes,* 35-49. Paris: Éditions Du Cerf, 1972.

Boyer, André. *Un demi siècle au sein du Mouvement Catéchistique Français.* Paris: Editions de L'Ecole, 1966.

——. *Pédagogie chrétienne.* Paris: Lethielleux, 1947 (1943).

Boys, Mary C. *Biblical Interpretation in Religious Education.* Birmingham, Ala.: Religious Education Press, 1980.

——. "Curriculum Thinking From a Roman Catholic Perspective." *Religious Education* 75, no. 5 (1980):516-27.

——. "Religious Education and Contemporary Biblical Scholarship." *Religious Education* 74, no. 2 (1979):182-97.

Brodeur, Raymond, ed. *Les Catéchismes au Québec 1702-1963.* Ste. Foy: Les Presses de L'Université Laval, 1990.

——. "L'enseignement religieux au Québec: Des programmes de classe!" In *Le défi de l'enseignement religieux: problématiques et perspectives.* Published Under the Direction of Marcel Aubert, Micheline Milot and Réginald Richard. In *Les Cahiers de recherches en sciences de la religion.* 9. 1988.

Brodeur, Raymond, and Jean-Paul Rouleau, eds. *Une inconnue de l'histoire de la culture: la production des catéchismes en Amérique française.* Ste. Foy: Éditions Anne Sigier, 1986.

Brown, Raymond E., and Sandra M. Schneiders. "Hermeneutics." In *The New Jerome Biblical Commentary,* 1146-65. London: Geoffrey Chapman, 1990.

Burke, Dennis J. *The Prophetic Mission of Henri de Lubac: A Study of His Theological Anthropology and Its Function in the Renewal of Theology.* Ph. D. Diss. Ann Arbor, Mi.: Published on Demand by University Microfilms International, 1968.

Carrier, Hervé. *Psycho-sociologie de l'appartenance religieuse.* 3d ed. Studia Socialia. Rome: Les Presses de L'univeristé Grégorienne, 1966.
Carter, G. Emmett. *The Modern Challenge to Religious Education.* New York: Sadlier, 1961.
Caster, Marcel van. *Catéchèse et dialogue.* Bruxelles: Editions de Lumen Vitae, 1966.
—. *Dieu nous parle: Structures de la catéchèse.* Bruges: Desclée de Brouwer, 1964.
—. *God's Word Today: Principles, Methods and Examples of Catechesis.* London: Geoffrey Chapman, 1966.
—. "Pour un éclairage chrétien de l'expérience." *Lumen Vitae* XXV (September 1970):429-46.
—. *The Redemption: A Personalist View.* Translated by E. O'Gormann and O. Guedatarian. Glen Rocks, N.J.: Paulist Press, 1965.
—. *The Structure of Catechetics.* Translated by E. J. Dirkswater, O. Guedatarian, and Mother N. Smith. New York: Herder and Herder, 1965.
Le catéchisme des provinces ecclésiastiques de Québec, Montréal et Ottawa. Québec, 1976 (1888) reprint of the 1944 edition.
Centre Documentaire Catéchétique. *Où en est l'enseignement religieux?* Paris: Éditions Casterman, 1937.
Charles, Eugène. *Le catéchisme par l'évangile.* Marseille: Éditions Publiroc, 1931.
Coderre, Gérard-Marie. Interview. LaPrairie (P.Q.): 7 January 1992.
—. "Le nouveau catéchisme de première année." *Communauté Chrétienne* 3 (May-June 1964):181-82.
Collaboration: OCQ—NORE. *Alive as He Promised: Student Text—Grade Six.* Toronto: Paulist Press, 1970.
—. *Alive as He Promised: Teacher's Manual—Grade Six.* Toronto: Paulist Press, 1970.
—. *Building the New Earth: Student Text—Grade Five.* Toronto: Paulist Press, 1969.
—. *Building the New Earth: Teacher's Manual—Grade Five.* Toronto: Paulist Press, 1969.
—. *Celebrate God's Mighty Deeds: Teacher Manual—Grade Two.* Toronto: Paulist Press, 1967.
—. *Celebrate God's Mighty Deeds: Student Text—Grade Two.* Toronto: Paulist Press, 1967.

WORKS CITED

——. *Come to the Father: Student Text—Grade One.* Toronto: Paulist Press, 1966.
——. *Come to the Father: Teacher's Manual—Grade One.* Toronto: Paulist Press, 1966.
——. *Gathered in Love: Teacher Manual—Grade Three.* Toronto: Paulist Press, 1967.
——. *Nous avons vu le Seigneur: Catéchisme des enfants de 9-10 ans, Livre de l'enfant.* Montréal: Librairie Beauchemin, 1967.
——. *Nous avons vu le Seigneur: Catéchisme des enfants de 9-10 ans, Guide du maître.* Montréal: Librairie Beauchemin, 1967.
——. *Préparer la terre nouvelle: Catéchisme des enfants de 10-11 ans, Livre de l'enfant.* Montréal: Centre Éducatif et Culturel, 1968.
——. *Préparer la terre nouvelle: Catéchisme des enfants de 10-11 ans, Guide du maître.* Montréal: Centre Éducatif et Culturel, 1968.
——. *Selon ta promesse, Fais-moi vivre, Guide du maître.* Montreal: Éditions de l'Iris, 1969.
——. *Selon ta promesse, Fais-moi vivre, Livre de l'enfant.* Montreal: Éditions de l'Iris, 1969.
——. *We Have Seen the Lord: Student Text—Grade Four.* Toronto: Paulist Press, 1968.
——. *We Have Seen the Lord: Teacher's Manual—Grade Four.* Toronto: Paulist Press, 1968.
Colomb, Joseph. *Aux sources du catéchisme, I: Au temps de l'Avent: la Promesse.* Paris: Desclée, 1946.
——. *Aux sources du catéchisme, II: De Noël á Pâques: la vie de Jésus.* Paris: Desclée, 1947.
——. *Aux sources du catéchisme, III: De Pâques à l'Avent: le Christ glorieux et l'histoire de l'Église.* Paris: Desclée, 1948.
——. *Catéchisme progréssif. I: Parlez Seigneur; II: Dieu parmi nous; III: Avec le Christ Jésus.* Paris: Vitte, 1950.
——. *La doctrine de vie au Catéchisme. I: Vie nouvelle et nouveau royaume; II: Combat spirituel et succès de l'Église; III: Portrait du chrétien et vie de charité.* Paris: Desclée, 1953-4.
——. *Plaie ouverte au flanc de l'Église.* Lyon: Vitte, 1954.
——. *Le Service de l'Evangile, I.* Paris: Desclée, 1968.
——. *Le Service de L'Evangile, II.* Vol. 2. Desclée. Paris, 1968.
——. "Teaching Catechism as a Message of Life." In *Readings in European Catechetics*, 119-38. Brussels: Lumen Vitae, 1962.
——. "The Use of the Bible in Religious Education." *Catéchèse.* April 1961.

Commission episcopale de l'enseignement religieux. "Communiqué (dealing with Errors in Religious Education)." *Catéchistes*, no. 33 (January 1958):85-86.

Comstock, Gary. "Truth or Meaning: Ricoeur Versus Frei on Biblical Narrative." *The Journal of Religion* 2, no. 66 (1986):117-41.

Congar, Y. *La foi et la théologie*. Tournai: Desclée, 1962.

Cormier, Marcel, and Alcide Clément. "Les sacrements en deuxième année: pourquoi?" *Communauté Chrétienne* 3 (May-June 1964):214-22.

Coudreau, François. "'Celebration' in Catechism and Catechesis." In *Readings in European Catechesis*, edited by G. Delcuve and A. Godin, 139-51. Brussels: Lumen Vitae Press, 1962.

Cremin, Lawrence E. "Curriculum Making in the United States." edited by William Pinar. In *Curriculum Theorizing: The Reconceptualists*. Berkeley: McCutchan, 1975.

Crowe, Frederick E. *Old Things and New: Strategy for Education*. Atlanta: Scholar's Press, 1985.

Cully, Iris V. "Problems of Bible Instruction in American Catechetical Literature." *Concilium* 53 (1970):128-39.

Cully, Iris V., and Kendig Brubaker Cully, eds. *Encyclopedia of Religious Education*. San Francisco: Harper & Row, 1990.

d'Aragon, Jean-Louis. "Marx Ou Satan?" *Relations* 385 (September 1973):252.

Darcy, Françoise, and Jean-Marie Beniskos. "Il y en a qui disent..." *Lumen Vitae* 26 (June 1971):257-68.

de Lubac, Henri. "Le mystère du surnaturel." *Recherches de Sciences Religieuses* XXXVI (1949):80-121.

—. *Petite catéchèse sur Nature et Grace*. Paris: Fayard, 1980.

—. Letter to the Author. In Denis J. Burke's *The Prophetic Mission of Henri de Lubac: A Study of His Theological Anthropology and Its Function in the Renewal of Theology*. Ph. D. Diss. Ann Arbor, Mi.: Published on Demand by University Microfilms International, 1968.

—. *Surnaturel: études historiques*. Paris: Aubier, 1946.

Deconchy, Jean-Pierre. *Le développement psychologique de l'enfant et de l'adolescent*. Paris: Editions Ouvrières, 1966.

Delcuve, Georges. "International Session at Nijmegen." *Lumen Vitae* 15 (1960):153-58.

Delcuve, Georges, and Albert Drèze. "Chronique internationale: Organismes internationaux—Le centre 'Lumen Vitae'." *Lumen Vitae* XIII (January-March 1958):159-68.

WORKS CITED 273

Delorme, Jean. *Lecture de l'évangile selon saint Marc*. Cahiers évangile. Paris: Éditions Du Cerf, 1972.

Derkenne, Françoise. *La vie et la joie au catéchisme, I: Introduction pédagogique*. Lyon: Éditions de L'Abeille, 1935.

——. *La vie et la joie au catéchisme, II: Introduction pédagogique*. Lyon: Éditions de L'Abeille, 1939.

——. *Vive le Seigneur, Livre Des Catéchistes*. Paris: Fayard-Mame, 1966.

Derrida, Jacques. "Différance." In *Critical Theory Since 1965*, edited by Hazard Adams and Leroy Searle, 120-36. Tallahassee: Florida State University Press, 1986 (1960).

Dewey, John. *Experience and Education*. New York: Collier Books, 1963 <1938>.

Dulles, Avery. "Faith and Revelation." In *Systematic Theology*, 92-128. Minneapolis: Fortress Press, 1991.

Duperray, Georges. "Le contenu de la catéchèse: vrai ou faux problème?" *Catéchèse* 49 (October 1972):485-98.

Eisner, Elliot W., and Elizabeth Vallance, eds. *Conflicting Conceptions of Curriculum*. Berkeley: McCutcheon, 1974.

Elias, J. L. "Values." In *Encyclopedia of Religious Education*, edited by Iris V. Cully and Kendig Brubaker Cully, 678-80. San Francisco: Harper and Row, 1990.

Erdozain, Luis. "The Evolution of Catechetics: A Survey of Six International Study Weeks on Catechetics." *Lumen Vitae* 25, no. 1 (1970):7-31.

Fargues, Marie. *La formation religieuse des enfants du peuple dans le milieu déchristianisé*. Paris: Spes, 1935.

——. *How to Teach Religion* [D'hier à demain, Le Catéchisme]. Translated by Sister Gertrude. Glen Rock, N.J.: Paulist Press, 1968 <1964>.

——. *Les méthodes actives dans l'enseignement religieux*. Paris: Éditions Du Cerf, 1934.

——. *Our Children and the Lord* [Nos enfants devant le Seigneur]. Translated by G. McIntosh. Notre Dame, Ind.: Fides, 1965 <1959>.

Fiorenza, Francis Schüssler. *Foundational Theology: Jesus and the Church*. New York: Crossroad, 1984.

——. "Systematic Theology: Tasks and Methods." In *Systematic Theology: Roman Catholic Perspectives*, vol. I, 5-87. Minneapolis: Fortress Press, 1991.

Fish, Stanley. *Is There a Text in This Class? The Authority of Interpretive Communities*. Cambridge, Mass.: Harvard University Press, 1980.
Fokkelman, J. P. *Narrative Art in Genesis: Specimens of Stylistic and Structural Analysis*. Assen: Van Gorcum, 1975.
Fossion, André. *La catéchèse dans le champ de la communication: Ses enjeux pour l'inculturation de la foi*. Cogitatio Fidei. Paris: Les Éditions Du Cerf, 1990.
Foucault, Michel. "What is an Author?" In *Critical Theory Since 1965*, edited by Hazard Adams and Leroy Searle, 138-48. Tallahassee: Florida State University Press, 1986 (1969).
Fournier, Norbert. "Canada." In *Dizionario di catechetica*, edited by Joseph Gevaert, 96-99. Leumann: Elle Di Ci, 1986.
—. "Catéchèse: Orientations Actuelles." *Monde Nouveau* XXVI (August-September 1965):265-66.
—. *Entre nous, catéchistes: Bulletin de liaison publié par l'Office catéchistique provincial*, no. Bulletin no:12 (February 1966).
—. "Pour une meilleure formation des catéchistes." *La vie des communautés religieuses* 20, no. 4 (1962):114-16.
Fowler, Robert M. *Loaves and Fishes*. In *SBL Dissertation Series*. 54. Chico: Scholars Press, 1981.
Fraas, Hans-Jürgen. "Katechismus I: protestantische Kirche (historisch bis 1945)." edited by Gerhard Müller. In *Theologische Realenzyklopädie*, vol. XVII, 710-22. Berlin: Walter de Gruyter, 1988.
Frege, Gottlob. *The Philosophical Writings of Gottlob Frege*. Translated by Max Black and Peter Geach, 56-78. Oxford: Oxford University Press, 1952.
Frei, Hans W. *The Eclipse of Biblical Narrative: A Study in Eighteenth and Nineteenth Century Hermeneutics*. New Haven: Yale University Press, 1974.
—. *The Identity of Jesus Christ: The Hermeneutical Basis of Dogmatic Theology*. Philadelphia: Fortress Press, 1975.
—. "The 'Literal Reading' of Biblical Narrative in the Christian Tradition: Does It Stretch or Will It Break?" In *The Bible and the Narrative Tradition*, edited by Frank McConnell, 36-77. New York: Oxford University Press, 1986.
Freire, Paulo. *Pedagogy of the Oppressed*. New York: Seabury, 1970.

WORKS CITED

Frye, Northrop. "from *The Critical Path.*" In *Critical Theory Since 1965*, edited by Hazard Adams and Leroy Searle, 252-64. Tallahassee: Florida State University Press, 1986 (1960).

Gadamer, Hans Georg. "The Elevation of the Historicality of Understanding to the Status of Hermeneutical Principle." From *Truth and Method*. In *Critical Theory Since 1965*, edited by Hazard Adams and Leroy Searle, 840-55. Tallahassee: Florida State University Press, 1986 (1960).

Gaudet, Robert. "Activités catéchistiques dans le diocèse de Joliette." *Le Séminaire* XX (September 1955):141-46.

Gesell, Arnold, and Francis L. Ilg. *The Child from Five to Ten*. New York: Harper, 1946.

Gilson, Etienne. *History of Christian Philosophy in the Middle Ages*. New York: Random House, 1955.

Godin, Henri, and Y. Daniel. *La France, pays de mission?* Paris: Éditions Du Cerf, 1943.

Gouin-Décarie, Thérèse. *Le Développement Psychologique de L'enfant*. Montreal: Fides, 1953.

Grant, Robert M., and David Tracy. *A Short History of the Interpretation of the Bible*. 2d ed. Philadelphia: Fortress Press, 1984.

Grasso, Domenico. "The *Good News* and the Renewal of Theology." In *The Good News Yesterday and Today*, edited by Wm. A. Huesman, 201-10. New York: Sadlier, 1962.

Grégoire, F. *Questions sur l'expérience religieuse*. Louvain: Public. Universitaire, 1957.

Greimas, Algirdas Julien. *On Meaning: Selected Writings in Semiotic Theory*. Translated by Paul J. Collins and Frank H. Perron. Theory and History of Literature, vol. 38. Minneapolis: University of Minnesota Press, 1987.

Grom, Bernhard. "Regard de l'étranger." *Relations* 385 (September 1973):253-55.

Hacking, Ian. *Why Language Matters to Philosophy?* Cambridge: Cambridge University Press, 1975.

Hamelin, Jean. *Histoire du catholicisme québécois*. Vol. 2. Montréal: Boréal Express, 1984.

Harvey, Julien. "Mémoire sur les Manuels de Catéchèse de l'OCQ: Grandes options des manuels." Unpublished Paper. October 1973. photocopy.

———. "Nos manuels de catéchèse: expérience et message." *Relations* 385 (September 1973):230-34.

Hirsch, E. D. *Validity in Interpretation*. New Haven: Yale University Press, 1967.

Hitz, P. *Evangile et catéchèse: problèmes de la catéchèse au secondaire*. Charlesbourg, Qc.: Editions Du Renouveau, 1972.

Hofinger, Johannes. "La formation catéchétique des missionaires prêtres." In *Renouvellement de la catéchèse: Rapports de la semaine internationale d'études d'Eichstätt sur la catéchèse dans les pays de mission*, edited by J. Hofinger, 405-21. Paris: Éditions Du Cerf, 1961.

—. "J.A. Jungmann (1889-1975): In Memoriam." *The Living Light* 13 (1976):354-56.

—. "Katechismus." In *Lexikon für Theologie und Kirche*, edited by Josef Hofer and Karl Rahner, 42-44. Freiburg: Verlag Herder, 1961.

—. "The Place of the *Good News* in Modern Catechetics." In *The Good News Yesterday and Today*, edited by Wm. A. Huesman, 169-84. New York: Sadlier, 1962.

Hofinger, Johannes, editor. *Renouvellement de la catéchèse*. foi vivante. Paris: Les Éditions Du Cerf, 1961.

Houyoux, Philippe. "La bible et les jeunes." *Communauté Chrétienne* 5 (September-October 1966):356-70.

Huizinga, Johan. *The Waning of the Middle Ages*. Garden City, N.Y.: Doubleday Anchor, 1954.

Johnston, George. "Should the Synoptic Evangelists Be Considered as Theologians?" *Studies in Religion/Sciences Religieuses* 21, no. 2 (1992):181-90.

Jungmann, Josef Andreas. *The Good News Yesterday and Today (Die Frohbotschaft und Unsere Glaubensverkündigung)*. 2d ed. New York: Sadlier, 1962 <1936>.

—. *Handing on the Faith: Manual of Catechetics*. New York: Herder and Herder, 1959.

—. "Theology and Kerymatic Renewal." *Lumen Vitae* 5 (April-September 1950):258-63.

Kasper, Walter. *Dogme et evangile*. Tournai-Paris: Casterman, 1967.

—. *Jesus the Christ*. Translated by V. Green. New Jersey: Paulist Press, 1977.

Kuhn, Thomas S. "Objectivity, Value Judgment, and Theory Choice." In *Critical Theory Since 1965*, edited by Hazard Adams and Leroy Searle, 381-93. Tallahassee: Florida State University Press, 1986.

Kürzinger, J. "Bibelbewegung." In *Lexikon für Theologie und Kirche*, edited by Josef Höfer and Karl Rahner, 344-46. Freiburg: Verlag Herder, 1961.

L'équipe catéchétique. "«Viens Vers le Père»: The New Catechism for the Province of Quebec—Its Presentation and Reflections on It After a Year's Experiment." *Lumen Vitae* 20, no. 2 (1965):244-64.

Laforest, Jacques. Interview. Laval University (P.Q.) 22 September 1992.

———. *La catéchèse au secondaire: étude du manuel Un sens au voyage.* Québec: Les Presses de L'Université Laval, 1970.

Langevin, Gilles. "Méthode de corrélation et anthropologie transcendentale—Paul Tillich et Karl Rahner." In *Religion et Culture: Actes du colloque international du centenaire Paul Tillich, Université Laval, 18-22 août 1986.*, Jean-Claude Petit et Jean Richard sous la direction de Michel Despland, 605-16. Québec: Les Presses de L'Université Laval, 1987.

Latourelle, René. "Révélation." In *Dictionnaire de théologie fondamentale*, Under the direction of René Latourelle and Rino Fisichella, 1134-89. Montreal: Bellaramin, 1992.

Lee, James Michael. *The Flow of Religious Instruction.* Dayton: Pflaum, 1973.

Lemaire, Paul. "Religion et morale au primaire." *Communauté chrétienne* 4 (May-June 1965):253-65.

Lemaire, Paul-M. "Le nouveau catéchisme: Ses implications théologiques et pastorales." *Communauté Chrétienne* 3 (May-June 1964): 183-93.

Lestringant, Pierre. *Le ministère catéchétique de l'Église.* Paris: Éditions «Je Sers», 1945.

Lévesque, Grégoire. Telephone Interview. Trois Rivières (P.Q.): Fall 1992.

Lindbeck, George A. *The Nature of Doctrine: Religion and Theology in a Post-liberal Age.* Philadelphia: Westminster Press, 1984.

Lonergan, Bernard J. F. *Insight: A Study of Human Understanding.* New York: Harper and Row, 1978.

———. "The Transition from a Classicist World-View to Historical-Mindedness." In *A Second Collection: Papers by Bernard J.F. Lonergan, S.J.*, edited by Wm. F. J. Ryan and B. J. Tyrell, 1-9. London: Darton, Longman and Todd, 1967.

Lubienska de Lenval, Hélène. *Éducation biblique: les plus beaux textes de la Bible.* Paris: Éditions de l'Élan, 1949.

—. *L'éducation de l'homme conscient*. Paris: Spes, 1956.
—. *L'éducation du sens liturgique*. Paris: Éditions Du Cerf, 1952.
—. *L'éducation du sens religieux*. Paris: Spes, 1960 (1946).
—. *La méthode montessori*. Paris: Spes, 1947.
—. *Trêve de Dieu*. Tournai: Casterman, 1959.
—. *L'univers biblique où nous vivons*. Paris: Casterman, 1958.
McKnight, Edgar V. *The Bible and the Reader: An Introduction to Literary Criticism*. Philadelphia: Fortress Press, 1985.
—. *Meaning In Texts: The Historical Shaping of a Narrative Hermeneutics*. Philadelphia: Fortress Press, 1978.
—. *Post-Modern Use of the Bible: The Emergence of Reader-Oriented Criticism*. Nashville: Abingdon, 1988.
Maier, Gerhard. *The End of the Historical-Critical Method*. St. Louis: Concordia, 1977.
Mangenot, E. "Catéchisme." In *Dictionnaire de théologie catholique*, vol. 2, cols. 1895-968. Paris: Librairie Letouzey et Ané, 1932.
Maréchal, J. *Etudes sur la psychologie des mystiques*. Bruges: Desclée De Brouwer, 1938.
Marlé, Réné. *Bultmann and Christian Faith*. Translated by Theodore DuBois. Westminster, MD: Newmann Press, 1967.
Marlé, René. *Herméneutique et catéchèse*. Paris: Fayard-Mame, 1970.
—. "A New Stage in French Catechesis." *Lumen Vitae* 36, no. 1 (1981):63-79.
—. "La préoccupation herméneutique en catéchèse—l'interpretation de l'expérience." *Lumen Vitae* XXV (September 1970):377-82.
Marsolais, Réginald. "Trois décennies de catéchèse au Québec." *Le Souffle* 49 (October 1974):64-72.
Metz, Johann Baptist. "Karl Rahner—ein theologisches Leben." In *Unterbrechungen: Theologisch-politische Perspektiven und Profile*, edited by G. Mohn, 43-57. Gütersloh: Taschenbücher Siebenstern, 1981.
—. *Pour une théologie du monde*. Translated by Hervé Savon. Paris: Editions Du Cerf, 1971.
Michael, J. P. "Die liturgische Bewegung." In *Lexikon für Theologie und Kirche*, edited by Josef Höfer and Karl Rahner, 1097. Freiburg: Verlag Herder, 1961.
Moitel, Pierre. "From Yesterday to Today in France: What is Changing in Catechesis?" *Lumen Vitae* 34, no. 1:41-61.

Moltmann, Jürgen. *The Crucified God: The Cross of Christ as the Foundation and Criticism of Christian Theology*. Translated by R. A. Wilson and John Bowden. New York: Harper and Row, 1974.

Montessori, Maria. *L'enfant*. Geneva: Éditions Gonthier, 1968 (1936).

Moore, Stephen D. "Stories of Reading: Doing Gospel Criticism As/With a 'Reader'" edited by Kent Harold Richards. In *SBL 1988 Seminar Papers*, 141-59. Atlanta: Scholars Press, 1988.

Moran, Gabriel. *Catechesis of Revelation*. New York: Seabury Press, 1973.

Mouroux, J. *L'expérience chrétienne: introduction à une théologie*. Paris: Aubier, 1952.

Nédoncelle, M. *Prière humaine, prière divine*. Paris-Bruges: Desclée de Brouwer, 1962.

Neufeld, Karl Heinz. "Karl Rahner." In *Dictionnaire de théologie fondamentale*, Under the direction of René Latourelle and Rino Fisichella, 999-1002. Montreal: Bellaramin, 1992.

Newcomb, T. W. *Social Psychology*. New York: Holt and Co., 1958 (1950).

O'Collins, Gerald. *Fundamental Theology*. New York: Paulist Press, 1981.

OCQ—Equipe. *Célébrons ses merveilles: Initiation chrétienne des enfants de 7-8 ans, Guide du maitre*. Québec: Éditions Pedagogia, 1965.

—. *Célébrons ses merveilles: Initiation chrétienne des enfants de 7-8 ans, Livre de l'enfant*. Québec: Éditions Pedagogia, 1965.

—. *Rassemblés dans l'amour: Catéchisme des enfants de 8-9 ans, Guide du maitre*. Québec: L'action Sociale, 1966.

—. *Rassemblés dans l'amour: Catéchisme des enfants de 8-9 ans, Livre de l'enfant*. Québec: L'action Sociale, 1966.

—. *Viens vers le Père: Initiation chrétienne des enfants de 6-7 ans, Livre du maître*. Montreal: Fides, 1964.

—. *Viens vers le Père: Initiation chrétienne des enfants de 6-7 ans, Livre de l'enfant*. Montreal: Fides, 1964.

—. "Bilan d'une enquête sur l'utilisation du nouveau catéchisme Viens vers le Père dans les diocèses du Québec." *Catéchèse* 7 (1967):103-14.

—. "'Viens Vers le Père': The New Catechism for the Province of Quebec." *Lumen Vitae* 20, no. 2 (1965):244-64.

OCQ—Équipe. "*Viens Vers le Père*—The New Catechism for the Province of Quebec: Its Presentation and Reflections on It After a Year's Experiment." *Lumen Vitae* 20, no. 2 (1965):244-64.

Office catéchistique provincial. "Rapport général sur l'enseignement religieux donné dans la Province de Québec, Canada." Report Prepared for intra-ecclesial use. Episcopal Offices of the diocese of Saint-Jean-de-Québec, June, 1958.

Penfield, W. F. "The Uncommitted Cortex: The Child's Changing Brain." *Atlantic Monthly*, no. 214 (1964):77-81.

Pinar, William, ed. *Curriculum Theorizing: The Reconceptualists.* Berkeley: McCutcheon, 1975.

Poland, Lynn M. *Literary Criticism and Biblical Hermeneutics: A Critique of Formalist Approaches.* Chico, Calif.: Scholar's Press, 1985.

Porter, Fernand. *L'institution catéchistique au Canada. Deux siècles de formation religieuse, 1633-1833.* Montréal: Les Éditions Franciscaines, 1949.

Pottmeyer, Hermann J. "Tradition." In *Dictionnaire de théologie fondamentale*, Under the direction of René Latourelle and Rino Fisichella. Montreal: Bellaramin, 1992.

Preus, James Samuel. *From Shadow to Promise.* Cambridge, Mass.: Belknap Press, 1969.

Provencher, Normand. "Modernisme." In *Dictionnaire de théologie fondamentale*, Under the direction of René Latourelle and Rino Fisichella, 875-79. Montreal: Bellaramin, 1992.

Racine, Louis. "The Child's Psychological Experience and His Evangelization: A Ground Yet to Be Covered." *Lumen Vitae* 22, no. 3 (1967):475-86.

———. *L'évangile selon Paul Tillich.* Paris: Les Éditions Du Cerf, 1970.

———. Interview. Sherbrooke (P.Q.): 15 December 1992.

Rahner, Karl. *Foundations of Christian Faith: An Introduction to the Idea of Christianity.* Translated by William V. Dych. New York: Seabury Press, Crossroads, 1978.

———. *Karl Rahner Im Gespräch.* Edited by P. Imhof and H. Biallowons. I. Munich: Kösel, 1982.

———. *Karl Rahner Im Gespräch.* Edited by P. Imhof and H. Biallowons. II. Munich: Kösel, 1983.

———. *Karl Rahner in Dialogue.* Edited and translated by Harvey D. Egan. New York: Crossroad, 1986.

—. *Revelation and Tradition*, translated by William O'Hara. In *Quaestiones Disputatae #17*. Montreal: Palm Publishers, 1965.
—. *Spirit in the World*. Translated by William Dych. New York: Herder and Herder, 1968.
—. *Spiritual Exercises*, 8. New York: Herder and Herder, 1965.
—. "Über die Erfahrung der Gnade." In *Schriften zur Theologie*, vol. III, 105-10. Benzinger Verlag: Einsiedeln, 1967 (1956).
Ranwez, Pierre. *Aspects contemporains de la pastorale de l'enfance*. Paris: Les Éditions Du Vitrail, 1950.
—. "Comment éveiller et développer le sens de Dieu chez l'écolier de 6 à 8 ans." *Lumen Vitae* XXV (September 1970):447-56.
—. "Le discernement de l'expérience religieuse chez l'enfant." *Lumen Vitae* 19 (1965):221-42.
—. "Typical Trends of the Contemporary Movement in Religious Training of Children." In *Readings in European Catechetics*, edited by G. Delcuve and A. Godin, 13-20. Brussels: Lumen Vitae Press, 1962.
"Rapport de la Réunion Des Responsables Diocésains de L'enseignement Religieux." Montreal, 1963.
Raymond, Gilles. "L'autorité de la foi sur les normes de l'éducation de la foi." In *Enseigner la foi ou former les croyants?*, 43-57. Montreal: Fides, 1988.
Ricard, Anne-Marie. "Note de Recherche sur la Production Du Catéchisme *Viens Vers le Père*." In *Une inconnue de l'histoire de la culture: la production des catéchismes en Amérique française*, edited by Raymond Brodeur and Jean-Paul Rouleau, 391-99. Ste. Foy: Éditions Anne Sigier, 1986.
Ricoeur, Paul. "'Anatomy of Criticism' or the Order of Paradigms." In *Centre and Labyrinth: Essays in Honour of Northrop Frye*, edited by Eleanor Cooke. Toronto: Toronto University Press, 1983.
—. *De l'interprétation*. Paris: Editions Du Seuil, 1965.
—. *From Text to Action* [Du texte à l'action]. Translated by K. Blamey and J. B. Thompson. Evanston, Ill.: Northwestern University Press, 1991.
—. *Hermeneutics and the Human Sciences: Essays on Language, Action and Interpretation*. Edited by John B. Thompson. Cambridge: Cambridge University Press, 1981.
—. "The Metaphorical Process as Cognition, Imagination and Feeling." In *Critical Theory Since 1965*, edited by H. Adams and L.

Searle, 424-34. Tallahassee: Florida State University Press, 1985 (1978).

—. "Philosophical Hermeneutics and Theological Hermeneutics." *Studies in Religion: Sciences Religieuses* 5 (1975):14-33.

—. *The Philosophy of Paul Ricoeur.* ed. Charles E. Reagan and David Stewart. Boston: Beacon, 1978.

—. "Preface to Bultmann." In *The Conflict of Interpretations: Essays in Hermeneutics*, edited by Don Ihde, 381-401. Evanston: Northwestern University Press, 1974.

—. "Qu'est-ce qu'un texte? Expliquer et Comprendre." In *Hermeneutik und Dialektik*, edited by R. Bubner et al., 181-200. Tübingen: J.C.B. Mohr, 1970.

Rondet, Henri. "La nouvelle théologie." In *Sacramentum Mundi*, edited by Karl Rahner, vol. 4, 234-36. Montreal: Palm Publishers, 1968.

Rouleau, Jean-Paul. "La production du catéchisme catholique, édition canadienne (1951): Une première tentative d'adaptation du discours de l'Église et du catholicisme québécois et canadiens-français à la culture moderne." In *Une inconnue de l'histoire de la culture: La productions des catéchismes en amérique française*, edited by Raymond Brodeur and Jean-Paul Rouleau, 315-53. Ste. Foy (P.Q.): Éditions Anne Sigier, 1986.

Routhier, Gilles. *La réception d'un concile.* Paris: Les Éditions Du Cerf, 1993.

Roy, C. E. *L'organisation catéchétique.* Paris: Casterman, 1938.

Rummary, R. M. *Catechetics and Religious Education in a Pluralist Society.* London: Our Sunday Visitor Press, 1975

Sacred Congregation of the Council. "Provido Sane Consilio." In *Acta Apostolicae Sedis*, vol. XXVII, 145-52. Vatican City, 1935.

Schnackenburg, Rudolph. *Le message moral du Nouveau Testament (Die sittliche Botschaft des Neuen Testaments).* Paris: Lepuy, 1963.

Schoedel, William R. *Ignatius of Antioch: A Commentary on the Letters of Ignatius of Antioch.* Edited by Helmut Koester. Hermeneia Series. Philadelphia: Fortress Press, 1985.

Schutz, Alfred. *The Phenomenology of the Social World.* Evanston: Northwestern University Press, 1967.

Ska, Jean-Louis. *Le passage de la mer: étude de la construction du style et de la symbolique.* Rome: Biblical Institute Press, 1986.

Splett, Jörg. "Nature: The Philosophical Concept." In *Sacramentum Mundi: An Encyclopedia of Theology*, edited by Karl Rahner et al., vol. 4, 171-72. New York: Herder and Herder, 1968-.

Sr. Marie de la Visitation. "Le Dieu de Jésus-Christ présenté aux enfants de 6-7 ans." *Communauté chrétienne* 2 (July-August 1963):269-78.

—. "Introduire un enfant dans le mouvement des relations trinitaires?" *Lumen Vitae* 21 (Sept. 1966):523-32.

Sr. Marie de la Visitation, Jean-Paul Bérubé, Marcel Caron, and Réginald Marsolais. "Présentation Du Nouveau Catéchisme." *Communauté chrétienne* 3 (May-June 1964):194-205.

Stuhlmacher, Peter. *Historical Criticism and Theological Interpretation of Scripture: Towards a Hermeneutics of Consent*. Translated by Roy A. Harrisville. Philadelphia: Fortress Press, 1977.

—. *Historical Criticism and the Theological Interpretation of Scripture*. London: SPCK, 1979.

"Systematic Theology: Tasks and Methods." In *Systematic Theology: Roman Catholic Perspectives*, edited by Francis Schüssler Fiorenza and J.P. Galvin, vol. I, 5-87. Minneapolis: Fortress Press, 1991.

Thiemann, Ronald F. "Response to George Lindbeck." *Theology Today* 43 (1986):377-82.

Tremblay, Paul. Interview. Montreal (P.Q.): Fall, 1990.

Valensin, Auguste. "'Introduction' to Lubienska de Lenval's *L'éducation du sens religieux*." 11-27. Paris: Spes, 1960.

Vancourt, R. *La phénoménologie de la foi*. Tournai: Desclée, 1953.

Vanhoozer, Kevin J. *Biblical Narrative in the Philosophy of Paul Ricoeur*. Cambridge: Cambridge University Press, 1990.

Verscheure, J. "Katholische Aktion." In *Lexikon Für Theologie und Kirche*, edited by Josef Höfer and Karl Rahner, 74-77. Freiburg: Verlag Herder, 1961.

Vimont, J. and J. Duperray. "Le sens de l'effort demandé aux catéchistes." *Catéchistes*, no. 33 (January 1958):87-90.

Vogels, Walter. *Reading and Preaching the Bible*. Wilmington, Del.: Michael Glazier, 1986.

Vorgrimler, Herbert. *Understanding Karl Rahner: An Introduction to His Life and Thought*. Translated by John Bowden. New York: Crossroad, 1986.

Wagner, J. "Liturgische Bewegung." In *Lexikon für Theologie und Kirche*, edited by Johannes Höfer and Karl Rahner, 1097-99. Freiburg: Verlag Herder, 1961.

Watson, Nigel. "Reception Theory and Biblical Exegesis." *Australian Biblical Review* 36 (1988):45-56.
Weigel, Gustave. "Gleanings from Commentaries on *Humani Generis.*" *Theological Studies* XII (1951):535-50.
White, Hayden. "The Historical Text as Literary Artifact." In *Critical Theory Since 1965*, edited by Hazard Adams and Leroy Searle, 394-407. Tallahassee: Florida State University Press, 1986.
Wink, W. *The Bible in Human Transformation*. Philadelphia: Fortress, 1973.
Wrede, William. *Das Messiasgeheimnis in den Evangelien*. Göttingen: Vandenhoeck und Ruprecht, 1963.

INDEX

A

accumulated wisdom 126, 132
ACEBAC 30
affective disposition 109, 113
Alive as He Promised 102, 115
American Revolution 74, 211
anthropology 163, 164, 169, 186, 202, 203, 246
Aquinas, Thomas 25, 67, 154, 172
Archiconfrérie... 39
ars interpretandi 10
articles of the Creed 10, 15, 99, 144, 183
assimilation of doctrine 128
Auerbach, Erich 102, 116, 240, 242, 243, 246
Augustine 20, 168, 169
Ayel, Vincent 80

B

Bal, Mieke 7
baptism 17, 18, 93, 99, 125, 168, 176
Barth, Karl 239, 240, 246, 247, 248, 249, 250, 252
Bauer, Arndt, Gingrich 9
Bauer, F.C. 212
Baum, Gregory 73, 74, 85, 158, 159, 160
Beaulieu, Alberte 38
Bellarmine, Robert 20
Bellinger, Gerhard J. 19, 20

Benedictine abbeys 28
Best, E. 207
Bibel und Liturgie 29
biblical criticism 6, 7, 11, 35, 202, 210, 212, 266
biblical hermeneutics 2, 8, 11, 12, 13, 60, 68, 88, 119, 200, 202, 218, 265
biblical interpretation 2, 5, 6, 9, 13, 145, 151, 157, 201, 204, 215, 234, 238, 239, 241, 242, 243, 247, 249, 253, 254, 255, 257, 264
biblical movement 26, 27, 29, 30, 43, 44, 153, 162, 187, 260
Binet, Alfred 50
Bishop Landrieux 42
Blais, Léo 92, 93, 94, 95
Bossard, J.H.S. 104
Bouillard, H. 56
Bournique, Joseph 79, 83
Boyer, A. 21, 49
Boys, Mary C. 66, 146, 162, 163
Brodeur, Raymond 21, 75, 76
Brown, Raymond E. 9
Building the New Earth 89, 101
Bulletin biblique 30
Bultmann, Rudolph 210

INDEX

C

Calvin _____ 17, 18, 67
Canisius, Peter _____ 18, 19 21, 22, 23, 26, 27
Caron, Marcel __ 38, 46, 83, 128
Carrier, Hervé _____ 104
Carter, G.Emmett _____ 15, 35
catechetical congress _____ 78
catechetical manuals _ 20, 21, 76
catechetical movement _____ 5, 13, 82, 88, 90,148, 166, 180
catechetical renewal _____ 13, 24, 25, 37, 39, 41, 42, 45, 49, 50, 58, 60, 64, 68, 74, 78, 81, 90, 91, 95, 102, 103, 106, 135, 150, 151, 155, 161, 162, 182, 184, 191, 194, 260, 261
catechetics _____ 4, 5, 14, 26, 27, 29,33, 39, 43, 49, 50, 58, 59, 60, 61, 63, 73, 75, 79, 80, 82, 86, 90, 96, 135, 151, 155, 161, 181, 187, 194, 195, 196
catechism _____ 1, 2, 3, 4, 5, 8, 11, 13, 14, 18, 19, 20, 41, 42, 43, 44, 45, 49, 51, 52, 55, 57, 58, 60, 69, 75, 76, 77, 85, 87, 88, 89, 94, 97, 100, 103, 107, 118, 124, 127, 129, 135, 142, 143, 148, 149, 150, 155, 180, 187, 190, 191, 192, 195, 196, 197, 198, 200, 202, 215, 235, 254, 259, 260, 261
Catéchisme canadien _____ 2
Catechismus Romanus _____ 19
catechumenate _____ 15, 17, 20, 71, 79
Catholic Action ____ 2, 7, 28, 29, 30, 31, 32, 194, 260
Catholic Reformation _____ 19
CCC _____ 89
CCD _____ 89
Celebrate God's Mighty Deeds _____ 89, 99
Célébrons ses merveilles ___ 89, 99, 100, 106, 114, 125, 130, 183,188, 191
Centre Documentaire Catéchétique _____ 64
Centre National _____ 43
Charles, Eugène _____ 42
Childs, Brevard _____ 206
Choquette Joseph _____ 80
Christian mystery _____ 88, 100
christology _____ 6, 120, 165, 167, 180
Church Fathers __ 17, 19, 21, 37
Cité Libre _____ 82
Claparède, Edouard ___ 50, 261
class celebrations _____ 28, 108, 121, 261
Cocceius, Johannes _____ 65
Coderre, Gérard-Marie _____ 75, 77, 83, 85, 87, 91
cognitive acquisition _____ 40, 48, 97, 109, 110, 113, 183, 184, 259

INDEX

Collin, G. _____ 109
Colomb, Joseph ____ 14, 15, 17, 19, 21, 26, 39, 40, 42, 43, 44, 45, 55, 57, 58, 61, 62, 63, 68, 71, 104, 109, 112, 135, 149, 150, 151, 155, 156, 157, 158, 160, 161, 163, 164, 165, 184, 187, 189, 190, 191, 196, 203, 261, 264
Come to the Father _____ 1, 2 89, 90, 95, 99, 108, 109, 110, 111, 118, 128, 193
compulsory education _____ 26
Comstock, Gary __ 226, 227, 231, 239, 240, 243, 244, 245, 247, 250, 251
consciousness _____ 224
Contin, Oscar _____ 80
conversion _____ 4, 27, 52, 57, 60, 67, 104, 117, 124, 144, 185, 218, 259
Coriden, James _____ 36, 37
Coudreau, François __ 39, 58, 78, 79, 81
Council of Trent _____ 19
Counter Reformation ___ 19, 20
Cousinet, Roger _____ 50
Creed _____ 10, 11, 15, 18, 94, 99, 143, 144,183
Cremin, Lawrence E. _____ 132
Crowe, Frederick _____ 132
Cullmann, O. _____ 66
Cully, Iris V. _____ 119
curriculum as content _____ 139
curriculum as process _____ 139
curriculum theory _____ 4, 14, 40, 42, 96, 134, 155, 261

D

d'Aragon, Jean-Louis ___ 3, 107
Daniélou, J. _____ 34, 35, 37
Darcy, Françoise _____ 124
das Katholische Bibelwerk __ 29
das Volksliturgischen Apostolat _____ 29
De catechizandis rudibus ___ 20
de Greeff, E. _____ 109
de Lubac, Henri _____ 14, 154, 167, 169, 170, 173, 182, 190, 203, 252
de-colonization _____ 24
Declaration of Independence 211
Deconchy, J.P. _____ 115
Decroly, Ovide _____ 261
Delorme, Jean _____ 97, 124, 125, 120, 156, 211
Derkenne, Françoise _____ 104, 184, 261
Derrida, Jacques _____ 217, 218, 221, 224, 232
Descartes, René _____ 219
Dewey, J. _____ 132, 133, 261
Die Frohbotschaft ___ 33, 34, 36
Dilthey, Wm. ___ 146, 199, 220
Divino afflante spiritu _____ 35
doctrinal formulæ _____ 4
doctrine _____ 11, 12, 15, 17, 22, 23, 27, 97, 98, 100, 105, 106, 108, 112, 118, 119, 120, 122, 123, 125, 127, 128, 130, 131, 135, 139, 143, 144, 145, 146, 148, 150, 151, 152, 153, 158, 160, 166, 168, 174, 176, 177, 179, 180, 183, 185, 188, 189, 190, 191, 192, 193, 194, 195, 199,

201, 212, 215, 233, 234, 235, 253, 254, 255, 256, 257, 262, 263, 264, 266, 267
dogma _____ 11, 12, 25, 36, 188, 189, 195, 203, 234, 254

E

ecclesial reform _____ 13
École active _____ 40, 45, 48, 49, 77, 183
ecumenical movement ___ 24, 35
education
 as achievement ____ 135, 138
 education as experience ___ 141
 education as message _____ 141
Educational theory _____ 5, 14, 55, 234
Eecclesial reform _____ 25
egocentrism _____ 112
Enlightenment _____ 20, 23, 152, 206, 211, 218, 221, 247
Erdozain, L. ____ 40, 65, 69, 70
Eucharist __ 18, 33, 86, 100, 125
exegesis _____ 8, 9, 17, 77, 153, 189, 223, 230, 246, 247, 254
Exercises in Silence _____ 111
experience model of curriculum _____ 98
experience as Anknüpfungspunkt... ___ 127
explanation and understanding _____ 222, 229, 230, 233, 234

F

faith _____ 4, 6, 10, 11, 19, 20, 22, 29, 33, 34, 36, 41, 42, 46, 51, 56, 57, 59, 60, 72, 92, 101, 102, 105, 110, 117, 118, 122, 123, 125, 135, 145, 147, 149, 151, 152, 153, 156, 157, 159, 160, 162, 167, 168, 170, 172, 174, 175, 176, 177, 178, 180, 186, 187, 195, 198, 201, 203, 204, 215, 219, 226, 228, 234, 236, 239, 241, 251, 254, 257, 266
Fargues, Marie _____ 21, 42, 49, 50, 53, 55, 69, 86, 139, 144, 180
Father Lussier _____ 76
Ferrière, Adolphe _____ 50
Fokkelman, J.P. _____ 206
Forget, Bishop _____ 77
Form Criticism _____ 237
Fossion, André _____ 69, 70, 71, 72, 162, 165
Foucault, Michel _____ 206, 217
Fournier Norbert _____ 39, 79, 82,
Fowler, R.M. _____ 7, 206, 207
Fraas, Hans-Jürgen _____ 18
Frege, Gottlob ___ 210, 220, 241
Frei, Hans W. _____ 65, 67, 226, 232, 238, 239, 240, 241, 242, 243, 244, 245, 246,

247, 248, 249, 250, 251, 252, 253, 255, 256, 257, 258, 265
Freire, Paulo _____ 134
Frère Untel _____ 85
Frye, Northrop ___ 222, 232, 251
fundamental theology 24, **37**, 179

G

Gathered in Love _____ 89, 100
Gignac André _____ 80
Gilson, Etienne _____ 131
Godin, Henri _____ 44
Goethe, J.W. von _____ 218
Grant, R.M. _____ 17, 35, 67, 113, 140, 217, 230,
Grasso, Domenico _____ 34
Greimas, A.J. _____ 206
Grom, Bernard _____ 130, 141, 184

H

Hamel, Edouard _____ 91
Hamelin, Jean _____ 28, 84
Hamman, Aimé _____ 80
Harris, William Torrey _____ 132
Harvey, Julien ___ 91, 107, 125, 189, 190, 193
Heidegger, Martin _____ 37, 148, 172, 218, 220, 221, 222, 223, 228
Heilsgeschichte __ 65, 66, 67, 68, 71, 162, 163, 195
Hell _____ 94, 124
Henripin Marthe _____ 82
hermeneutics _____ 8, 9, 10, 13, 14, 68, 98, 119, 202, 206, 207, 208, 216, 218, 219, 223, 224, 225, 232, 245, 246, 256, 260, 264, 265
hermeneutics of suspicion ___ 13, 219, 225, 256
heuristics _____ 8
Hirsch, E.D. _____ 208, 209, 210, 211, 253
historical criticism _____ 237
Historical critics _____ 208, 210
historical setting of Jesus __ 121
History of Salvation _____ 26
Hitz, P. _____ 91
Hofinger, J. ___ 34, 61, 68, 163
Hooker, M.D. _____ 207
Houyoux, Philippe _____ 38
Hubert, R. _____ 109
Huizinga, J. _____ 16
human sciences _____ 25, 27
human subject _____ 5, 62, 148, 153, 164, 190, 195, 216, 218, 220, 221, 222, 223, 224, 228, 265
Husserl. E. _____ 219, 220, 221, 223, 224

I

identity _____ 6, 9, 60, 66, 74, 84, 85, 120, 121, 244, 245, 248, 249, 250, 251
ideology _____ 74, 211
Ignatius of Antioch _____ 1, 2, 3
implied author _____ 226
Initiation chrétienne _____ 2, 46, 87, 100, 201
intellectual midwifery _ 126, 263

intellectualist strain _____ 58
interiority _____ 45, 46, 111, 114, 118
International Catechetical Meetings _____ 64

J

J.L. Elias _____ 136
Jeffery, Martin __ 38, 89, 90, 110
Jesus of Nazareth _ 73, 101, 121, 122, 161, 164, 176, 181
Johnston, George _____ 207
Jungmann, J.A. _____ 33, 34, 36, 41, 44, 68, 163

K

Kant, Immanuel _ 136, 181, 219
kerygma ____ 33, 41, 67, 70, 250
kerygmatic theology _____ 32, 34, 81, 187, 195
Kierkegaard, S. __ 100, 214, 216
kingdom of God _____ 30, 228, 229, 231, 236, 250, 251, 255, 266, 267
Kuhn, Thomas _____ 207
Kürzinger, J. _____ 29

L

La nouvelle théologie _____ 27
language of events _____ 102
...of symbolic gestures _____ 102
learner _____ 105, 126, 134, 135, 136, 138, 139, 141, 144, 146, 147, 164, 22
legalism _____ 21
Leo XIII _____ 30
Lestringant, Pierre _____ 18
Letter to the Romans _____ 1, 2
Lindbeck, George A. _____ 246
linguistics _____ 10, 227
Liturgics _____ 27
Lohfink, Norbert _____ 6
Lonergan, Bernard _____ 36, 37, 137, 142, 154
Lord's prayer _____ 15
Lubienska de Lenval, _ 106, 110, 120, 184, 233, 261 185
Lumen Vitae _____ 23, 99, 109, 124, 127, 130, 148, 162, 165, 173, 182
Luther _____ 17, 18, 19

M

Magisterium _____ 56, 94, 118, 153, 156
Maier, Gerhard _____ 208
maieutic process _ 126, 128, 263
manipulables _____ 141
Marlé, René _____ 6, 9, 10, 12, 22, 23, 58, 69, 188, 189, 195, 216, 218, 219, 225, 248, 249, 250, 254
Marsolais, Réginald ____ 38, 46, 65, 83, 128
Martucci, Jean _____ 79
McGrory, Barry _____ 38
meaning behind the text ____ 14

225, 227, 238, 240, 254, 264
meaning in front
  of the text ___ 14, 206, 218, 227, 228, 231, 233, 238, 250, 255, 264, 267
meaning in
  the text itself ___ 14, 264
memorization ___ 53, 55, 73, 94, 108, 185,
méthodes actives ___ 40, 49, 50, 55, 191, 261
Michael, J.P. ___ 28
Middle Ages ___ 15, 16, 17, 24, 33, 131, 230
mirabilia Dei ___ 100, 174, 191
mnemonic devices ___ 15
Moltmann, Jürgen ___ 116
Mondésert, J. ___ 35
Montessori, M. _ 46, 52, 86, 102
Moore, Stephen D. ___ 206
Moses ___ 112, 145, 164, 191
Munich Method ___ 40, 41

N

Nachgeschichte ___ 212
narrative criticism ___ 219, 237
Neo-Scholasticism ___ 10, 23, 67, 153, 154, 172, 187, 191, 192, 195, 260
Newcomb, T.W. ___ 104
Nocent, Adrien ___ 79
noematics ___ 8
NORE ___ 90
Nous avons vu le Seigneur _ 38, 89, 101, 115, 119, 120, 122, 149, 150, 201, 213, 214, 233, 254

O

OCQ-Équipe ___ 2, 98, 99, 100, 103, 116, 190
OCQ-NORE ___ 2, 99, 101, 102, 213
ONC ___ 90
O'Neill, Louis ___ 80
ontology ___ 223

P

Palestine ___ 101, 115, 145, 213, 214, 233
Parsch, Pius ___ 28, 29
Penfield, Wilder ___ 53
Pesch, R. ___ 207
philosophy of education ___ 98, 143, 261
Piaget, Jean _ 50, 108, 109, 261
pictorial dimension
  to understanding ___ 110
Pius X _ 28, 30, 31, 35, 154, 260
Pius XII ___ 28, 31, 35, 154, 260
Poppe, E.J.M. ___ 40
Porter, Fernand ___ 21
Pottmeyer, Hermann J. ___ 10
preaching ___ 8, 11, 16, 17, 18, 21, 34, 70, 104, 123, 163, 213, 248, 256, 257, 264, 266
Préparer la terre nouvelle _ 89, 101, 192
progressive revelation ___ 98, 145, 189
prophoristics ___ 8
psychology ___ 5, 8, 10, 13, 26, 37, 39, 42, 48, 49, 55, 57, 59, 69, 96, 97, 103, 107,

109, 115, 128, 143, 148, 155, 156, 161, 163, 166, 187, 195, 196, 260

Q

Quinet, Charles _____ 40, 49

R

Racine, Louis _____ 127, 128 139, 180, 266
Rad, Gerhard von _____ 66, 226
Rahner, Karl _____ 14, 28, 34, 37, 151, 152, 154, 167, 170, 171, 172, 173, 174, 175, 176, 177, 178, 179, 180, 181, 182, 184, 186, 192, 193, 194, 196, 198, 203, 204, 205, 231, 246, 264, 265
Ranwez, Pierre _____ 43, 48, 49, 59, 60, 61,109, 173, 184, 185, 261
Rassemblés dans l'amour _____ 89, 100
rationalism _____ 21, 61, 159
Reader Response Theory _____ 7
reading ability _____ 112
Reception Aesthetics _____ 7
Reception Theory _____ 7
Redaction Criticism _____ 237
Reformation _____ 11, 15, 18, 19, 20, 33, 35, 100, 119, 152, 168, 178, 211, 216, 241, 247, 251, 252
Relations _____ 3, 95, 107, 130
Renaissance _____ 216, 237
revelation _____ 2, 3, 6, 14, 36, 55, 56, 60, 70, 71, 72, 73, 92, 98, 150, 151, 157, 158, 159, 160, 161, 163, 164, 165, 167, 170, 171, 172, 174, 175, 176, 177, 180, 181, 182, 187, 188, 189, 191, 192, 194, 195, 196, 197, 199, 102, 115, 118, 123, 127, 200, 201, 203, 204, 205, 231, 234, 239, 246, 248, 249, 250, 251, 252, 253, 254, 256, 257, 262, 263, 264, 265, 266, 267
Revolution _____ 20, 74, 211
Rezeptionstheorie _____ 7
Ricoeur, Paul _____ 137, 146, 216, 218, 219, 223, 232, 239, 251, 254, 265
rocognitive hermeneutics __ 224
Rondet, Henri _____ 27
Routhier, Gilles _____ 7
Roy, C.E. _____ 16, 21
Rummary, R.M. _____ 22
Ryle, Gilbert _____ 240

S

sapiential and notional language _____ 102
Schmaus, M. _____ 34
Schneiders, Sandra M. _____ 9
Schoedel, William _____ 1, 2

Schreiber, J. _____ 207
secularization __ 20, 25, 27, 267
See, Judge, Act _____ 30
semiotics _____ 225, 237
sense of wonder _____ 99, 112, 113, 137
sensus litteralis _____ 230, 238, 241, 246
singing _____ 108, 261
Sister Marie de la Visitation _ 38 39, 45, 46, 83, 86, 113
Ska, J.-L. _____ 206
sociology _____ 10, 26, 37, 69, 97, 103, 161
Source Criticism _____ 237
Sources chrétiennes _____ 35
spiritual content of bible ___ 113
Stolz, A. _____ 34
Stuhlmacher, P. _____ 208
subjectivism _____ 5, 34, 150
Summa _____ 18, 33
supernatural _____ 6, 51, 56, 59, 62, 154, 159, 167, 169, 170, 173, 252

T

Ten Commandments _____ 18
Gospel encounters of Jesus _ 121
text Criticism _____ 237
the Talk _____ 108, 111
theme sheets _____ 103
Theological Renewal _____ 32
Thiemann, Ronald _____ 248, 249, 250
Thomism _____ 5, 81, 153, 154, 187, 190, 194, 195
Tracy, David _____ 17, 140, 216
Tradition _____ 10, 11, 28, 35, 102, 107, 118, 123, 129, 139, 141 143, 144, 146, 147, 149, 151, 154, 156, 167, 171, 175, 181, 182, 186, 194, 196, 199, 201, 202, 203, 231, 234, 239, 252, 253, 254, 257, 263, 265, 266, 267
traditional method _ 22, 53, 133
Tremblay, Paul _____ 38, 63
Tridentine
  style catechisms ___ 100, 143
Trinitarianism _____ 2, 55, 56
truth
  of correspondence _____ 209, 220, 222, 227, 228
ultramontanist sympathy ___ 31
urbanization _____ 25
Urs von Balthasar _____ 34
use of OT and NT _____ 146

V

Vagaggini, J. _____ 116, 117
values in education __ 11, 29, 53, 121, 122, 136, 138, 141, 142, 143, 145, 156, 162, 163, 204, 211, 247,
van Caster, Marcel __ 39, 79, 80, 83, 162, 163, 164, 165, 187, 191, 261
Vatican (Councils etc.) _ 13, 26, 56, 57, 75, 83, 89, 107, 123, 151, 154, 166, 170, 181, 192, 252, 260
Verkündigungstheologie _ 32, 34, 67, 172, 195
Verscheure, J. _____ 30
Vimont, J. _____ 62

Vogels, Walter — 237, 238
VVLP—Year 1 — 89, 107
VVLP—Year 4 — 101, 201, 213, 214, 254
VVLP—Year 5 — 101
VVLP—Year 6 — 89, 101, 102, 107

W

Watson, Nigel — 7
We Have Seen the Lord — 89, 99, 101, 115, 119, 120, 121, 123, 214
White, Hayden — 206, 207
Wink, W. — 208
Wirkungsgeschichte — 212
Wrede, Wm. — 120